The Delta Project

The Delta Project

Discovering New Sources of Profitability in a Networked Economy

Arnoldo C. Hax
and
Dean L. Wilde II

palgrave

First published 2001 by
PALGRAVE
Houndmills, Basingstoke, Hampshire RG21 6XS and
175 Fifth Avenue, New York, N.Y. 10010
Companies and representatives throughout the world

PALGRAVE is the new global academic imprint of
St. Martin's Press LLC Scholarly and Reference Division and
Palgrave Publishers Ltd (formerly Macmillan Press Ltd).

ISBN 0–333–96245–1 hardback

This book is printed on paper suitable for recycling and made from fully managed and sustained forest sources.

A catalogue record for this book is available from the British Library.

Cataloging-in-Publication Data is available from the Library of Congress

Editing and origination by
Aardvark Editorial, Mendham, Suffolk

10 9   8   7   6   5   4   3
10 09 08 07 06 05 04 03 02

Printed in Great Britain by
Creative Print & Design (Wales) Ebbw Vale

*To our families, the sources of much love, joy,
encouragement and support*

The Haxes: Neva Sr., Neva Jr., and Andres

The Wildes: Cécile, Audrey, Emilie, and Alexander

CONTENTS

Contents

List of Figures

LIST OF TABLES

PREFACE

The Delta Model is a fresh approach to business strategy development and strategic management in today's increasingly networked economy.

The prevailing feature of the new economic milieu is the pervasiveness of networks – both the familiar networks of physical assets and real goods flows – power grids, supply chains, and airline routes – as well as those born of the information age – virtual corporations, global financial systems, communities of interest, and the Internet. The rise of networking has proven to be as central and disruptive an industry force as the development of the standardized assembly line and the introduction of motive power. Economic networks have altered the nature of competition, amplifying the relationships between customers and suppliers, enabling the development of new business models for competitors, and fostering the roles of new participants as complementors. Networks have created externalities to the conventional economic marketplace that have fundamentally changed – and will continue to redefine – the rules for business success.

Existing frameworks for business strategy, rooted in the old economy, did not anticipate the changes to the competitive landscape wrought by the forces of networking. More than 20 years ago, Michael Porter, perhaps the most influential thinker in business strategy, drew lessons from the industrial economy to construct a valuable framework for competition which still dominates both the teaching and practice of strategy today. Porter introduced the notion of strategy based on Low Cost or Differentiation, and framed competition as a rivalry in which the participants must leverage their relative power over that of their competitors, customers, and suppliers in order to achieve sustainable advantage. More recently, Prahalad and Hamel popularized another influential framework, the Resource-Based or Core Competencies model of business strategy. This perspective asserts that firms enjoy high levels of profits because of the unique tangible and intangible assets they appropriate and instantiate in their products and services, which are thus differentiated from those of their competitors. Both frameworks represent significant contributions to the field of strategic thinking, and, indeed, both are widely taught and applied in practice throughout the world today. However, neither perspective addresses the significant role of economic networks in today's competitive environment nor the new sources of strategic advantage that such networks have empowered.

The Delta Model was developed to account for the more complex economic forces and business relationships in today's networked environment, and draws upon the lessons learned from today's business successes. Derived from the more recent experience of the networked digital economy, it renders an integrated framework that defines new sustainable strategic positions and the organizational processes required to achieve them, while unifying the concepts embodied in the existing 'classic' paradigms of business strategy. The underlying theme of the Delta model is that strategy – in both the new and old economy – may be, and in many cases should be, formulated on the basis of bonding as opposed to rivalry. It expands the strategic tableau to include customers, suppliers, competitors, substitutes, and complementors (firms that deliver products and services which significantly enhance a company's own offerings). It recognizes and describes how customer and complementor relationships can create strong bonds to the customer – independent of the product or service that the company sells. It explicitly links strategy with execution – the necessary processes, metrics, and adaptations which constitute the day-to-day actions of a business. And it acknowledges that more businesses today fail due to gaps in execution than in strategy, and explains why.

Bonding is not a new force; we find it in the old economy, but it has become more prevalent in the new economy due to the common digital language and pervasiveness of the network. But to pursue bonding effectively requires more than simply a new mission statement, or selling the current portfolio of goods and services online. It requires a reorientation of the firm so that it acquires and acts on a deep understanding of its customers' activities and its complementors' economics. Most firms are anchored in their product economics, their internal activities and those of their suppliers. This is reflected in their processes, which are exhorted to pursue lower cost, faster delivery, and better features. All commendable goals, but insufficient to gain bonding.

Bonding requires redefining metrics to evaluate the market along new dimensions that represent value to the customer or complementor. It requires attention to Granular Metrics, because each customer and complementor is different and the values associated with each are wide ranging. Finally, it requires that the entire organization is hardwired to an Adaptive Process involving structured tests and experiments, so that individuals can respond to a changing market. Reserving the privilege of change to senior management alone restricts a large organization to the nimbleness of a battleship, able to respond only to incremental budget variances or to five-year plans. Successfully adopting the new strategies enabled by the networked economy requires sweeping change throughout a company. It requires a new strategic framework that reflects these demands.

The Delta Model is a practical framework for competing in the new economy. It is integrated from strategy to execution:

- It captures three essential forms of competitive position.
- It explains how these positions are translated into a Strategic Agenda.
- It describes how processes and tasks are aligned to that agenda.
- It defines the metrics to track progress.
- It shows how to adapt to the inevitable uncertainties in the market.

The Delta Project describes the journey that leads us along the full discovery and implementation of the concepts surrounding the Delta Model. After you have read this book, we wish you a safe and prosperous trip.

ARNOLDO C. HAX
DEAN L. WILDE II

Acknowledgments

We owe acknowledgment and profuse thanks to the many people who contributed to the production of this book. First and foremost we have to recognize our own institutions, MIT and Dean & Company. In fact throughout the working of this book, both places became quite intertwined in our lives. Dean Wilde, the Chairman and Founder of Dean & Company, became a Visiting Lecturer at Sloan School, and actively participated in course development and teaching related to the Delta Model. Arnoldo Hax, the Alfred P. Sloan Professor of Management at the MIT Sloan School, became a Board Member of Dean & Company, and took part in consulting activities with the firm. Both places contributed enormous intellectual inspiration and professional support.

Many years ago at MIT, we initiated a dialogue among some senior executives and faculty members at the Sloan School to identify the issues and challenges that managers were facing. The senior managers participating were Skip LeFauve, CEO of Saturn; Gerhard Schulmeyer, then CEO of Asea Brown Boveri and now President and CEO of Siemens Corporation; Iain Anderson, CEO of Chemical Coordination at Unilever; Judy Lewent, CFO of Merck; and Bert Morris, Chief Executive of Operations at National Westminster Bank. The faculty members were Charles Fine, Arnoldo Hax, Henry Jacoby, Thomas Magnanti, Robert McKersie, Stewart Myers, John Rockart, Edgar Schein, Michael Scott Morton, and John Van Maanen. We explored in depth the forces confronting business worldwide to determine whether current frameworks responded to modern issues. This initiative we called the Delta Project and it was the foundation of our own reflections on how to respond effectively to these challenges and led to a new framework we call the 'Delta Model.'

Over 70 graduate students conducted research theses on the Delta Model, looking at its application to different industries and companies, and comparing it to other frameworks. Each of these added substantially to our thinking and to the robustness of the Delta Model. In particular we would single out the following theses which we've used in selected chapters of the book. C. C. Lee's, 'An Application of the Delta Model: Developing Strategies for Singapore Post,' provided the basis for the discussion on the Singapore Post Office, in Chapter 9. Patrick Preux's, 'Customer Targeting, Sustainable Competitive Advantage and Core Competencies,' we used for some portions of the customer targeting discussion in Chapter 7. Robert Browning and Winfried Holz's, 'The Virtual Utility: Strategic Choices for Utilities in the Restructured Electric Industry,' was the basis of Chapter 11. We would especially like to thank Jordan Siegel, a Ph.D. student at Sloan, who also cheerfully took on the burden of editing the complete book, and who also offered many refinements of the Delta Model concepts and their relationship to other management frameworks.

From Dean & Company, Jim Smist is the most accomplished master in using granular metrics to conceive of and drive strategy, and his pioneering work in this area contributed to the foundation for our work. Moray Dewhurst with his typically outstanding intellectual rigor has helped us refine and distil the Delta Project ideas to their essence. Chris Bennett helped along multiple dimensions, with our writing style, with our understanding of many technology sectors and with the subtler aspects of lock-in. Ware Adams has helped to develop many of the concepts in the real world via our consulting practice, and introduced the application of the Delta Model to the energy industry. Mark d'Agostino was involved in our formative stages and should be credited for the initial construction of the bonding continuum. Michael Echenberg dedicated many long days to the careful editing of the entire book, and helped to originally cast the Internet chapter. All the professionals at Dean & Company contributed to the development and applications of the Delta Model concepts through their consulting work in the pragmatic and formidable world of business.

We also thank Stephen Rutt, the Publishing Director at Palgrave, and his entire team, particularly including Linda Norris at Aardvark Editorial. Stephen was a delightful partner who provided the personal attention, patience, and support we so desperately needed.

Our colleagues, clients, and friends, are often unsung heroes and they deserve special praise. They initially signaled to us the deficits in the existing management frameworks. They live and breathe the challenge and exhilaration of day-to-day management in very complex and changing environments. All of them share an intellectual desire to comprehend the driving forces that were acting upon their business and that were so deeply affecting their personal lives.

Last, but not least, we are indebted to our families who not only endured our long days, then months, and then years of endless collaboration on this book, but indeed supported us. When there was no light at the end of the tunnel, they provided a candle. And, when our pride occasionally exceeded the circumference of our britches, they gently deflated our girth. Our relationships with our families define the deepest form of bonding, and they are the spring of our accomplishments.

Every effort has been made to trace all the copyright holders but if any have been inadvertently overlooked the publishers will be pleased to make the necessary arrangements at the first opportunity.

LIST OF ABBREVIATIONS

AMD	Advanced Micro Devices
ARPA	Advanced Research Project Agency
ASP	Application service provider
CISC	Complex instruction set computing
CPU	Central processing unit
CRM	Customer relationship managment
DARPA	Defense Advanced Research Project Agency
DEC	Digital Equipment Corporation
DRAMS	Dynamic random access memory semiconductors
DSL	Digital subscriber loop
EBIT	Earning before taxes and interest
ERP	Enterprise resource planning
GE	General Electric
IP	Internet protocol
IPO	Initial public offering
ISP	Internet service provider
IT	Information technology
LANs	Local area networks
M/B	Market-to-book value
MVA	Market value added
NPV	Net present value
NSI	National Starch
OEM	Original equipment manufacturer
OS	Operating system
P&G	Procter & Gamble
PDA	Personal digital assistants
RISC	Reduced instruction set computing

ROA	Return on assets
ROE	Return on equity
SBU	Strategic business unit
SLA	Service level agreement
TCP	Transport control protocol
VAR	Value-added reseller
WAP	Wireless application protocol
WSJ	*Wall Street Journal*
WSJI	Wall Street Journal Interactive

The world is in the midst of what an economic historian of the future is going to call the third industrial revolution (steam being the first and electrification the second). This revolution is based upon technological leaps forward and interactions among six key technologies – microelectronics, computers, telecommunication, new man-made materials, robotics, and biotechnology. In revolutionary periods strategies have to change but, more importantly, the way that firms think about strategies has to change.

Analysts often make a distinction between what they call the new and the old economy. It is a mistaken distinction. Everyone in the old economy is going to use the new technologies. Everyone is going to have their business revolutionized by the new technologies. Everyone is on the road to joining the new economy. The differences are the speeds with which different industries are joining the new economy.

Every business firm should imagine that they are in the music business. MP3 has been invented. Young people can freely copy music. The Napsters can be legally put out of business for copyright infringement but no one can stop millions of young people from freely exchanging music. It may be illegal but it is going to happen. How does one sell music when it can be gotten without having to pay? If this problem cannot be solved within five years, there won't be a professional music industry. Hundreds of millions of dollars' worth of sales will come to an end. Such problems concentrate the attention.

If this were your problem, what would you do? It is your problem in the sense that every industry is going to face a similar problem even if the problem emerges more slowly than in the case of music.

Internet sales are going to slowly turn our biggest industry, retailing, upside down. In personal computers and airline tickets they have already done so. More than half of airline ticket sales are now electronic. Retail computer stores are fast disappearing. In finance online financial service firms have grabbed a rapidly growing 16 percent market share. Some parts of traditional retailing will survive – but which?

Everyone has to prepare to defend their economic turf. Everyone has an opportunity to conquer new economic turf. But what are the right defensive and offensive strategies?

A new business model must be developed if you are in the music industry. The new technologies must be used to defeat the new technologies. Maybe the answer is the modern equivalent of the juke box – a device where one pays for plays and is automatically charged on a debit card for every listen. The listener never buys a CD – the digital code to the music. Maybe the answer requires new laws governing intellectual property rights. Maybe for a time working together with other firms in the industry will be far more important to profitability than competing with them. But whatever the answer, survival requires new strategy thinking.

In revolutionary times no one knows what will work. Since no one knows what will work lots of things have to be tried and many will fail. Do retail customers want cheaper products via the Internet or the human interactions possible in a conventional store – entertainment shopping? In all likelihood they sometimes want one sales mode and sometimes want the other. Maybe they want to be treated like a king when they buy their Armani suits at a store with a lot of service. But at the same time they want their underwear online at the cheapest possible price. Maybe they don't want to go shopping in the heat of summer but love the Christmas shopping experience in the winter. What would Christmas be without the crowds, the music, the lights, and the elbows in the ribs? It wouldn't be Christmas.

The possibilities all require new strategic thinking. The opportunities to conquer new markets and the probabilities of failure are both higher than they used to be.

Electronic B2B markets will bring about similar changes in business-to-business sales. Traditional supplier–OEM relationships will survive in some places and be broken in others. New electronic sales relationships will emerge. Impersonal auction sales (I don't care who the seller is, I just want the cheapest possible price.) will dominate for some components. What is the right strategy for both seller and buyer when these new forms of relationship are possible?

The breakthroughs in communications that permit networking are just a small part of the overall economic revolution now underway, but they are profound when it comes to dealing with customers since they allow the business firm to surround the customer with webs of communication. Instantaneous continuous interactions are possible. How do I work out strategically the right set of interactions to bond the customer to my firm, my products, and my services?

How do I competitively position myself? How do I translate these positions into a strategic agenda? How do I align process and tasks to this agenda? What are the right metrics to track progress? How do I deal with the inevitable uncertainties?

The Delta Project provides a path for working out the answers. The best products, total customer solutions, system lock-ins can each play a role. But which, or which combination, is going to add the greatest market value? What core competencies should I develop in this new economy? What are the measures that will focus attention on the variables that lead to short- and long-term economic success?

Too often a simple focus on short-term economic variables does not lead to long-term economic success. How does General Electric cannibalize a successful division (vacuum tubes) to open up a new division (transistors and semiconductors)? It didn't. How does WalMart open up an Internet store when its success would mean the huge costs of closing down many of its conventional stores? It closed its Internet store in October 2000.

Strategically new organizations may have an advantage in revolutionary periods. But how should old firms strategically respond? One can work out economic scenarios where the right, most profitable, answer is to have a strategy for going out of business and essentially slowly selling off the franchise. But no one wants to accept this answer.

In any industry the profits earned per dollar of sales differ enormously as one moves along the value-added chain. Within a profitable industry there are very profitable and zero profit places to be. When technological revolutions occur the most profitable places move. In computers they have moved from assembly (IBM, DIGITAL twenty years ago) to components (INTEL, MICROSOFT today). How does one figure out where these profit points are moving in one's own industries and then implement a strategy for moving one's firm to these points?

With the new technologies increasing marginal returns and external networking effects are becoming much more pervasive than before. In electronic finance the costs of serving 20 million customers are not much higher than the costs of serving 10 million customers. Whatever one believes Microsoft did or did not do, its actions were not what gave it its large market share. It was the networking effects. You and I want to use the same computer operating system even if it is not the best or the cheapest system.

Diminishing costs and networking effects are leading to what has been called the bar bell economy. Strategic consulting companies will tell you that your firm has only two options. It can be a big global player doing everything everywhere (Goldman Sachs in finance) or a small, highly specialized, fast on its feet niche player (Long Term Capital Management). But what your firm cannot be is the mid-sized national bank or auto manufacturer. In autos it is widely believed that within fifteen years there will only be six to eight players and we already know the names of four – General Motors, Ford, Toyota, Volkswagen. The only question is who are the other two to four. This is why Mercedes buys Chrysler, Renault buys Nissan, and Fiat sells out to General Motors. But are these widely held views the right strategic dilemma. Are there really only two options?

It is important to understand that the world was more globalized a century ago that it is now. In 1900 the world was full of colonial empires. Britain was running half the world – India, Nigeria, South Africa, Egypt Australia, Canada, Burma. The French, Germans, and Japanese each had their empires. America was running Cuba and the Philippines. Governments led the march to globalization and companies followed. These political empires were dismantled in the aftermath of WWII.

The emerging globalization of the 21st century is very different. Companies are creating a global economy with national governments generally lagging behind and often resisting. Improvements in transportation and communication technologies are producing this global economy. Profit-maximizing business firms must search the globe for the most profitable places to sell their products and the lowest costs places to produce their products.

Global economies are not national economies just as national economies are not local–regional economies. Each requires a different strategic approach. In a global economy without global government strategies have to be developed to handle situations where there will be no laws or governments to protect one's rights. The chief area of conflict is going to be the defense of intellectual property rights. No global legal system protects the firm's most valuable assets in a knowledge-based economy.

In the process of globalization governments are losing many of their powers to regulate their economies. If firms don't like one nation's system of regulations, they just move their activities to different countries. Here again a different strategic approach is required. Systems of government regulation are not taken as given but viewed as a selection of restaurants where one has to choose where one wants to eat based upon the menu offered.

Economic revolutions are both great opportunities and great threats. Challenging WalMart with conventional retail stores is very difficult. They are the best at using that technology. Challenging them over the Internet is much easier. They have no advantages from their past experiences and have the handicaps of being tied to their current stores. An opportunity exists that did not used to exist.

At the same time new technologies can destroy whole industries. If the fuel cell were to work (something that depends upon advances in man-made materials) as an electrical power device, ninety percent of the demand for oil would disappear. A new hydrogen energy economy would emerge to take its place, but that new hydrogen economy based on solar power and sea water may not be dominated by the old oil companies. Most of their technologies for finding and processing oil would become irrelevant in this new hydrogen economy.

There has never been a better time for rethinking how one does strategic thinking and fortunately we have Hax and Wilde to chart the way – to take us on a voyage of exploration.

LESTER THUROW
December 2000

CHAPTER 1

The Delta Model: The End of Conventional Wisdom

The Delta Model encompasses a set of frameworks and methodologies that we have developed in recent years to help managers articulate and implement effective corporate and business strategies. It grew from our conviction that the world of business has been experiencing transformations of such magnitude that the existing managerial frameworks have become either invalid or incomplete. A fundamental force in these transformations has been the emergence of the networked economy. The most obvious manifestation of this networking is the Internet. Networks have enabled a degree of bonding between customers, complementors, and suppliers that has changed the drivers of profitability and, consequently, the landscape of strategy.

Bonding: The Driving Force in Strategy

A firm owes itself to its customers. They are the ultimate repository of all the firm's activities. At the heart of management and, certainly, at the heart of strategy, resides the customer. We have to serve the customer in a distinctive way if we expect to enjoy superior performance. The name of the game is to attract, satisfy, and retain the customer. The conventional method for doing this is to offer a superior product – through some combination of cost, quality, features, and speed.

Classic strategy frameworks emphasize a product orientation. They pit competitor against competitor in a rivalry where the outcome is determined by who has the best product. Consequently, old economy companies are typically consumed by a product-centric mindset. There is often a product-silo mentality that permeates the organization. Companies in the old economy tend to commoditize the customers by offering standardized products, through mass distribution channels, making limited attempts to recognize and satisfy individual customer needs. Frequently, the point of contact with the client organization is the client's purchasing department through a conventional salesforce (its own or another's) commissioned to sell products or services. This institutes an arm's length relationship that inhibits any deep knowledge being nurtured and developed.

The physical nature of distribution channels themselves present barriers that block the firm from its final consumers. Michael Dell thought that he was simply reducing costs when he decided to skip the wholesale and retail channels and deal directly with the customers. However, we discovered that this new business model opened up a world of intelligence and information that could be put to use in offering customized solutions to key customers that could have not been generated under the old distribution scheme.

The intimacy and connectivity of a networked economy offer opportunities to create competitive positions based upon the structure of the customer relationship itself, independent of the product. A business can establish an unbreakable link, deep knowledge, and close relationship that we refer to as *customer bonding*. These bonds can be directly formed with the customer, or indirectly formed through the complementors that the customer wishes to access. Both are powerful sources of margin and sustainability. The bonds represent investments made by customers and complementors in and around the business' product. The investments include things such as learning how to use the product, incorporating customer-specific data, customized interfaces to the product, among others. These are external to the product itself and are enabled by a networked economy. With this understanding comes a recognition that competition based upon the product alone misses entirely a primary force driving profitability. Bonding emerges as a central force in shaping strategy.

We have observed that most companies, even those in consumer-oriented industries, lack the intimate customer knowledge needed to address this issue properly, or they are so absorbed in a product-centric mindset that it can be a challenge to relate to this kind of strategic thinking.

At the same time, we find companies so intoxicated by the new technology that they are lulled into a false sense that the technology is the strategy, rather than a powerful tool that can enhance bonding. The bright light of technology blinds them from the customer or complementor, and the value proposition is also product based.

Whether you are in the old or new economy, the customer and complementor should be at the center of your strategy. The Delta Model enables this positioning by providing a management framework that sets strategy which incorporates bonding.

Table 1.1   Contributions of the Delta Model

Contribution:	Goal:	Implication:	Method:
The Triangle	Opening the mindset to new strategic positions	The best product does not always win	Three distinct strategic options: ■ Best Product ■ Total Customer Solutions ■ System Lock-in
Adaptive Processes	Linking strategy with execution	Execution is not the problem, linking to strategy is	Execution is captured through three Adaptive Processes: ■ Operational Effectiveness ■ Customer Targeting ■ Innovation whose roles need to change to achieve different strategic positions
Aggregate Metrics	Measuring success	Good financials do not always lead to good results	Aggregate performance metrics need to reflect each of the Adaptive Processes and their role based upon the strategic position ■ Product performance ■ Customer performance ■ Complementor performance
Granular Metrics and Feedback	Discovering performance drivers	Managing by averages leads to below average performance	Business is nonlinear. Performance is concentrated, particularly when it involves bonding. Granular Metrics allow us to focus on underlying performance drivers, to detect variability, explain, learn, and act

The Delta Model: A Brief Overview

We believe that the Delta Model offers four major contributions essential for addressing the new economy. If taken as a whole, the total model constitutes a new approach and a new discipline for strategic management. The four contributions are the Triangle, Adaptive Processes, Aggregate Metrics, and Granular Metrics and Feedback (Table 1.1).

The Triangle: Opening the Mindset to a New Set of Strategic Options

Our foremost concern in defining the strategy of a firm or business is to decide on the relevant strategic positioning. This should capture the essence of how the firm competes and serves customers in its relevant marketplace.

There are three distinct strategic options, which offer very different approaches to achieve customer bonding. They are depicted graphically through a triangle (Figure 1.1). We have chosen the Triangle to display the different strategic positions not simply because it is a visual icon that is easy to remember, but also because it represents the letter Delta, which means transformation.

The *Best Product* (BP) positioning builds upon the classical form of competition. The customer is attracted by the inherent characteristics of the product itself, either due to its Low Cost, which provides a price advantage to the customer, or due to its Differentiation, which introduces unique features that the customers value and for which they are willing to pay a premium. The products tend to be standardized and unbundled. The customers are generic, numerous, and faceless. The central focus of attention is the competitor, who we are trying to equal or surpass. Competitive advantage rests upon product economics and the internal supply chain, which provide the engine for efficient product production. Innovation is centered on the internal product development process. The liability of this

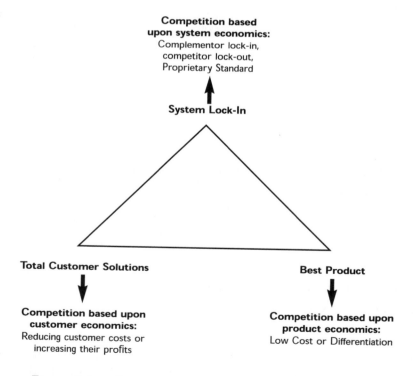

Competition based upon system economics:
Complementor lock-in,
competitor lock-out,
Proprietary Standard

System Lock-In

Total Customer Solutions

Competition based upon customer economics:
Reducing customer costs or
increasing their profits

Best Product

Competition based upon product economics:
Low Cost or Differentiation

Figure 1.1   Business model: three distinct strategic options

approach is that it generates a minimal amount of customer bonding, hence making the incumbent firms most vulnerable to new entrants. Its obsessive concern with competitors often leads to imitation and price war, resulting in rivalry and convergence; the worst of all situations. In spite of the inherent limitations of this strategic position, it is by far the most widely adopted, and the default position for those businesses that do not deliberately consider other strategic options.

The *Total Customer Solutions* (TCS) strategy is a complete reversal from the Best Product approach. Instead of commoditizing the customer, we seek a deep customer understanding and relationship that allows us to develop value propositions that bond to each individual customer. Instead of developing and marketing standardized and isolated products, we seek to provide a coherent composition of products and services aimed at enhancing the customer's ability to create their own economic value. Instead of concentrating inwardly on our own supply chain, we seek to develop an integrated supply chain that links us with key suppliers and customers. Instead of focusing on competitors and imitating them, we redefine the ways to capture and serve the customer by putting together an overall set of corporate capabilities, also sourcing from proper external parties, that enhance our product offering. We are outwardly driven; customer economics is our guide. Strategy is not war with our competitors; it is love with our customers. What would you rather do, make war or make love? The innovation process is not oriented toward the design of standardized products; it is aimed at initiatives with our key customers for the joint development of distinctive products.

The *System Lock-In* (SLI) strategic option has the widest scope; it includes the *extended enterprise* – the firm, the customers, the suppliers, and most importantly, the *complementors*. A complementor is a firm engaged in the delivery of products and services which enhance our own product and service portfolio. The key to this strategic option is to identify, attract, and nurture the complementors. They are typically external, but may also be internal to the corporation, particularly in large and diversified organizations. These complementors are rarely detected and exploited effectively. That is why a System Lock-In strategy has to start with the full corporate scope – not just for one product or business – and has to continue with the identification and incorporation of all the key external players that can become complementors. The customer continues to be the central focus, but now we extend the enterprise to the fullest. We look at the overall system supply chain, not just the supply chain for our product, and harness the innovation percolating throughout the system as a whole. The richness and depth of complementors supporting your product or service lock your product into the system and lock-out the competition. De facto Proprietary Standards are one way to achieve System Lock-In. Microsoft is the most public example. Personal computer users are compelled to buy Microsoft's Windows operating system because it has the widest selection of available software applications. Over 100,000 applications are designed to work with Windows, whereas Apple's Macintosh operating system has one quarter that number. If you want to use the latest or most esoteric software, you had better have Windows on your computer. Correspondingly, if you are a software company that wants to reach the most customers, you had better write your application to work first (or only) with Windows because it is the operating system on the most computers. This creates a powerfully positive and self-reinforcing feedback loop – people choose Windows to gain access to the most applications, applications providers choose Windows to reach the most people. Once Microsoft achieved a slight edge, it became the clear choice. The system tolerates no meaningful second place.

Distribution channels are often a key consideration for System Lock-In positioning, particularly for old economy companies. By owning or restricting access to distribution channels, competitors can be locked out. Brands can be a means to this end. Coca-Cola creates higher turnover for retailers than lesser brands, motivating the retailer to give Coca-Cola more shelf space, which further enhances the brand, further improving its turnover, and so on. There are several routes to System Lock-In. A company that achieves this position exercises an enormous amount of power. However, a System Lock-In position is not always possible; there are necessary conditions. Foremost among these is that the value of the product to a customer should significantly increase as the product is used by others. Microsoft is valuable primarily because it is used by the majority of the PC users; the *Yellow Pages* is valuable because it is used by most shoppers; eBay is valuable because it is used by the vast majority of online auction buyers; and the list goes on. This leads to a self-reinforcing value proposition. After attaining it, there are additional challenges to a System Lock-In position: how to sustain it and exercise this power in an ethical way that does not create excesses of monopolistic behavior.

In a Best Product position the value proposition to the customer is the product and its attributes are independent of the customer. In a Total Customer Solutions position, the value proposition to the customer is enhanced by the interaction between the customer and the product, which leads to bonding with existing customers. In a System Lock-In position, the value proposition to the customer is enhanced by interaction with other customers, which leads to bonding with existing and new customers. Bonding reflects externalities beyond the product itself.

Value Creation by Each Strategic Option: Empirical Evidence

Economic returns differ markedly by strategic position. We collected empirical evidence from over 100 companies occupying a range of strategic positions. Our sample included the examples used in this book plus additional firms drawn from the Fortune 500 whose corporate-wide strategies could be clearly categorized as emphasizing one of the three alternatives in the Triangle. The Delta Model applies to companies pursuing different options in their different business units, but because such companies have blended the overall performance measures which then resist clear analysis, we pulled them from the sample. Moreover, our sample is selected from established (and hence old economy) firms with longstanding records of performance in order to avoid the speculative and volatile valuations that are a current part of the Internet marketplace at the time this book was written.

The acid test in terms of the merits of each option is the economic value that the companies are able to create for their shareholders. We use two common, and very popular, measures of performance: market value added (MVA) and market-to-book ratio (M/B).

Market value added measures the difference between a company's total market value of equity and debt and its book value, which is the total amount that investors of equity and debt have contributed to the company. This metric has received increasing currency as a key indicator to rank performance. In particular, *Fortune* magazine and *The Journal of Applied Corporate Finance* use it as the leading gauge of financial attainment. On this measure, System Lock-In businesses produce an MVA, which, on average, is over four times that of Best Product companies; Total Customer Solutions firms generate over 1.5 times the MVA of Best Product organizations. The results are shown in Table 1.2.

The market-to-book ratio compares the value that shareholders place on the business based upon their assessment of the expected future cashflows relative to the past resources that have been committed to the business. In other words, if a total of $1 million has been invested in a business that today is valued at $2 million, then the market-to-book ratio is 2. Obviously, the strategy and execution of the business has a multiplier effect that creates the additional value. The empirical data shows that the System Lock-In companies have an M/B ratio that is on average twice as large as

Table 1.2   Value creation by each strategic option: empirical evidence

	Number of firms	Market Value Added			Market-to-Book Value		
		Mean	Standard deviation	Index	Mean	Standard deviation	Index
Best Product	74	14.26	16.57	1.0	5.88	9.33	1.0
Total Customer Solutions	67	22.38	28.14	1.6	7.29	7.7	1.2
System Lock-In	16	57.15	48.67	4.0	11.98	5.86	2.0

the Best Product companies. The Total Customer Solutions companies have an average M/B that is 20% higher than that of the Best Product firms (Table 1.2).

We have found a significant financial premium for companies that can achieve a Total Customer Solutions position, and a further enhanced premium for those attaining System Lock-In. However, there are important caveats. This conclusion reflects the performance of companies that have successfully arrived at these positions, it does not account for those that have attempted and failed. There may be added risk and greater difficulty in reaching for the brass ring of System Lock-In or the annuities attached to Total Customer Solutions. Furthermore, while there are striking rewards that can draw you to new strategies, we are not implying that the strategic answer for all companies is the same.

The Various Dimensions of the Triangle – Beware the Product-centric Mindset

Table 1.3 provides a summary of the managerial differences among the three strategic positionings of the Triangle. Many companies implicitly follow the practices of the Best Product position. In fact, these actions are often praised as 'best practices' that should be applied by all companies. These include total quality management, reengineering, time-based competition, benchmarking, and so on. Best practices are a by-product of a product-centric mentality. Table 1.4 makes clear the consequences of adopting, without much reflection, a Best Product position. We are not suggesting that a Best Product strategy cannot be the most appropriate one, as there are excellent companies which are truly extraordinary in every conceivable dimension of performance which are part of that vertex of the Triangle. What we want to warn against is the passive adoption of this strategy without considering other alternatives.

Table 1.3   The various dimensions of the Triangle

Competitive Positioning	Best Product	Total Customer Solutions	System Lock-In
Strategic Focus	*Product* The business, its Industry and its competitors	*Corporation* The firm, its customers, and its suppliers	*The extended enterprise* The firm, its customers, its suppliers, and its complementors
Relevant Benchmarking	Competitors	Customers	Complementors
The Customer Value Proposition	*Product focus* Product economics	*Customer focus* Customer economics	*System focus* System economics
Product Offerings	Standardized products	Customized bundle of products and services	Portfolio of products and services extended by complementors
Relevant Supply Chain	*Internal supply chain*	*Integrated supply chain* Suppliers, the firm and the customers	*System supply chain* Suppliers, the firm, the customers, and the complementors
Relevant Channels	Generic channels, mass distribution	Targeted direct channel	Channels to complementors and customers
Impact on Brands	*Product orientation* Brand explosion	*Brands harmonized around the customer* Coherent portfolio of brands	*Brands harmonized around the system* System economics
Innovation Focus	Internal product development	Joint product innovation with customer	Open architecture, complementors as key investors
IT Role	*Internal support* E.g., SAP	*Customer and supplier support* E.g. e-business and e-commerce	*Total network support* E.g. e-system
Degree of Customer Bonding	*Very small* Depends exclusively on the product characteristics	*Potentially high* Reinforced by customization and mutual learning	*Potentially the highest* Reinforced by competitor lock-out and complementor lock-in

The danger of 'functional silos' is well known. The fact of the matter is that functions rarely act as silos. By their very nature they are obliged to exercise a high degree of synergy in an organization. If, in a functionally structured company, you are in charge of R&D, you are supposed to care for all the innovation issues across all the products in your company and it is hard to do otherwise; likewise, if you are in charge of finance, human resources, manufacturing, and so forth. Product-centric business units are the prevalent silos in today's organizations. These often represent parochial territory that prevent a firm from intelligently using all its capabilities and creatively serving the customer as effectively as it could.

If you look at Table 1.3 under the 'Best Product' column, you can immediately visualize the narrow cascade of responses that are associated with this option. The strategic focus is the single product; the relevant benchmarks are the competitors; the customer value proposition is dictated by the internal product economics; the product offering is standardized; the relevant supply chain is internal; the channels are generic and mass-driven; the product orientation leads to an explosion of disconnected brands; the innovation process is self-centered; the IT role, which is so critical to management today, deals with internal information. As a result, this brings a feeble degree of customer bonding and a rather conventional view of the business, which might limit creativity. It is a fundamentally inwardly oriented strategy, with its outside view centered on competitors. With this perspective in mind, you can see how this is totally divorced from a network-based Internet economy.

Contrast the Best Product option with the Total Customer Solutions positioning. You can envision the significant enrichment in scope and content that takes place. The strategic scope now looks across the corporation, not just a single product or business; the relevant benchmarks are of the customer's activities, not just the competitors'; the customer value proposition is dictated by the customer's economics, not just the product's internal economics; the product offering is often customized, rather than standardized; the relevant supply chain includes the customer, as well as the supplier; the channels are targeted and direct, not wholesale through mass channels; the customer solution orientation leads to a harmonization of brands; the innovation process emphasizes joint development with the customer, not just the typical stand-alone R&D center; the role of IT is to use the broadly available Internet protocols and infrastructure to inextricably link the customer to the firm, rather than to use proprietary internally oriented software. In the end, these actions create strong bonds to existing customers and generate assets and skills for the customer and the firm that are unique to that relationship. The firm benefits from innovation by the customer as well as from their own efforts. This is an outwardly oriented strategy, centered on the customer. In contrast with the Best Product strategy, this position is enabled, if not dependent, on the network-based Internet economy.

When we adopt the System Lock-In strategic positioning, we have to extend our perspectives even further. The strategic scope now covers the entire system including complementors that accompany, augment, or enhance your product, even though they may not be in the same 'product' industry; the relevant benchmarks necessarily encompass the complementor; the customer value proposition is focused on the system, not just on what the product does on its own; the product offering entails the portfolio of applications extended by complementors; the relevant supply chain also includes the complementors; the channels to customers and complementors are massive, direct and indirect because our share will dominate the system; the brand is harmonized around the system, a la Intel inside or Microsoft compatibility; the innovation process harnesses the creative juices of a multitude of complementors; the role of IT is to support the integration, efficiency, and compatibility of the complementors; the entire system benefits from a common network interface. In the end, the system is bonded to the product. It attracts new customers to the product as well as adhering to existing customers. This strategy is centered on the system, particularly the complementors.

A System Lock-In position can best develop when the industry is undergoing major transition, such as induced by new technology, deregulation, and globalization. In these situations, the traditional integrated competitors often become disaggregated into component pieces. New standards and exchanges then emerge to help reconnect the newly fragmented elements.

The Adaptive Processes – How to Genuinely Link Strategy and Execution

John S. Reed, the past Chairman of CitiGroup, once said:[1] 'A CEO has just two jobs, decide what to do and making it happen. And, ninety percent of the job is making it happen. When you are running a company execution becomes everything.' To guide managers in the 'what to do' question, the Triangle dramatically expands the sources of profitability to describe three distinct choices for strategic positioning: Best Product, Total Customer Solutions, and System Lock-In.

'How to make it happen' depends first and foremost on the proper alignment of the core activities of the business with the chosen strategy. Alignment is the operative term. Each strategic position of the Triangle generates a different set of tasks and activities. Our research suggests that the primary obstacle in execution is not working harder, with less error, faster, or smarter, but is failing to align the activities of execution with the specific requirements inherent in the desired strategic position of the business.

To accomplish this goal, we identified the three business processes that capture the essential tasks of execution. The core activities of the firm are embodied in three processes:

1. Operational Effectiveness (OE) – the production and delivery of goods and services.
2. Customer Targeting (CT) – the management of the customer interface.
3. Innovation (I) – the process of new product development.

Collectively we call them Adaptive Processes, to emphasize the changing nature of the tasks. Figure 1.2 represents the interactions that exist between the Triangle which is critical to define the changing role of each Adaptive Process and among the processes themselves, since each one influences the other.

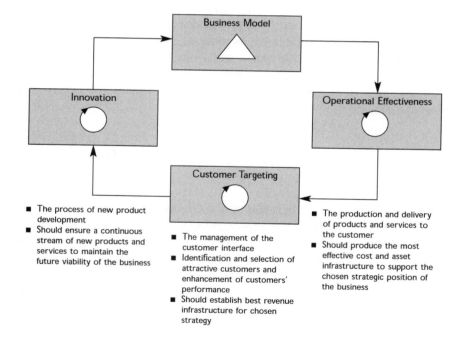

Figure 1.2   The Adaptive Processes: linking strategy with execution

Table 1.4   Role of the Adaptive Processes in
supporting the strategic options of the Triangle

		STRATEGIC POSITIONING		
		Best Product	**Total Customer Solutions**	**System Lock-In**
ADAPTIVE PROCESS	Operational Effectiveness	*Best Product Cost* ■ Identify product cost drivers ■ Improve stand-alone product cost	*Best Customer Benefits* ■ Improve customer economics ■ Improve horizontal linkages in the components of total solutions	*Best System Performance* ■ Improve system performance drivers ■ Integrate complementors to improve system performance
	Customer Targeting	*Target Distribution Channels* ■ Maximize coverage through multiple channels ■ Obtain low-cost distribution ■ Identify and enhance the profitability of each product by channel ■ Maximize product share	*Target Customer Bundles* ■ Identify and exploit opportunities to add value to key customers by bundling solutions and customization ■ Increase customer value and possible alliances to bundle solutions ■ Select key vertical markets ■ Examine channel ownership options ■ Maximize customer share	*Target System Architecture* ■ Identify leading complementors in the system ■ Expand number and variety of complementors ■ Establish channels to complementors, as well as customers ■ Consolidate high share with complementors
	Innovation	*Product Innovation* ■ Develop family of products based on common platform ■ First to market, or follow rapidly – stream of products	*Customer Service Innovation* ■ Identify and exploit joint development linked to the customer value chain ■ Expand your offer into the customer value chain to improve customer economics ■ Integrate and innovate customer care functions ■ Increase customer lock-in through customization and learning	*System Innovation* ■ Create customer and system lock-in, and competitive lock-out ■ Design proprietary and open architecture – Complex interfaces – Rapid evolution – Backward compatibility ■ Facilitate complementor as well as customer innovation on our platform

Strategy is not effective if kept at an abstract level. The Adaptive Processes spell out in detail their unique supportive role for each of the three strategic positions in the Triangle. Figure 1.2 summarizes these roles.

What we find particularly alarming is that in practice most managers implicitly define each process according to a Best Product strategy. Namely, Operational Effectiveness seeks to establish an internally efficient cost infrastructure; Customer Targeting seeks maximum coverage through distribution channels; and Innovation seeks the speedy development of the firm's products aided by appropriate platforms and first-to-market expectations. As recognized in Table 1.4, the situation is starkly different when the Adaptive Processes support the TCS and the SLI strategic options.

In the TCS strategy, the key objective of Operational Effectiveness is the maximization of customer value, and this can only be achieved through consideration of the combined value chain of the firm and its customers. Customer Targeting is aimed at developing individual customer bonds, by structurally enhancing the interface with the customer and by creating assets in the customer's knowledge of your product or services. Innovation aims for the development of a composition of customized products jointly with the customer.

In the SLI strategic position the role of each process again changes. Now Operational Effectiveness is concerned with enhancing the overall system performance, often by consolidating strong partnerships with complementors. Customer Targeting attempts to consolidate a harmonized system architecture through a network of complementors and complementor interfaces. The ultimate goal of Innovation is to develop and appropriate an industry standard, facilitating a broad range of applications.

Once more, a primary objective is to raise the awareness of the product-centric mentality and to expand the alternatives open to managers. Rivalry and competition may not be the winning strategies.

Aggregate Metrics

Just as activities need to vary by strategy, so do the measures of success. Performance measurements and quantifiable indicators are essential for the development, execution, and monitoring of the desired strategy. The Delta Model aligns performance metrics to the strategic options selected, and recognizes that these metrics will be fundamentally different depending on the strategic position they intend to support.

There are two types of metrics. First, we need Aggregate Metrics to give us the overall, integrated view of the business and the firm's performance. Second, we need Granular Metrics that will allow us to decipher the fundamental performance drivers.

The Aggregate Metrics we will highlight are a direct by-product of the Adaptive Processes. Since these processes are the instruments for the execution of each strategic option, they also serve as guidelines to define the strategy performance. Table 1.5 provides a summary of a selected set of generic metrics according to Adaptive Processes and strategic options.

Table 1.5   Performance metrics for the business drivers of the Delta Model

		STRATEGIC POSITIONING		
		Best Product	**Total Customer Solutions**	**System Lock-In**
ADAPTIVE PROCESS	Operational Effectiveness (cost drivers)	▪ Cost performance – Unit cost – Life cycle cost – Variable and total cost ▪ Cost drivers ▪ Quality performance ▪ Degree of differentiation	▪ Customer value chain – total cost – total revenue and profit ▪ Customer economic drivers ▪ Impact on customer profit due to our service vs. competitors	▪ Description of system infrastructure ▪ Total system costs/revenues ▪ Complementor's investments and profits ▪ Complementor costs of adhering to your standard ▪ System performance drivers
	Customer Targeting (profit drivers)	▪ Product market share ▪ Channel cost ▪ Product profit – by product type – by offer – by channel ▪ Profit drivers	▪ Customer share ▪ Customer retention ▪ Our profitability by customer – individual and by segment ▪ Customer bonding – switching costs	▪ System market share ▪ Our share of complementors – % of investments tied to our proprietary standard ▪ Our profit by complementor
	Innovation (renewal drivers)	▪ Rate of product introduction ▪ Time to market ▪ Percent of sales from new products ▪ Cost of product development ▪ R&D as % of sales	▪ Relative involvement in customer value chain ▪ Percent of product development – from joint development – customized ▪ Degree of product scope – current vs. potential bundling	▪ Switching costs for complementors and for customers ▪ Rate of product development ▪ Cost of competitors to imitate standard

Of course, specific tailor-made metrics could and should be introduced in each individual business situation.

The Aggregate Metrics intrinsic to the Adaptive Processes stand in contrast to the conventional measures of success, which focus on financial measures, such as return on equity (ROE), return on assets (ROA), earning before taxes and interest (EBIT), and so on. Financial metrics are the ultimate manifestation of overall past performance and are critical, but they are poor predictors of future performance and provide few clues regarding the performance of the tasks of execution. Correspondingly, the Aggregate Metrics inherent in the Adaptive Processes reflect the top line performance of execution. Granular Metrics (discussed next) are necessary to understand the performance drivers and are indicators of future performance. While not yet broadly applied in industry, the idea of incorporating non-financial metrics is well established. The Delta Model provides an integrated framework that naturally gives rise to the appropriate metrics and describes how these change according to the distinct strategic positions.

Notice that the various processes assume metrics related to their defined charters: Operational Effectiveness is the depository of the cost drivers; Customer Targeting, of the profit drivers; and Innovation, of the renewal drivers. Also notice that the BP options are product oriented; TCS, customer oriented; and SLI, system oriented. However, most firms today only concentrate their attention on product-oriented opportunities. It is yet another manifestation of the pervasive product-centric mindset.

Granular Metrics and Feedback

To fully appreciate the necessity of Granular Metrics in a management framework for the new economy we should return to the fundamental force enabling new strategic positions – bonding. Bonding is remarkable because it is self-reinforcing. Where cost-based competition grows more difficult with each incremental improvement (and exhibits diminishing returns), bonding is an attractive force that naturally accelerates under its own power. There are a variety of popular terms used to describe this phenomenon ranging from increasing returns to viral effects. The essential characteristic is a positive feedback loop among market participants (end-users, suppliers, complementors) that is inherent in certain strategic positions. For example, eBay is the beneficiary of buyers wanting to shop at the market exchange with the most sellers, and sellers preferring the exchange with the most buyers. This is a positive feedback loop that creates a Dominant Exchange, leaving little room for competitors to occupy the same space. The same feedback can occur in the individual bonding to a customer. For example, customers using Schwab's One Source account learn how to use a range of its services, from checking and credit cards to charitable donation services. They also customize these services as they use them, such as adding money wiring or bill paying vendors. This learning and customization further induces the customer to invest even more in the Schwab service, further enhancing the unique bond between the customer and Schwab.

From feedback emerge three distinctive properties – nonlinearity, concentrations, and sensitive dependence. Nonlinearity is evident in the eBay exchange example; growth in users creates an exponential growth in the value of the exchange. If only four people used this exchange to buy and sell there would be the possibility of twelve different transactions (each user can buy or sell from the three others). Adding another user expands the number of possible transactions to twenty (possible transaction pairs equal n, the number of users, multiplied by n − 1, the number of users addressable by any one user). Six users expand the possibilities to thirty, seven expand the possibilities to forty-two, eight to fifty six, and so on. Contrast this to a conventional retailing relationship where each additional shopper visiting a store simply adds one more transactional possibility. Feedback creates an exponential (n^2), or nonlinear relationship. Nonlinear systems exhibit massive concentrations. Concentrations in cost, where a small portion of activities drives a disproportionate amount of effort; or in profits, where a small number of customers account for a vast majority of the earnings; or in collateral assets, where a small number of key complementors are central to the value proposition of the system. In a nonlinear world, managing by averages is at best misleading, and at worse dysfunctional. Furthermore, these concentrations are subject to sensitive dependence, as seemingly minor and detailed factors are magnified through a nonlinear system to yield huge consequences. Granular Metrics are necessary to succeed in this environment:

- They can identify the natural economic concentrations and inherent variability in business.
- They represent the performance drivers, which often occur at the detailed intersection of the three dimensions highlighted in the Delta Model: product, customer, and complementor.
- They enable a customized response at a customer and complementor specific level, which is so critical to secure bonding.

Granular segmentation is central to the effectiveness of the Adaptive Processes because it enables one to focus, detect variability, explain it, learn from it, and act. This in itself constitutes a response mechanism that is an important part of each Adaptive Process and is necessary in order to continually adapt strategy and to self-direct the day-to-day tasks of execution.

The forces of the new economy take us full circle, from bonding as strategy to Granular Metrics as the tools to manage bonding. Our research shows that a management framework must integrate the large with the small. There are profoundly new strategic positions for a business to consider, and execution must wrestle with specific details to realize these new sources of profitability.

How We Organized the Book

The book is organized to take the reader step by step through the Delta Model. This first chapter provides a brief overview of the integrated framework. Since a key message of the Delta Model is the need for an integrated plan of attack, this is a critical chapter to show how the pieces come together to yield more than the sum of its parts. Alignment of strategy with execution is a fundamental element of the Delta Model, and this is essential when attempting to reposition a business to take advantage of bonding and the forces of a networked economy. Incumbent firms are entrenched in the product-centric mindset, a legacy of the industrial era, and shifting position requires a change in activities, processes, and metrics.

Chapter 2 describes the Triangle and contrasts it with the most influential and current management frameworks, Porter's framework of Competitive Advantage and the Resource-Based View. The current frameworks for business strategy are rooted in the old economy and did not anticipate the changes to the competitive landscape wrought by the forces of networking. They are correct, but incomplete, and the Delta Model is a necessary complement. The networked economy has made bonding a pervasive force. Bonding is a continuum and leads to eight distinct ways of achieving the strategic positions in the Triangle.

In Chapters 3, 4 and 5, we describe in detail the strategic positions in the Triangle, and the eight ways to achieve them. Competing as a Best Product is achieved through Low Cost or Differentiation, the traditional options in strategy. We have observed three ways to achieve Total Customer Solutions: Redefining Customer Experience, Horizontal Breadth, and Customer Integration. There are also three ways to achieve a System Lock-In position: Restricted Access, Dominant Exchange, and Proprietary Standard.

In Chapter 6, we look at a case example to understand how to set a Strategic Agenda. Fifteen years ago Motorola was the leading corporation in the world for the semiconductor industry. By 1997, they had dropped to number 5 with a mere 6% of the market share. The case describes the transformation that is taking place within Motorola to recapture its leadership. The Delta Model is the driving intellectual force behind this strategic repositioning.

The case diagnoses the current situation, defines the new strategic position of the business, describes the mission statement, and the required Strategic Agenda. It demonstrates how the Delta Model can be implemented in a complex and high stakes situation.

In Chapter 7, we begin to link execution with strategy. We define the three Adaptive Processes and analyze extensively the changing role of each process to support each strategic position. Not surprisingly, we uncover that the common interpretation of the processes implicitly assumes that they are intending to support the Best Product strategy. This stands in stark contrast to the very different nature of the processes when properly pursuing a Total Customer Solutions or System Lock-In strategy.

In Chapter 8 we examine the Internet industry through the lens of the Delta Model. Most analysts admit that they do not know how many companies in the Internet industry will make money. At the same time, they all recognize the new infrastructure as a clear and persistent threat to the incumbent firms who do not adopt some e-business strategy. Whereas many categorize companies as 'content', or 'B2B' (business to business), or 'B2C' (business to consumer), or 'infrastructure', the more relevant dimensions from a strategy (and profitability) perspective are Best Product, Total Customer Solutions, and System Lock-In. We learn important lessons for the dot.coms and the incumbents.

With the strategy defined and the tasks aligned, in Chapter 9 we address the question of how to measure success, that is, metrics. The Delta Model presents a complete set of Aggregate Metrics that cover dimensions well beyond the financials. The alignment of the strategic position with the processes points to the proper design of aggregate measures.

Without denying the significance of Aggregate Metrics, they are not enough. In Chapter 10 we introduce Granular Metrics to close the loop on bonding. Complex businesses cannot be run with a handful of Aggregate Metrics alone, Granular Metrics are necessary to identify the natural concentrations of value, to reflect the underlying performance drivers, and to customize the bonds with individual customers and complementors. We show how companies integrate Granular Metrics into experimental feedback mechanisms as part of their Operational Effectiveness, Customer Targeting, and Innovation processes in order to respond to the market. The Delta Model can generate profound and deep change in a company, as is the case when attempting to move from one vertex to another vertex in the Triangle. This transformation brings us into unknown territory full of risks and uncertainty. Experimentation and testing are imperative when facing fundamental transformation, it enhances our knowledge and improves the odds of success. Failures are rife in the design of any grand plan, so you have to structure the business to learn systematically from them.

Chapter 11 describes the transformation of an entire industry. The Delta Model is particularly suited to the demands of the new economy, whether or not the Internet is central to the transformation. The transformation of the electric utility industry is being initiated by deregulation, although technological forces also play a role. This transition is similar to the one that has occurred in other industries including the computer industry, financial services, and telecommunications. Deregulation and technology apply a 10X force to the existing monolithic entities, fragmenting them and rotating the industry from a vertical to a horizontal structure. New companies enter each level of the value chain, competing with the fragmented residual businesses of the established participants. Standards and exchanges often emerge to facilitate the interoperability of the disaggregated parts. Each new business is best suited for very different strategic options, as is evident from the Delta Model.

Chapter 12 unifies the various frameworks of strategy. The most celebrated and influential frameworks of strategy – Porter's Competitive Advantage and the Resource-Based View of the firm – are insightful guides to developing strategy, but they are fundamentally incomplete. They fail to explain the new sources of profitability and do not serve as an effective guide to define superior strategic options in our new and complex environment. The Delta Model complements the perspectives of the existing frameworks, extends them to encompass new economic forces, and provides the integrative glue that results in a unified framework.

Note

1.   MIT Tech Talk, April 29, 1998.

CHAPTER 2

The Triangle: Strategy Based upon Bonding

An effective business model needs to meet two criteria. First, the model should be able to explain how businesses and firms achieve superior financial performance. This is the *descriptive* side of the model. By observing the actual performance of a collection of businesses and applying the basic concepts implicit in the model, we can understand better the heterogeneity in firm performance. Second, and perhaps more important from a practical point of view, is the *normative* side of the model. The framework should provide guidelines and tools that will help to create a winning strategy and support the successful implementation of that strategy. The existing business models are at best incomplete in both dimensions. Why is this so?

In spite of the enormous proliferation of competing schemes in the business strategy literature, there are just two fundamental paradigms that have emerged as most influential in the last two decades. First, Competitive Advantage, as proposed by Michael Porter[1] from the Harvard Business School in the 1980s, and, second, the Resource-Based View[2] of the firm that evolved during the 1990s. A more elaborate description of these frameworks is provided in Chapter 12.

Porter's arguments are drawn from the work of organizational economists who place the industry as the central focus of strategic attention. According to Porter's framework, structural characteristics of a firm's industry best explain variations in firm performance. In other words, Porter sees good industries, such as pharmaceuticals, where most players enjoy high margins, and he sees bad industries, such as trucking, where most participants suffer from low profitability. The industry is an organization of activities that generates economic 'rents.' To gain access to the highest rents, a firm needs to position itself properly by accumulating bargaining power against competitors, suppliers, and customers, and by erecting entry barriers against substitutes and new entrants. These tasks constitute the five forces made famous by Porter, to which we return at the end of the chapter.

A company in an industry with few competitors, thousands of competing suppliers, millions of eager customers, high barriers to entry (perhaps because government patents exclude new entrants), and no possibility of another company's product substituting for its own has satisfied the first requirement for a promising strategy. It has found what should be an enormously profitable industry. Now all the company must do is position itself as the dominant competitor in order to control the lion's share of the industry's profits. Using the language of economics, a successful firm is one that appropriates monopolistic rents. In other words, in the industry as a whole or in a segment of the industry, the firm establishes itself as the dominant (or sole) competitor.

The logical conclusion from this perspective is that there are only two ways to compete: through Low Cost or product Differentiation. Most managers in the 1980s became familiar with Porter's taxonomy. Cost leadership is achieved through the aggressive pursuit of economies of scale, product and process simplification, and significant product market share that allows companies to exploit experience and learning effects. Differentiation calls for creating a product that the customer perceives as highly valuable and unique. Approaches to Differentiation can take many forms: design of brand image, technology, features, customer service, and dealer networks.

From Porter's perspective, strategy is about defeating competitors through fierce rivalry, battling customers and suppliers with bargaining power, and creating obstacles for new participants. In a single word, strategy is war. Furthermore, the exclusive strategic positions of Low Cost and Differentiation are centered on product economics. The resulting mentality of this approach, which is widely apparent in the business world, has enormous implications that we will address later.

Instead of looking at the industry as the source of profitability, the Resource-Based View of the firm argues that the attention should turn to the firm. Instead of seeking profitability at the intersection of the products and markets, the Resource-Based View looks for value derived from resources, capabilities and competencies. Instead of relying on monopoly rents, premium returns depend upon what economists refer to as 'Ricardian rents.' What makes one firm different from another is its ability to appropriate resources that are valuable, rare, and difficult to substitute or imitate. The roots of this perspective go back to David Ricardo,[3] a British economist who lived in the early 1800s. Ricardo tried to explain variations in farm profitability by pointing to differences in the supply of fertile land. Proponents of the Resource-Based View had the insight to recognize that management skills, information capabilities, and administrative processes can also be regarded as scarce factors able to generate Ricardian rents.

The Resource-Based View has drawbacks in a practical setting because of the inherent ambiguity in what constitutes a unique resource. Several attempts have been made to catalog and list competencies. In the end, most sound generic and superficial. By emphasizing the supply side of the firm's activities the Resource-Based View carries an inward bias, concentrating exclusively on the internal capabilities of the firm, and a desire to achieve competitive advantage in a zero-sum game. In a single phrase, this perspective argues that strategy is real estate.

Expanding the Strategic Options

The conventional strategic options have to be expanded to explain the new sources of profitability observed in today's economy. By adding to the options, we complement Porter's model, which offers Low Cost and Differentiation as the only genuine strategic positions. With regard to the Resource-Based View of the firm, each strategic option in the Delta Model calls for a distinct set of resources and capabilities. This provides resource-based implications in a very tangible and practical setting. The central actor in Porter's model or in the Resource-Based View is the competitor. Low Cost and Differentiation help a firm to beat competitors by improving the firm's product economics; hence we call this orientation 'Best Product.'

The Best Product strategy continues to be relevant; however, the problem is that in the current environment it does not describe all the ways that companies compete, nor is it always the most effective strategic position. Two companies illustrate this point.

Microsoft has its supporters and detractors, but on one point everybody agrees – it has been a phenomenal business success. It is perhaps *the* model for success for a modern business in a complex environment. By 2000, Microsoft had created half a trillion dollars of market value in excess of debt and book equity. It beat the all-powerful IBM at its own game, and it created the richest man in the world in the process. Did it do this by having the Best Product? Microsoft does not have a 90% share of the market for PC operating systems because of low price. While Microsoft may have an effective cost infrastructure, no one would argue that the company's position was based on being a low-cost provider. At the same time, few would argue that their operating systems, and most certainly the MS DOS product that fueled their dominance, had the best features or were the easiest to use. Many would say Apple had, and perhaps still has, the best set of differentiated features. Nonetheless, Microsoft is unambiguously the market leader. The source of their success is a strategy that is not Best Product, but one that is supported by the economics of the system as a whole. We label this position 'System Lock-In.' Customers are attracted to Microsoft's operating system because more companies write applications for it than for any other operating system. These companies are critical complementors to Microsoft, and the complementors rather than the product are the explanation for Microsoft's success.

MCI WorldCom is a small telecommunications company with an impressive market value. Over a 15-year period, MCI WorldCom grew from nothing to over $70 billion in market value, with about $36 billion in annual revenue by 2000. How did a small company do this? The predominant activity at MCI WorldCom's Jackson, Mississippi headquarters is acquisition – WorldCom has acquired over 30 companies since its inception in 1985. The focus of the acquisitions has not been to create the product with the lowest cost, but, to expand the breadth of the company's products from long distance, to include local services through the acquisition of MFS and Brooks Fiber, Internet access through the acquisition of UUNet and ANS, and data services through the acquisition of WilTel. MCI WorldCom now enjoys a small product market share across many products. The focus of the acquisitions was not on product differentiation. In fact, each of the products could almost be considered commodities in light of the competitive situations in their respective industries. Nevertheless, MCI WorldCom created enormous value by pursuing a unique strategy. Instead of choosing a Best Product strategy, MCI WorldCom chose to focus more on the customer's total needs. We label this position 'Total Customer Solutions.' The central actor is now the customer, and the objective is to improve the customer's economics rather than the internal product economics.

The two strategies of Total Customer Solutions and System Lock-In produce a new business model that details how to compete successfully in the 21st-century economy.

The Triangle: Three Distinctive Strategic Options

The Triangle represents a business model that fills a significant void in the development of strategic thinking. It offers three potential options as distinct sources of profitability for a business: Best Product, Total Customer Solutions, and System Lock-In (Figure 2.1). Each option concentrates its attention on a different actor. Best Product attempts to outrun the competitors. Total Customer Solutions seeks a relationship that enhances the customers' performance and resulting profitability. System Lock-In attempts to attract complementors by providing mutually beneficial opportunities that enhance system performance, ultimately locking in customers and locking out competitors.

The primary message from the Triangle is that bonding is a powerful source of profitability. Our research has led us to two observations. First, bonding is a continuum. We can cut the Triangle at the Best Product point and extend it into a straight line ending at the System Lock-In point. Bonding is most feeble at the Best Product point, especially when the business is ambiguously aiming for some mixture of Low Cost and Differentiation. Bonding is strongest at the point of System Lock-In. Second, bonding is the adhesive between a business and its customers and complementors, thus highlighting two participants beyond competitors that require comprehensive and in-depth understanding. From the customer perspective, we all know intuitively that customer relationships are crucial, but the economics

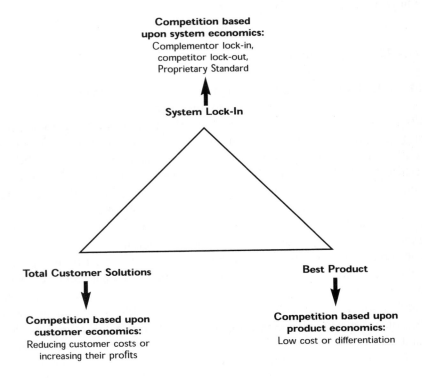

Figure 2.1   Business model: three distinct strategic options

and structural alternatives of that relationship have not traditionally been included in the strategy framework itself. As far as the complementors are concerned, even the concept is foreign to most companies.

The Bonding Continuum: The Various Degrees of Product, Customer, and System Bonding

Bonding is a primary element in the description of each of the three distinct strategic positions in the Delta Model. It is so central to the achievement of competitive advantage that it deserves close examination. Bonding is a continuum that extends from the first loyalty that a customer feels toward a product to a full lock-in with Proprietary Standards.

We have identified four stages in the bonding continuum as character-ized in Figure 2.2. A successful Best Product business should generate a dominant design. Total Customer Solutions draws upon customer lock-in. System Lock-In utilizes the most complete form of bonding enabling competitive lock-out as well as customer lock-in.

The Dominant Design

In the first stage, dominant design, customers are attracted to a product because it excels in the dimensions they care about. If the product posi-tioning is one of Low Cost, it is the low price that draws the customer. If the strategic positioning is one of Differentiation, it is the features or services that accompany the product that attract the customer. In an embryonic industry without a commonly accepted product design there is typically an enormous amount of experimentation that occurs in the offers of various competitors. This product variety eventually consolidates to a common design, one that has the features and characteristics that people learn to expect from that product type. This emerging dominant design captures the common requirements of many types of users for a particular product, although it may not exactly meet the requirements of a particular segment of the customer base. All products in that category are typically compelled to emulate the dominant design because it plainly exhibits the dimensions that consumers expect and use in comparison shopping. In this regard the domi-nant design is a generic and standardized offer as opposed to customized.

The competitor generating this design captures the first element of loyalty from customers, as well as the benefits of first mover advantage. As an example, IBM enjoyed the benefits of a dominant design with its PC, which

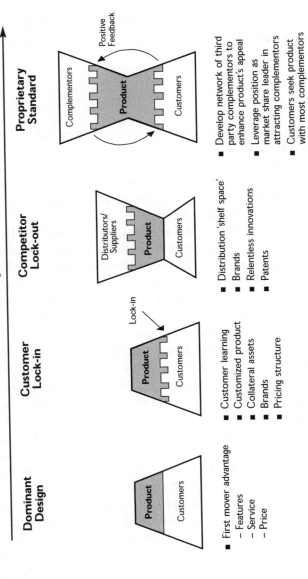

Figure 2.2 Bonding continuum

included a TV monitor, a standard disk drive, the QWERTY keyboard, the Intel chip, an open architecture, and the MS DOS operating system. They came together to define the ideal PC for the market, which would later have to be emulated by every other PC-compatible manufacturer in the market, if they wanted to be quickly accepted by the customer.

The bonding at this extreme is feeble. Customer loyalty is to the attributes of the product and they swiftly switch to a different provider when offered superior attributes.

Customer Lock-in

After dominant design, the first degree of bonding is customer lock-in. In this instance, customers may initially be attracted to a product due to its attributes but are then retained due to a host of externalities that are created as the customer uses the product. The switching costs are not infinite, but there are barriers to change that go well beyond the product itself. Customization and learning are the primary tools for creating customer lock-in.

In the consumer market for financial services, customized bundles of services provide a compelling example. Merrill Lynch first introduced customer management accounts, but Fidelity and Schwab quickly followed suit. These accounts are tailored to the circumstances of the user; characteristics of bill payment, brokerage, mutual fund investments, IRA accounts, charitable donation services, credit cards, and checking are customer specific and managed by the customer. Moving an account is a laborious activity for the consumer involving restating a number of customized preferences and variables that creates a high switching cost for the customer.

Customization is a trend with a long history, but it is usually presumed to be an effort by the manufacturer to tailor a product to meet the needs of a narrow segment, or perhaps just one customer. This practice has value in differentiating an offer, but it does not create bonding. Bonds are created when the customer produces the customization. Customization is analogous to writing an application. The more applications you write based upon a particular service, the more you have invested in the service and the more difficult it is for you to switch products. For example, personalized web pages on the Yahoo! portal create lock-in. After investing the time to construct pages with the information you want to see, you are considerably vested in the service. Even if a better portal comes along, you will hesitate to re-create this sunk cost. The new economy is bringing the tools for self-service to individual customers, making it possible to expand bonding by customization.

The origins of Digital Equipment Corporation (DEC) provide a good example of customer lock-in in an embryonic industry. During the 1950s a group of engineers headed by Ken Olson produced the first minicomputer. Working out of a modest warehouse in Maynard, Massachusetts, they started a technological revolution, and without knowing it they were seriously challenging the most formidable competitor in the computer industry, IBM. DEC was singularly driven by technology. Their engineers were given great freedom to both propose and follow through their innovations. There was an unprecedented stream of new computers, with one breakthrough after another. They produced over 15 new versions in less than six years. Out of this process came two significant sources of competitive advantage. First, it was difficult for the competition to pass this moving target. DEC was always ahead and moving faster. Second, there was the considerable investment that DEC users were making in customized software development. The first minicomputer, the PDP-1, was dedicated to satisfying the computer needs of single users who were experiencing the frustrations and delays of sharing a mainframe facility. The PDP-1 immediately attracted the interest of engineers and scientists working on their own specific problems that needed fast and effective computational capabilities. DEC was not addressing generic business applications, such as payroll, inventory, and accounting, which were the bread and butter of mainframe computers at that time. As a result, customers had to develop their own tailor-made software applications. Most importantly, all DEC computers were compatible with each other; therefore legacy software could run on the new generation equipment. The DEC architecture was not open, as are personal computers today that are assembled from commonly available components, so competitors not only had to match the technical features, but also had to be compatible with the existing software base. In just 10 years, DEC became the second largest computer company in the world.

Learning also adds to customer lock-in. For example, once you learn how to operate the Microsoft Excel spreadsheet application, there is a significant effort in switching to another spreadsheet program. This has been a sustaining force behind Microsoft's market share in the spreadsheet market. Additionally, there is great benefit to be derived from customer proximity, as it allows the service provider to better understand the customer and appropriately customize the service, but, as importantly, it encourages the customer to learn how to get the most from the service. As a result, the bonding increases over time and a newcomer finds it very hard to break into a relationship that has developed mutual investments and benefits to both parties. EDS and National Starch both excel in working closely with and jointly developing products with the customer.

Intuitively, customer relationships have long been considered to be valuable. Customer lock-in results from formalizing a structure to these relationships that becomes a valuable asset to the customer going beyond the product itself. A brand can sometime become this asset when the product is unfamiliar and the functionality unknown. The assurance of support from a well-known corporation can dissipate doubts about product performance and encourage repeat purchases.

An example is Motorola's entry into the cellular business. Motorola had had a terrible experience in the consumer segment, which had left a big scar in the mind of top management, due to its exiting the TV business, which was acquired by the Japanese and transformed into the very successful Quasar brand. Bob Galvin, CEO of Motorola at that time, had purposely decided to get out of the business. The business press presented this transformation as an example of a business badly managed by a U.S. corporation that was turned around by the Japanese, using their superior management methods. Motorola vowed never to reenter the consumer industry. However, years later, Motorola made breakthrough developments in cellular technology and a debate raged as to whether they should commercialize this capability. They eventually decided to introduce a product and it became the dominant design. They quickly gained a reputation in wireless technology for high quality. Motorola's collateral assets in brand name and distribution were critical to this success. This success was repeated when Motorola entered the paging industry, where it claimed the dominant design with the aid of collateral assets, and in particular the brand, built in the cellular business.

Price structure can also influence bonding. The two most innovative marketing programs in the 1980s were the frequent flyer program, which was initiated by American Airlines, and the 'Friends and Family' promotion of MCI. They were widely acclaimed because they created some lock-in for traditional commodity businesses. The frequent flyer program encourages flyers to continue using the same airline in order to accumulate sufficient frequent flyer points to earn a free flight. MCI's Friends and Family awarded discounts to customers who were calling other MCI customers on this same program, making it more difficult for customers to leave and adding to MCI's growth.

Competitor Lock-out

Locking out the competitor is the next step in bonding. There can be a thin line between customer lock-in and competitor lock-out. In the first case, a company seeks to make certain that, once it acquires customers, it is very hard for them to switch to an alternative competitor. In the second case, a company attempts to create significant barriers for competitors trying to enter the business.

Four forces can contribute to competitor lock-out, as shown in Figure 2.2. The first is based upon the restrictions imposed by distribution channels. Physical distribution channels, in particular, have limits on their ability to handle multiple product lines. At the extreme end of the spectrum you have channels that carry only one product, such as soda fountains which serve only one brand of soda. If Coca-Cola captures the channel, Pepsi is preempted from that specific market, and vice versa. Although they are a less extreme example, supermarkets have similar constraints on shelf space. Retailers are sensitive to the profits they can earn per square foot of shelf space, and this profit is a function of profit margin and inventory turnover. The brand that moves the most products generates the most profit per square foot.

In constrained environments, brands can lead to competitor lock-out. They create customer demand that causes retailers to stock the branded product, at the expense of other competitive products. In turn, the shelf presence further accentuates demand for the brand, because people buy the products that are most visible and available to them. This reinforcing loop causes brands to be an effective tool for consolidating share and creating competitive lock-out, particularly when the industry structure includes constrained physical distribution channels. Brands have less leverage in industries that emphasize direct or virtual channels such as telemarketing, direct mail, or e-commerce.

In the new economy, physical distribution may decline, but other physical constraints to market access may emerge. Broadband access to consumers may not be infinite, and those who own the physical plant may have to prioritize who gets access, not necessarily to keep it for themselves but to assign it to the Internet service that gets the most usage. Compact wireless devices may represent very tight real estate. Some applications, such as wavelet compression for wireless video, may be better installed as chips rather than as software. Manufacturers, such as Nokia and Ericsson, or service providers, such as Verizon or SBC, may be compelled to make slots and installation available only to the few brands with the broadest appeal. And of course, availability will make these brands even more appealing to the customer.

Patents, of course, can also provide for competitor lock-out. Clearly, patents are a factor driving the attractive margins in the pharmaceutical industry, the archetype of a patent-based industry. Participation in a patent-based industry, however, is not without challenges. Often a significant portion of the length of the patent is consumed before the product is released to the market because of the time required to conduct trials and to seek FDA approval. It is not unusual for half the patent's life to expire before the product is introduced to the market. This dilemma is compounded when patents are required in a number of countries, each with different requirements for documentation, languages, testing, legal compliance, and so on. In this situation, speed is a key factor in realizing competitive lock-out.

Proprietary Standards

Proprietary Standards are at the extreme of the bonding continuum. They represent the fulfillment of the most demanding objectives. If a firm is able to reach and sustain this position, the rewards are immense. It is easy to presume that this would be associated with the most dominant of the three positions in our business model. However, there are significant obstacles to creating this bond. First, it is not always possible to develop a standard in every market segment. Second, even if a standard can be developed, it might not be possible to appropriate it by a single firm. Finally, not all firms have the capabilities to obtain a Proprietary Standard. It is a question of fit.

Unfortunately, the term 'standard' is a common one that is used loosely today in a variety of contexts. It can refer, among other things, to a level of performance, the dominant design of a product, or a protocol agreed to by some designated consensus group. When we refer to a de facto Proprietary Standard we have a very specific definition in mind that describes a particular business model for generating profit. There are a number of criteria that must be met to create a de facto Proprietary Standard. This cascading set of characteristics is shown in Figure 2.3.

The ability to create a standard typically occurs as an industry is transformed. With computer operating systems, new standards and new owners of the standards emerged with the mainframe, minicomputer, and microcomputer – perhaps it will again occur with the Internet. The *Yellow Pages* has System Lock-In and it was impossible for competitors to create a new *Yellow Pages* standard in a stable and well-defined market. When the industry eventually transforms, perhaps with the advent of electronic yellow pages, opportunities will again emerge to create new proprietary standards. With the enormous value of the System Lock-In strategic position in mind, management needs to be alert to industry changes and the window of opportunity they may bring.

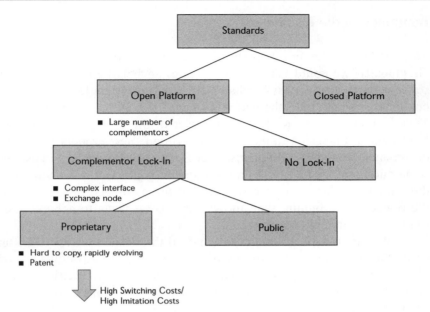

It should be based on a platform or architecture open to complementors. Its power is directly proportional to the number and variety of complementors it can attract. The Microsoft operating system has over 100,000 software applications; Novell has over 4000; each *Yellow Pages* book has thousands of advertisements; HMOs contain thousands of doctors; MasterCard has millions of cardholders and hundreds of thousands of merchants. If there are only a few complementors, the switching costs of moving them to a different standard are low. If there are many complementors who are able to bring innovation and attention to a wide span of the market, the customer will find the system more valuable and the standard more essential.

There should be lock-in between the standard and the complementors' products. This may be a result of the interface between the complementor's product and the standard, referred to as the application program interface in the case of a PC operating system. A complex interface between a complementor's products and the interface can make it expensive for the complementor to design its product around multiple standards. The number of tools and capabilities the standard provides the application often drives its complexity. The bond may also be the result of the standard being a natural exchange, one that occurs more comprehensively and efficiently at one locus point rather than several. The *Yellow Pages*, eBay, and the stock exchanges are natural exchange points. For example, if you are selling General Electric stock you will want to go to the exchange with the most likely buyers of GE stock, and vice versa.

It must be proprietary so that there is a way to appropriate the economic rents of the system. The QWERTY keyboard layout is a standard with tremendous lock-in, but one that is easily copied by others. A standard can become proprietary because it is hard to imitate by competitors. The Intel chip is hard to copy, but Advanced Micro Devices (AMD) attempts to do this. Intel's challenge, thus far successfully met, is to provide frequent upgrades to the chip (from 386 to 486 to Pentiums I, II and III) that keep AMD continually trailing the evolving standard.

Figure 2.3   The requirements for a Proprietary
Standard or Dominant Exchange

Bonding and the Triangle

The bonding continuum maps to the strategic positions on the Triangle. Graphically, we could take the continuum, anchor the dominant design starting point at the Best Product vertex of the Triangle and wrap the continuum around until the end point meets the System Lock-In vertex. This is shown on Figure 2.4. Each corner of the Triangle emphasizes a fundamental dimension to the strategic position: Best Product is centered on product economics, Total Customer Solutions is oriented to customer economics, and System Lock-In rests upon complementor economics. At the same time, there is richness in each of these corners, as suggested by the bonding continuum, that allows for several ways to achieve these fundamental strategic positions.

Competing as a Best Product is achieved through Low Cost or Differentiation, the traditional options in strategy. It is this product-centric history which is embedded in each process, activity, and metric for most businesses. It is a legacy that can be the biggest hurdle to changing strategic position.

We have observed three ways to achieve Total Customer Solutions. The first is by Redefining Customer Experience in a way that considers the full experience of the customer from the point of acquisition through to the complete life cycle of ownership of the product. Saturn, the car company, and Digital Island, a web hosting company, distinguish themselves on this dimension. The second way to achieve customer lock-in is by pursuing Horizontal Breadth. You provide a complete set of product and service offerings that fulfill the entire customer need. The bonding results from a single invoice, single point of contact, learning the breadth of customer needs, and, most importantly, through customization of this bundle by the customer. Examples include MCI WorldCom, Fidelity, Schwab, E*TRADE, and Amazon. The third way is through Customer Integration, which effectively substitutes for or leverages activities currently performed by the customer. In its most extreme form this is outsourcing such as done by EDS and other IT firms. In its more subtle form, it represents a complex web of connections with the customer that enhance their ability to do business and to use your product, as exhibited in the selling and servicing relationship between Dell and its biggest customers.

There are also three ways to achieve a System Lock-In position. The first is referred to as Restricted Access. In the case of customer lock-in, it is hard for acquired customers to switch to an alternative supplier. In the case of Restricted Access, there are significant barriers for competitors to even compete for the acquisition of customers. The competitors are deprived of

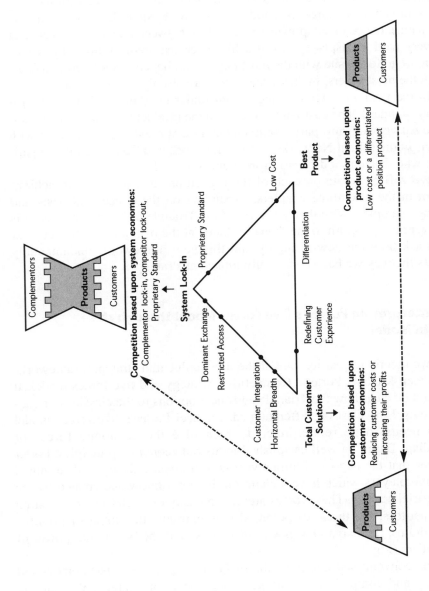

Complementors | **Products** | **Customers**

Competition based upon system economics:
Complementor lock-in, competitor lock-out, Proprietary Standard

System Lock-In

Proprietary Standard

Dominant Exchange

Restricted Access

Customer Integration

Horizontal Breadth

Total Customer Solutions

Competition based upon customer economics:
Reducing customer costs or increasing their profits

Products | **Customers**

Low Cost

Differentiation

Redefining Customer Experience

Best Product

Competition based upon product economics:
Low cost or a differentiated position product

Products | **Customers**

Figure 2.4 Bonding and the Triangle

access to the customer because the channel has limited capacity to handle multiple vendors. This is the situation for the Walls ice cream cabinets located in small stores throughout Europe. These cabinets are given, free of charge, to small stores and are kept fully stocked by Walls. Due to space constraints there is no room for competitors to install a second cabinet.

Dominant Exchange is another route to System Lock-In. With an exchange, the company provides an interface between buyers and sellers that is very hard to displace, once it achieves critical mass. With eBay, sellers want to go to the site with the most buyers and buyers want to go to the site with the most sellers. In effect, customers are also the complementors.

In the final and extreme stage of customer bonding we have a Proprietary Standard. The customer is drawn to the product because of the extensive network of third party complementors that are designed to work with your product. Real Networks, Palm, Microsoft, and Cisco are all competitors who thrive as a de facto Proprietary Standard.

We will elaborate on each of these positions and the ways to achieve them in the next three chapters, expanding on the conceptual basis and using examples. With this overview of the Triangle in mind, however, it is appropriate to return to the theme initiated at the beginning of this chapter and ask how the new economy and this new framework fundamentally alters the way we have historically looked at strategy.

Reinterpreting Porter's Five Forces Model through the Delta Model

As we mentioned earlier, one of the most influential strategic frameworks has been Michael Porter's Competitive Strategy and five forces model. It should be clear how the Triangle adds new options to the classic strategies of being Low Cost or Differentiated. Michael Porter's five forces model also needs to be reinterpreted to recognize the economic forces of bonding. Based on well-established industrial economic principles, Porter argues that the degree of attractiveness of a given industry is determined by five players which have a claim on the economic value created by the industrial activity. These forces are: the intensity of rivalry among existing competitors, the threat of potential new entrants, the threat of possible substitutes, the bargaining power of buyers, and the bargaining power of suppliers (Figure 2.5).

The conventional interpretation of Porter's framework has emphasized rivalry and competition as the key components of strategy. We start by analyzing the industry in which we are in, namely the one that is shaped

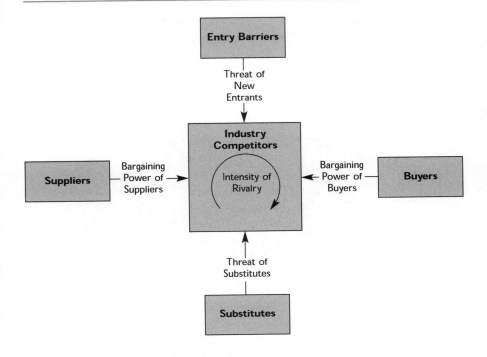

Figure 2.5   Porter's five forces model

by our competitors. Not only are we concerned with the incumbent firms, but also with those who could enter either directly or indirectly, by means of substitutes. In addition, we are concerned with the amount of wealth that can be appropriated by our buyers or suppliers. The strategic focus is internal, the prevailing climate is friction, and the way to win is by defeating and outsmarting those who could have a claim on the industry wealth. Whether Porter intended it or not, the legacy has been a product-centric mentality; strategy is war.

Let us put to work the lessons of the Delta Model to reinterpret Porter's five forces in a fundamental new way that will move us out of the Best Product positioning toward Total Customer Solutions and System Lock-In. (Figure 2.6). The trick is not to take the industry as given. Think of the five forces as a way to identify actions which will lead to a very strong positioning for you, and for all of your relevant partners: customers, suppliers, and complementors. The following process emerges.

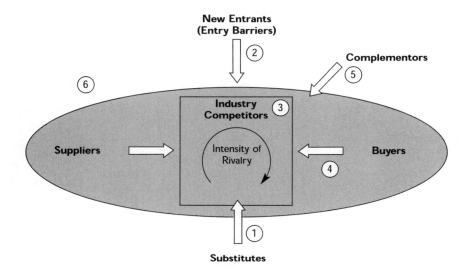

1. Create a powerful 10× force to change the rules of the game. Reject imitation of competitors, a product-centric mentality, and a commoditization mindset.

2. Generate significant barriers around the customer through a unique customer value proposition based on deep customer segmentation, and customer and consumer understanding.

3. Do not use competitors as a central benchmark to guide your strategic actions. The key industries to concentrate on are those of your customers, suppliers, and complementors. Strategy is not *war* with your competitors; it is *love* with your customers, suppliers, consumers, and complementors.

4. Develop and nurture the integrated value chain with your key suppliers and customers. Bring in all the power of B2B and B2C to accomplish this objective. This is critical for customer lock-in.

5. Add a new player: the *complementors*. Seek complementor support and investment in your business. Make them key partners in seeking the delivery of Total Customer Solutions. Extend the unique value proposition to include complementors, as well as suppliers. This is the key for obtaining complementor lock-in, competitor lock-out, and ultimately, System Lock-In.

6. If your customers, suppliers, and complementors are numerous and fragmented you could also provide them with state-of-the-art management practices and a wealth of information and intelligence that they could never acquire otherwise. Your lock-in will be admirably enhanced.

Figure 2.6   Reinterpreting Porter's five forces through the Delta Model

① Search for the 10X Force

In his book *Only the Paranoid Survive*, Andy Grove, the Chairman of Intel, introduces the concept of the 10X force. This goes well beyond assessing the potential substitute product in a given industry, and requires searching for a change of such magnitude that it will transform the rules of competition and the playing field. This is a 10X force because it is an order of magnitude larger than the existing forces in the industry. This concept is both provocative and, at times, quite practical. It requires a completely open mind, rejecting the stereotypes of the industry, not emulating, not taking anything for granted, and, above all, rejecting the product-centric mentality and commoditization mindset.

② Generate Barriers Around Your Customers

Do not think of barriers to entry as those forces that prevent an outsider from penetrating the overall industry. Rather think about building barriers around your key individual customers so as to establish customer lock-in. This is not based on abusive behavior; on the contrary, it is built on a relationship so strong and so mutually beneficial that both parties will never break apart. The key to achieve this position is to gain a deep customer and consumer understanding through careful segmentation and targeting. Having acquired this knowledge we can develop unique economic value propositions to the customer, which is the source of the barriers to change. It is interesting to note that it is not your industry knowledge that is most critical to achieve this state of relationship with the customer. It is rather the customer's industry that is most relevant. You need a deep knowledge of the profit and cost drivers of your customer so that your capabilities and product offerings measurably enhance your customer's performance.

③ Your Competitors Are Not the Relevant Benchmarks

This could be seen as heretical; after all, your competitors are at the center of Porter's five forces. We do not suggest that you should ignore your competitors. Study them intensely. From this you can learn both what to do and what *not* to do. If you use them as an across-the-board, unquestioned benchmark, your standards will decline. Merck, a pharmaceutical company, collects extraordinarily detailed competitor intelligence, because they want to be informed of their competitors' actions but not simply to follow or imitate. As we have said before, competitor imitation leads towards commoditization and congruency which is the opposite of leadership.

It is not your industry that is the most relevant when you pursue a Total Customer Solutions or System Lock-In strategy. The key industries that you need to comprehend are those of your customers and complementors. It is the overall system and how to influence it that is critical.

④ Develop and Nurture the Integrated Value Chain

Your customers and your suppliers are your natural partners that you need to cultivate around the jointly structured value proposition to your customer. Those relationships can be greatly enhanced by the use of e-business and e-commerce technology. The chain of interrelationships often extends beyond the customer to include the end-user and complementors (Figure 2.7).

If you do not reach the consumer directly, you have to make a concerted effort to have as much understanding of the end-user as possible. The consumer, the end-user, the ultimate payer in the chain is absolutely critical. With today's technology, it is possible to understand individually each and every one of the consumers and tailor services to his or her needs in a highly customized way.

⑤ Add a New Player: the Complementors

Why has Microsoft been so successful? Because Bill Gates has an army of people working for him who are not on his payroll. These are the complementors: software producers, content developers, and a cadre of professionals whose primary work is to extend the usefulness of the Windows

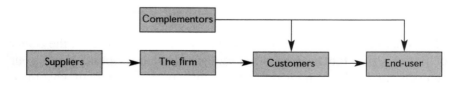

Figure 2.7   The full integrated value chain

operating system. Suppliers and customers are critical to achieve customer lock-in. Complementors go even further; they are the instruments for seeking competitor lock-out and System Lock-In. In order to achieve this, you need to:

- Identify key potential complementors (many of whom could be in your own backyard, as other businesses in your company portfolio that have not been integrated into a well-conceived corporate, not business, strategy).
- Make the complementors into your loyal partners, by providing them with a mutually exciting value proposition.
- Have them invest in your business.
- Make the relationship stable and longlasting.

⑥ Fragmented Industries Offer Big Opportunities

If your customers, suppliers, and complementors are numerous, fragmented, and somehow 'ignored' by the top industry players, you could have a golden opportunity to serve as the 'glue' in bonding the industry together and emerge as a key powerful leader.

The beauty of network technology is that one can access directly the fragmented players and create a virtual entity that could enjoy the economies of scale that have been otherwise reserved for the major players. Also, one could provide them with state-of-the-art managerial capabilities that would have been impossible to acquire under the old economy.

The Required Resources and Capabilities for the Delta Model

Besides Porter's framework, the other influential school of thinking in strategy has been the Resource-Based View of the firm. This postulates that firms enjoy high levels of profits not because of the intrinsic characteristics of the industry in which they compete, but rather due to the resources and capabilities that they are able to appropriate. The primary limitation of the Resource-Based View of the firm is its inherent vagueness. Proper resources and capabilities do constitute a basis for competitive advantage, but it is hard to assess pragmatically the nature of these resources and how they will be used to make money. We believe that anchoring the competitive position on resources puts 'the cart in front of the horse.' We need to know where we want to go, before we decide how to get there.

We will point out in later chapters how the Delta Model sets the Strategic Agenda and defines the critical processes to achieve the desired strategic position in the Triangle. By directly linking strategy to execution, the Delta Model answers the question of critical resources and capabilities. Even at a generic level, however, the Delta Model suggests a small list of desirable capabilities that will allow a firm to develop a new business model more in tune with today's challenges.

1. First and foremost, you need a deep understanding of the customer obtained via a detailed segmentation and supported by Aggregated and Granular Metrics.
2. This understanding should also be extended to critical suppliers and complementors. Do not get trapped in your industry trends alone.
3. The implementation of the new business model is frequently available due to the Internet and its associated technologies: e-business, e-commerce, e-systems. The appropriation of this skill is essential.
4. Create the dynamic and entrepreneurial environment of risk taking and reward sharing originated by the professional challenges associated with the 'new technologies.'
5. The ultimate output is the development and implementation of unique and exciting value propositions for all the key players: customers, consumers, suppliers, and complementors. The first mover advantage is important, but the value of intelligent moves is overwhelming.

Of course, we need to complement these capabilities with all the conventional and traditional skills associated with good management. We have purposely emphasized only those that are required by this new business model.

Reflections

The Best Product Does not Always Win

Neither Microsoft nor MCI WorldCom win in the marketplace by being Low Cost or Differentiated. These and a growing number of companies sustain themselves by bonding with the customer or the system. Product economics is secondary. Unfortunately, most businesses are caught in the Best Product mindset, or as a senior executive recently exclaimed: 'We are trapped by the smoke stack mentality.' A lot has been said about the dangers of the silos that are often created around the functions in an organ-ization. The pursuit of independent product lines is subtler and therefore a more insidious problem, but it has equal dangers. It focuses the mind on the product and the Best Product options. The Triangle has the remarkable capacity to expand managers' perspectives. It encourages a creative strategic dialogue that uncovers the potential for playing the game a different way that yields different and often better results.

Strategy as Love versus Strategy as War

Most strategic thinking has military as well as economic roots. It is not surprising that 'rivalry,' 'conflict,' and 'power' are commonly used terms. The essence of strategy, according to the conventional view, is to beat your competitors. Surprisingly, in this way of thinking, the customer is at best someone to be bargained with rather than embraced. As we have stated throughout this chapter, our key concept in strategic positioning is bonding – with the goal of attracting, satisfying, and retaining customers. The new options we advance – Total Customer Solutions, and System Lock-In – abandon the 'competitor as enemy' mindset. The new mindset focuses on partnering with customers and complementors with the ulti-mate aim of captivating rather than capturing them.

Notes

1. Michael E. Porter's primary work on competitive positioning is in his books, *Competitive Strategy* (New York: Free Press, 1980) and *Competitive Advantage* (New York: Free Press, 1985).
2. The seeds for this view originated in the work by E. Penrose, *The Theory of the Growth of the Firm* (Oxford: Basil Blackwell, 1959). This approach was substantially developed among others by B. Wernerfelt, 'A resource-based view of the firm', *Strategic Management Journal*, Vol. 5, pp. 171–80, 1984; J.B. Barney, 'Firm resources and sustained competitive advantage', *Journal of Management*, Vol. 17 pp. 99–120, 1991; M. Peteraf, 'The cornerstones of compet-itive advantage: a resource-based view', *Strategic Management Journal*, Vol. 14, No. 3, pp. 179–92, 1993. C.K. Prahalad and Gary Hamel popularized the approach in their now classic paper, 'The core competence of the corporation', *Harvard Business Review*, May–June, 1990, pp. 71–91.
3. Ricardo, D. *Principles of Political Economy and Taxation* (London: J. Murray, 1817).

CHAPTER 3

The Best Product: Winning through Costs and Features

The Best Product position builds upon the classic forms of competition through Low Cost or Differentiation. In this case the relevant economic drivers are centered on the value chain of the product or service. Products tend to be standardized and unbundled. Companies pursuing this strategy have the primary objective of improving the efficiency of their own supply chain, which is the machine that delivers the product. Customers are likely to be considered faceless and generic and to be served through mass distribution channels. Innovation is focused on the renewal of the product line. In the best case, the firm has a common product platform that supports the rapid development of a stream of products enabling 'first-to-market' positions and the establishment of the so-called dominant design.[1] Best Product emerged as a strategic position from the industrial era and is the default strategic option for the majority of firms today. Best Product businesses attract customers by the intrinsic characteristics of the product itself. This is the position where a company has the least to do with its customer, hence making the incumbent firms more vulnerable to new entrants. After all, if the customer is attracted by the superiority of your product, then the customer will desert you if a new superior product appears in the marketplace.

There are two fundamental ways to achieve a Best Product position: through Low Cost, which provides a price advantage to the customer, or through Differentiation, which offers unique features that the customer values beyond mere price. Throughout Chapters 3, 4, and 5 we will illustrate the appeal of a well-executed Best Product, Total Customer Solutions, or System Lock-In strategies through examples of old and new economy companies. The old economy examples provide a useful perspective because they have proven the profit model over the course of time. The new economy examples are necessary because they indicate the growing prevalence of bonding as way to compete, and the use of new technology to do this. Figure 3.1 shows the positioning of selected companies from both the old and new economy pursuing a Low Cost and Differentiated strategy. Let us look at several of these.

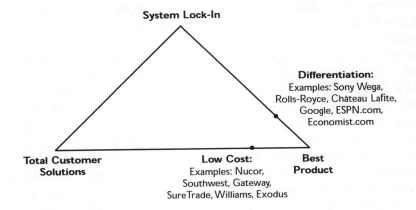

Figure 3.1   The Triangle: options for strategic planning

Achieving Best Product Positioning through Low Cost

Nucor,[2] in the steel industry, and Southwest, in the commercial airline industry, are great examples of companies that have successfully achieved a Low Cost position in the old economy. As a result of their effective Best Product strategies, both thwarted the progress of the incumbent firms in their industries and became clear leaders. These two examples also invalidate the conventional belief that industry structure drives profitability. Industry is not a good indicator of company performance. While these companies were accumulating extraordinary value to their shareholders, their corresponding industries – steel and commercial airlines – were stagnating.

Nucor Corporation will soon be the nation's largest steel producer, likely to pass US Steel early in the 21st century. Nucor chose a classic Best Product strategic position with the objective of being the lowest-cost producer in the steel industry. The company has costs that are $40–50 per ton cheaper than the modern, fully integrated mills. Its sales per employee are $550,000 per year, compared to $240,000 for the industry. Nucor achieved this performance through a single-minded focus on product economics.

Nucor is a Best Product company that excels in seeking the lowest-cost position. According to John Correnti, Nucor's former CEO, their low-cost position is due 80% to culture and 20% to technology. Across the corporation there is a strong alignment between the objectives, processes, and metrics that are critical to the strategy, namely to be Low Cost. The congruency in objectives becomes clear as we look across each activity in their business.

Measurements critical to a low-cost producer are collected and openly shared from the CEO, to the plant manager, and down to the first level employee. At the smallest unit of production, which is a team of 40–50 people that take in scrap steel at one end and produce a roll of steel at the other, measurements are on constant display showing the output for that shift. The fundamental metric is 'quality tons of steel produced.' Faulty steel that is sent back by the customer is subtracted from production. The metrics, however, become quite sophisticated in sorting out the cost drivers. For example, at the production level they account for thinner gauge steel, because it is harder to produce, and for new equipment, because there are learning effects and break-in periods. This theme of quantitative measurement continues up the organizational hierarchy. At the department level, all the functional costs are measured in absolute and per unit terms. The most aggregated levels of performance reside at the plant, where each of the 23 facilities is evaluated on its return on assets, and, of course, again at the corporate level where the firm's overall financials are judged by return on equity.

The metrics are not just an abstract number. They are significant drivers of compensation and rewards; hourly employees receive two-thirds of their total pay from bonuses based upon these metrics. Their base pay is low for the industry, but the total compensation is well above the competition – and there is no limit. When they first initiated the program, management was concerned with recalibrating the bonus compensation levels, but decided to let the compensation grow lock step with productivity so that people would not be demotivated because of the 'moving goal posts.' During industry downturns, management shares the pain with the workers. In an industry characterized by massive layoffs, Nucor broke with tradition by having management salaries decline more dramatically than the salaries for the line worker, and limiting hours so that layoffs would be reduced. Besides building morale, this adds to the flexibility of the plant because of the wage variability. It also encourages flexibility in work roles. Employees are expected to work in a broad range of activities and they rush to help to relieve any bottlenecks that form in the production line. They extensively outsource the ancillary activities in the plant; in a plant workforce of 400–450 people, about 80 may be contractors that work on site who are cheaper and can be redeployed when volume declines.

Nucor extensively benchmarks itself against the industry, particularly with a view towards the new entrants such as Chaparral Steel. They compare the metrics in order to understand relative costs and new ways to improve further their own productivity.

Nucor is quick to adopt new and risky technology. For example, they were the first to introduce compact strip production (CSP) technology developed by SMS Corporation. This is a custom technology that allows Nucor to cast directly thin slabs, which then require less rolling. While other competitors caught up with the technology, Nucor has been able to maintain its productivity advantage because of the lead time in experience. This was a $500 million bet for Nucor. It was made at a time when they had $570 million in assets. When Ken Iverson, the CEO at that time, was asked if he could sleep well at night while going through that traumatic period, he replied: 'Oh yes, I slept like a baby. I woke up every half an hour and started to cry.'

Nucor has removed the obstacles to experimentation. The philosophy of Ken Iverson was 'good managers make bad decisions.' He said, good managers get it right only 60% of the time, so everyone has to keep a check on mistakes and should be forgiving. He further elaborated that good managers do not target 100%, because then they are not taking enough risk in seeking higher returns. They recruit smart people, but not necessarily those with a background in steel making, in order to stimulate creative thinking. Correspondingly, training is on the job and limited, there are no job descriptions, and you certainly do not have to follow the manual. One equipment supplier was aghast at a recent visit to a Nucor plant. The machine they installed was supposed to run at 100 tons/hour, and it was running at 140. The 5-horsepower oscillator had been replaced with one having 15 horsepower and the hoses had been doubled in their diameter. Many other adjustments had been made to squeeze the last ounce out of production.

To further encourage experimentation, the vast majority of the decisions are decentralized down to the divisions, plants, and departments. The metrics and incentives give everyone a common objective and managers are trusted to run their team as they see fit. There is coordination from corporate headquarters, but, with only 22 people including clerical support at the corporate office, there is no room for micromanagement. The extent to which they value this decision-making freedom is apparent in their purchasing practices. A supplier recently offered a 30% discount on electrodes, a significant cost element in electric furnaces, if Nucor decided to purchase from this vendor for all its divisions. Nucor rejected the offer because, by imposing this decision, the plants would end up having less freedom, and accountability to manage and experiment with their costs.

Nucor does not put much emphasis on paperwork, but they are rigorous about evaluation. A recent $8 million investment was proposed on one sheet of paper with two paragraphs and room for a signature. On the other hand, management does not sign off on just anything. They put more emphasis on the actual results tested elsewhere in the system rather than on speculative upfront analysis. Each organizational unit effectively serves as a laboratory to test, measure, learn, and, finally, rollout different work practices and investments.

The measurements, both weekly and monthly, are broadly shared. People in the department of one plant can look at the performance of the same department in another plant. If their productivity is lower, they have a keen interest in improving it. Almost everyone in a plant has traveled to another site to get help, or to learn better practices. They are now extending this approach so that hourly people are beginning to visit customers to understand better their problems and requirements.

Before new management took over Nucor in 1966, the stock market valued the company at just $14 million. Thirty-three years later, deft managers have used a successful Best Product strategy to take Nucor to $4.5 billion in market value. This represents 19% compounded annual growth in market value, which is spectacular in any industry, let alone steel (Figure 3.2).

Perhaps even more to the point, Nucor's performance can be compared to the steel minimill's average performance of only 6% in that time period. While Nucor saw skyrocketing profits, 25 minimills were closed or sold between 1975 and 1982.

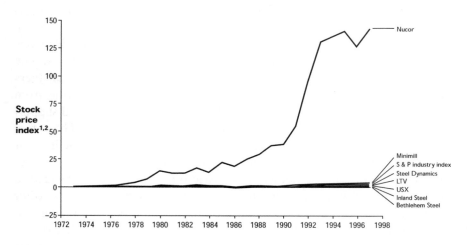

Notes
1. Base year is 1973 (=1.00)
2. Closing date stock prices were used except for index starting after 1973 where IPO stock prices were used

Figure 3.2   Stock performance comparisons among
Nucor, minimill and integrated steel companies

Southwest Airlines provides another example of a well-conceived Best Product strategy achieved through a relentless focus on product economics. Part of this drive was based on reducing the product scope and defeaturing service. When Southwest started its operation, it excluded baggage handling, passenger ticketing, advance reservations, and hot food. The only thing Southwest did not eliminate, it seemed, was the flight itself. The incumbent carriers took for granted that these features were an inherent part of travel service. In the end, Southwest proved that these items were not worth their cost for many customers.

The activities Southwest continued to perform were done in ways quite different from the established airlines. The airline emphasized shuttle flights that efficiently utilized an aircraft on repeated trips between two airports, rather than imitating the full service carriers that use hubs and spokes. Southwest concentrated on the smaller and less congested airports surrounding large cities. The airline reduced the costs of maintenance and training by relying almost exclusively on the Boeing 737. Each and every activity throughout Southwest Airlines resonates with a low-cost, product-oriented position. Furthermore, each employee is motivated to meet the strategic goals, since Southwest gives stock to employees and implements human resource policies that encourage the workforce to act like owners.

In both examples, the new companies had an advantage over the existing firms by basing their success on radically low-cost strategies. A new organization may find it easier to redefine how traditional business activities are performed. Existing firms have embedded systems, processes, and procedures that are obstacles to change and that carry a heavy cost infrastructure. Think of how many successful small companies have penetrated well-established industries and have promptly reached a position of cost leadership with a more narrowly defined product. We can look beyond Nucor and Southwest; to Gateway in personal computers; and to Williams in telecommunications. All these companies show the same pattern: they narrow the scope of their offering relative to the incumbents, they defeature the product, and they collapse the activities of the value chain by eliminating some activities and outsourcing others. Then, they carry out the remaining activities in a manner different from competitors, with the desire that this will lead to distinctively low costs. Doing things the same way as everyone else, they have concluded, is no way to achieve superior performance.

While the new economy offers great potential for customer bonding through Total Customer Solutions and System Lock-In, as we will show later, it also has its fair share of Best Product businesses. SureTrade, 'the ultimate in no-frills, bare-bones online trading,'[3] is a clear illustration.

SureTrade's strategic position is solidly Best Product with a focus on Low Cost rather than Differentiation. The company's own press release announcing its launch provides the clearest evidence:

> In an unprecedented competitive move which sets a new price and quality standard for securities trading on the Internet, the brokerage firm SureTrade, Inc. today said it would charge $7.95 per trade to buy or sell up to 5000 shares of stock ... These commissions are the lowest available from any NASD member brokerage firm.

In a host of industry surveys, it is consistently touted for its Low Cost. They stress its low-cost, 'no-frills' approach to online investing. Some online financial services do offer the frills. E*TRADE, for example, provides games, shopping, credit cards, discussion groups, and partnerships with content providers. SureTrade and E*TRADE have chosen different strategies for reasons that correspond to their different situations. E*TRADE is a stand-alone firm aiming to become a full service financial services provider. SureTrade, on the other hand, is a subsidiary of Fleet Financial, already a full service financial service provider.

Exodus is another example of a high flying Internet-based Best Product company. They pioneered the web site hosting business by offering colocation facilities. Colocation provides real estate, security, backup power, and redundant broadband access to the Internet in data center locations around the world. There are huge scale economies to these services, making it difficult for a single company to do it alone affordably. In effect, Exodus provided the scale-related functions of web and data hosting, allowing the customers and their software vendors to focus on the more individual and customized jobs regarding web design, server and storage maintenance. Web hosting is becoming a huge market, and as it grows companies are positioning themselves on different corners of the Triangle. Some remain focused on Best Product, but as we will note later some are moving to Total Customer Solutions positions by providing managed web hosting services assuming all the equipment, maintenance, and sometimes design elements. Others are even attempting to create some System Lock-In by providing data centers that are at the nexus of multiple ISP (Internet Service Provider) backbones, essentially serving as an exchange or gateway between the backbones. This provides the additional functionality of moving traffic between backbones based upon congestion. They hope that content providers and ISPs will want to congregate at these nodal exchanges where everyone else is.

Achieving Best Product Positioning through Differentiation

A Best Product position relies upon attracting the customer through the characteristics of the product itself. Differentiation offers something beyond price that is truly distinctive. It can be features, such as with the Sony Wega television, that boasts distinctive features unmatched by competitive products by merging the technical prowess of Japanese Sony with the singular design of the German Wega. It can also be image, such as with Dom Perignon champagne or the Rolls-Royce automobile, that is a symbol of class and success. Or, it can be unique quality, as embodied in the Château Lafite red burgundy wine.

Differentiation persists as a strategy in the new economy and is exemplified by Google. This is an Internet search engine based on what may be considered a better feature – searching for content on the web and ranking its relevance to the user according to the number of significant links to other web pages. It is relatively easy for a user to switch between search engines if a better product comes along. Yahoo! proved this recently by dropping Inktomi as it general search engine to begin using Google.

As another example in Differentiation, ESPN.com has made itself the primary Internet destination for enthusiasts seeking news, commentary, and statistics about every major spectator sport. It has done so by being 'first to market' among sports sites and by focusing on the quality of its product. ESPN was in fact one of the first major 'traditional' media outlets of any sort (news, sports, entertainment, and so on) to develop an online presence. And those that followed – including sports-focused competitors CNNSI.com (a joint venture between CNN and Sports Illustrated) and CBSsportsline.com – copied its dominant design.

In this option, success may be straightforward, as expressed in the proverbial saying, 'build a better mousetrap and the world will beat a path to your door.' But beware, someone else will inevitably build an even better mousetrap and the customer will abandon you. Success in this instance is fragile, and bonding is at a minimum.

Fighting the Commodity Mentality – The Case of Codelco

The commodity mentality assumes that certain products cannot possibly be differentiated and, therefore, the only meaningful way to compete in those cases is to achieve a low-cost structure. Price becomes the determinant force to attract and retain the customer. This in turn focuses all the managerial efforts to 'beat the competitors', which generates a continuous rivalry and price war that ends up adversely affecting all the industry players. This becomes more than a state of the industry, but also a state of mind that is self-fulfilling. Once you begin competing on price as a Best Product then you have to eliminate costs which are superfluous to that position, customers consequently identify you as a commodity and you are left with the capabilities to compete only on price. One company caught in this vicious cycle was Codelco, the Chilean copper company that runs the largest and most successful copper corporation in the world. Codelco is blessed with owning the Chuquicamata mine, the largest open pit copper mine with the most concentrated deposits.

We were confronted with this issue in a most dramatic way when asked to assist Codelco. The original request for our services was to help in a comprehensive review of the Codelco organizational structure. In fact, we were explicitly asked *not* to look into Codelco's strategy. The strategic direction of Codelco was not an issue, as it was perfectly clear that this was defined by consistent and relentless efforts to improve operational effectiveness. The strong, unchallenged belief was that copper was a commodity – after all, can anyone claim that Chilean copper is in any way superior to American, Mexican, or Zambian copper? The resulting attitude was to concentrate on investments in order to generate continuous cost improvements, as well as exploration initiatives to maintain copper reserves.

Within these premises, Codelco was doing exceedingly well, playing strictly according to a Best Product strategy. With annual revenues of $3 billion it was the largest copper producer in the world. Most importantly, its profit margins were so outstanding as to outperform even the pharmaceutical industry – a feat unparalleled in the mining industry. In fact, from 1990 to 1995, Codelco had average margins of 14%, against 7% of the copper industry and 13% of the pharmaceutical industry.

As with many commodity managed businesses, Codelco had minimal effort allocated to marketing and sales. Surprisingly for a $3 billion in revenue company, it only had six salespersons on its payroll and a very limited number of buyers. Contracts were negotiated every year for ingots, plates, sheets, and so on. Rather than salespeople, they were order takers who routinely renewed long-term established contracts. The buyers transformed raw copper into semielaborate products that in turn were resold to further intermediaries. As a result of this practice, Codelco was totally removed from the final applications of its products. In a fundamental way Codelco was completely disconnected from the end-users and consumers of its products. For Codelco, and for most commodity producers, competitive advantage resided exclusively in the cost infrastructure.

In early 1998 the Triangle was presented to Codelco's top executives. In its applications to the copper industry they recognized the false premises under which they had been operating. Codelco had historically been mistaken about their competitors. While it might be true that they competed with other copper producers in the purchase of mines and other properties, the true competitors were the aluminum, plastic, and fiber optics producers representing major substitutes for copper. The aluminum industry had been particularly aggressive and successful in this respect. In what was a major blow against copper manufacturers, aluminum producers were successful in substituting aluminum for copper in auto-mobile radiators, despite the fact that copper delivers superior conduc-tivity. The aluminum industry has been remarkably effective in studying the uses of its product. The president of Alcoa visited the head of General Motors to ascertain their needs and promote the use of aluminum. Alcoa, in a move sympathetic to a Total Customer Solutions strategy, jointly designed with auto manufacturers new products and technologies to benefit the car industry through the use of aluminum. Of even more concern was that this extraordinary event took most copper producers by surprise. They were unaware of the aluminum manufacturing options, revealing once more how distant the copper producers were from their users. While copper, in itself, may be an undifferentiated product, at some point in the value chain even this commodity is converted into a differ-entiated product in the eyes of the customer.

These considerations led Codelco to realize that copper producers should move quickly and decisively away from the Best Product corner of the Triangle toward the other two corners. The Total Customer Solutions position brings unknown and unattended customers into focus. The System Lock-In position calls for the recognition of the overall system in which the copper producers operate, to organize their activities more closely to promote the demand of copper worldwide, and to allow the identification and attraction of complementors in the pursuit of these tasks.

How could you possibly create System Lock-In in a market for raw materials? The potential is illustrated with concrete versus steel in Britain. During World War II steel production was channeled into military activities and consequently concrete emerged as a dominant material for buildings. The participants in the building industry were forced to organize around the use of concrete. This included the firms providing electrical installa-tion, architects, contractors organizing the building process, firms special-izing in the delivery of mechanical instruments and parts, institutions overseeing fire safety, subcontractors dealing with building maintenance, and the individual laborers with skills in material handling. All these groups have become strong complementors for concrete in the building industry. All these parties developed an infrastructure around concrete that reinforced its use because of the high switching costs of using new materials. This bias toward concrete has continued despite the fact that steel may be fundamentally superior to concrete based on cost and performance. Without a war, or some natural disaster, it requires a focused effort to change the concrete lock-in. British Steel has now been exploring how more steel can be incorporated into building design. For the same floor area the height of the building can be 10% lower with steel, thus reducing operating costs for mechanical and electrical systems. Because there can be fewer service obstructions, room partitions can be changed easily. Easy access to services provides less expensive maintenance and upgrading. Steel is also more fire resistant. Having a better product will not be enough, however; the challenge for British Steel is to get complementors to invest in steel, and then to invest in products made by British Steel.

While we are not implying that Codelco should abandon its commitment to maintaining the leadership position as a low-cost producer, we are saying that this is not sufficient. The efforts have to be expanded both as a firm and as an industry leader. From the firm's point of view, Codelco immediately started the strategic evolution through the vertices of the Triangle, as depicted in Figure 3.3.

Codelco has expanded its relationships with large end-users to improve the mutual knowledge of each other, to gain a better understanding of the current and future needs, to aim at fruitful joint product developments, and to increase lobbying in favor of the copper industry as a whole. Since some of these companies are also suppliers of Codelco, such as Siemens, ABB, and GE, there was immediately a basis for mutual, beneficial relationships.

The new approach constituted an enormous change in Codelco's direction, including the attitudes of their senior executives. Codelco's CEO had never in the past engaged in any direct conversations with his counterparts in the major end-user companies. In fact, there was a sense that there was nothing that they could meaningfully talk about. All that changed, and Codelco's CEO became an outspoken leader of the industry, seeking institutional and personal exchanges around the world. These contacts soon materialized into meaningful contracts with Alcatel in high voltage underground cables, and local area networks (LANs) premises copper cables; marketing studies with KME for the introduction of copper-nickel break lines in the car industry in Europe; and exploratory agreements with ABB, Electrolux, Carrier, GE, and Siemens.

Next Codelco turned its attention to reactivate ICA – the international copper association – that grouped all the key copper manufacturers. The

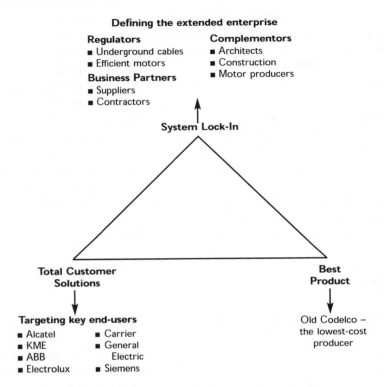

Figure 3.3   The expansion of Codelco's strategy

organization had been exceedingly passive, limited by a lack of mandate and an anemic budget. Codelco worked to establish a new paradigm within the copper industry, consistent with its business-oriented style of management. A major breakthrough occurred at the end of 1999 when Codelco led the other major copper producers in reformulating the mission and Strategic Agenda of ICA. The agreement was to focus on stimulating the demand for copper in industries sharing a high potential consumption (residential and commercial construction; power generation, transmission and distribution; car manufacturing; tele/data communications; and motors), and in the most attractive geographical markets, including Brazil, China, India, and Eastern Europe.

Adopting the lens of the System Lock-In perspective, there are important lessons for Codelco. As the leader in its industry, Codelco should assume an influential role in increasing global copper consumption. In the United States, around 190 kgs of copper is used on average in every home, and around 19 kgs is used in making every car. Across countries, we find enormous variation, however, in terms of copper consumption. Among the developed countries, Belgium consumes 40.4 kgs per person, while Austria consumes only 2.9 kgs. The United States stands at 9.8 kgs. The disparity exists even when we examine specific applications. The consumption of copper in water pipelines is 1.6 kgs per person in England and only 0.2 kgs in Japan. Likewise, consumption of copper in roofing is 0.8 kgs per person in Germany and only 0.2 kgs in the U.S.A. Clearly, these differences beg the question of what system effects could create such a disparity and they suggest that copper is not just used more but has different applications. By understanding how customers find value across a range of applications, Codelco could begin to increase worldwide demand for copper. With the full support of all the major copper producers, ICA should seize enormous opportunities for the industry to identify and promote more extensive uses of copper.

Reflections

Commodities Only Exist in the Minds of the Inept

The case of Codelco is quite instructive. Taking the premise that commodities only exist in the mind of the inept, we could not have picked a better illustration than copper, which is widely regarded as a commodity product 'par excellence.' The trouble with the commodity mindset is that it only looks at the product as the cause of the undifferentiated business. It misses the critical test which is the customer and the complementors. Although copper as a product would be a commodity, the users of copper are far from being undifferentiated. Their needs and their business opportunities are unique. The lessons of Codelco are obvious: do not just look at the product and competitors, look also at the customers and complementors and you will realize how much more room for creativity exists and how a business doomed to compete for low costs can be repositioned to compete for profits.

Notes

1. For a further discussion on the dominant design, see James N. Utterback, *Mastering the Dynamics of Innovation* (Boston, M.A., Harvard Business School, 1994).
2. 'Nucor at Crossroads', Harvard Business School, Case 9–793–9.
3. From *Fortune*'s 1999 Investor Guide.

CHAPTER 4

Total Customer Solutions: Winning through Relationships

The Total Customer Solutions option is a complete reversal of the Best Product approach. It is based upon creating a strong bond with the customer. Rather than supplying faceless customers through mass distribution, Total Customer Solutions players learn as much as they can about each customer in order to provide customized solutions. Rather than leaning on product economics, they thrive by engineering customer economics. Instead of offering independent products, they put together a bundle of products and services aimed at solving a wide array of customer needs.

The way in which Total Customer Solutions players address their internal processes is also different. They do not look at their supply chain in isolation, seeking to optimize its internal efficiency; rather, they focus on their supply chain in combination with that of their customer. Often it is important to expand the internal activities in order to enhance the link with customers and suppliers. The Internet is instrumental in bringing the customer, as well as suppliers, closer. Instead of using mass distribution channels that generate little loyalty, Total Customer Solutions players turn to alternative, nontraditional, and direct channels when possible.

These creative companies also learn to redesign their innovation process. They do not exclusively emphasize renewing their products, but rather establish joint product development with their target customers. This close interaction with customers also leads to mutual learning where the customer learns about the intricacies of the offer and the company learns how the customer applies their service or product. Sometimes the learning is embodied in people, sometimes in systems, such as when preferences and usage patterns are recorded from interactions on the web. These relationships often bring in additional third parties that complement their product bundle. Customization and mutual learning lead to bonding that cannot easily be replicated by competitors.

This strategy calls first for the proper segmentation of the customer base, with a clear set of priorities to identify the relative importance of each customer. It also requires a profound and intimate knowledge of the

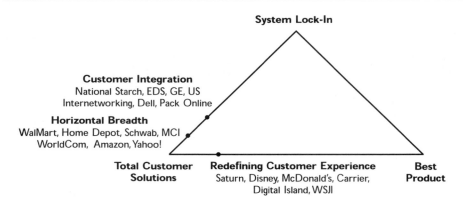

Figure 4.1   The Triangle: options for strategic planning

client's business and how it relates to your own business. It necessitates a more intense reciprocal learning from each party leading to mutual respect and trust based upon concrete dual benefits. The ultimate output of this strategy is an individual value proposition tailor-made for each customer and aimed at enhancing the customer's cost, revenue, or profit position. Whereas the prevalent measure of performance for the Best Product position is product market share, customer market share (or share of wallet) becomes the most relevant for this option.

There are three ways to achieve Total Customer Solutions (Figure 4.1). The first, Redefining Customer Experience, is by altering the relationship with the customers from the point of acquisition through to the complete life cycle of ownership. Saturn and Digital Island are examples. The second way to achieve Total Customer Solutions is through Horizontal Breadth. This provides a more complete set of products and services around the customer's needs. Examples include MCI WorldCom, Fidelity, and Amazon. The third way is through Customer Integration. This can take the form of outsourcing or facilitating activities otherwise performed by the customer.

Achieving Total Customer Solutions by Redefining Customer Experience

Saturn, a U.S. division of General Motors, redefined its customer relationship in the auto industry, and, whether or not it is perceived overall as a financial success, is clearly one of the most creative managerial initiatives in the last decade. Saturn managers departed from a Best Product strategy in that they explicitly decided at the outset *not* to have a product that was different from that of the leading competition. Saturn abandoned a product focus and turned their attention to improving the customer's full life cycle experience.

When General Motors finally decided to enter the small car segment of the auto industry, they realized that they could not successfully manufacture and market a small car within the overwhelming bureaucracy of the traditional General Motors. What they did instead was to start anew, far from Detroit in Spring Hills, Tennessee, and reinvent the business with an orientation toward the customer.

As any American buyer knows, purchasing a car can be one of the most unpleasant shopping experiences. What Saturn did was to structure the business with the customer in mind. They did not do this by focusing upon the product characteristics, but looked instead at the way the product was acquired and used by the customer.

Initially, Saturn made a deliberate decision to design a car that would produce a driving experience as similar to that of the Toyota Corolla or Honda Civic as possible. Saturn targeted the satisfied customers of these Japanese car manufacturers and wanted to make an easy transition to Saturn. Their car, they decided, should not be different from those of their leading competitors.

The key challenge that Saturn faced was in convincing the American consumer that a U.S. manufacturer could provide as good a product in the small car segment as a Japanese manufacturer. When Saturn entered this segment in 1989, Japanese manufacturers completely dominated the market. Seemingly in deference to Henry Ford Jr., who used to say 'small cars, small profits,' American manufacturers had been altogether absent from the small car segment.

To make matters worse, the American car industry significantly lagged behind the Japanese in quality and suffered from a poor image across the board. Saturn ran blind focus groups, centering on satisfied owners of Japanese cars in California – because that was the most critical market to capture. The focus groups indicated that 80% of the people would pick Saturn from among a dozen different models. However, when the nameplates were displayed, the first question was 'What is Saturn?' When told that it was an American car company, most potential buyers immediately had an adverse reaction.

To overcome this problem, Saturn broke with the auto industry by offering a remarkable deal: 'Satisfaction guaranteed, or your money back, with *no* questions asked.' They demonstrated their commitment to the customer in several ways. Perhaps the most dramatic one is when they implemented – for the first time in the history of the auto industry – a 'full car' recall. They replaced the complete car, not simply a component. Furthermore, they issued this recall within two weeks of first finding symptoms of a problem. In fact the problem they encountered did not originate at Saturn. It was a defective antifreeze liquid provided by a supplier that had the potential to damage the engine as well as the radiator.

Incidentally, few customers took Saturn up on its guarantee by returning their car after driving it for one month. 'No questions asked' was the most difficult promise for dealers to keep. Instinctively, they wanted to ask the customer why the car was being returned, but because their curiosity could detract from their customers' experience, they maintained strict discipline. Saturn sought to build a culture around making the customer experience as pleasant as possible.

The next step was to restructure the dealer channel itself. Saturn undertook a comprehensive evaluation of the dealership network; they chose their dealers from the list of the top 5% of dealers in America regardless of the brands they represented. Saturn targeted them and offered extraordinary terms, which also included a major commitment on the dealers' part to learn the Saturn culture with in-depth, long stays in the Saturn manufacturing facilities, and to make multimillion dollar investments in the dealership infrastructure. Saturn also made large investments in dealer support with an advanced information system linking the customer with dealers and suppliers to ensure rapid customer service and with a 24-hour road service capability (offered free of charge to the customer). Many things happened in the formation of this new dealer behavior. First, and not just symbolically, Saturn changed the term 'dealer,' with the implicit connotation of negotiation and harassment, to the term 'retailer,' which connotes loyalty and fairness in customer actions. Next, Saturn instituted a no-haggling policy. Every car, and every accessory in the car, had a fixed price throughout America. In fact, retailers helped to educate the customer on the features and price of the car and on how the car compared to competing models. Additionally, Saturn established a complete rezoning and expansion of the 'retailer' areas, thus limiting competition and allowing a more effective use of a central warehouse that would be shared by a circle of Saturn dealers to reduce their inventory and related costs.

Not surprisingly, the customer response was overwhelming, creating what has become a cult among Saturn owners. For seven years in a row now, Saturn has received the highest customer satisfaction rating in the industry as rated by J.D. Power and Associates, a rating even higher than those of all the luxury car makers – Lexus, Mercedes, BMW, and so on. The high customer satisfaction is a phenomenal accomplishment for a car that retails for about one quarter of the price of most luxury cars. Saturn's most powerful advertising channel became the 'word of mouth' of pleased customers, proving that a customer focus could be at least as strong a way to achieve competitive advantage as a product focus.

In essence, Saturn's competitive position was not centered on the product, but on providing the customer with a bundle of experiences and services unsurpassed by any of its direct competitors. They lowered the customer's cost of buying and owning a car through actions independent of the product itself.

How to Redefine the Customer Experience

To take this approach to a Total Customer Solutions position you need to understand fully how customers interact with a product or service and then creatively redefine this experience to the benefit of the customer. This often involves looking extensively at all the interactions with the customer that were previously marginalized (for example sales, billing, customer care) or at customer usage that was normally out of your purview (for example the end as well as the beginning of a product or service life cycle). The business should establish a relationship with the customer rather than a transaction. This continued presence allows the customer to learn more about your service as well as gain confidence in the promised outcome; these are assets that are not readily transferable to another competitor with a similar offering. Products can be evaluated prior to the purchase, making it easy for a customer to switch when offered new alternatives, but experiences are learned and can only be evaluated after the purchase. The business should establish multiple interfaces with the customer. A product is sold by the salesman to the person responsible for procurement. The product experience is shared by many individuals across many situations, from when the product is financed, registered in financial ledgers, used, upgraded, repaired, sold, and replaced. The companies cited below further illustrate these methods.

Other Illustrations of Redefining Customer Experience

Carrier, one of the world's largest air conditioning, heating, and refrigeration companies, is positioning itself to redefine the customer experience. Heating and cooling units have long been sold as products, and the customer would take the ultimate responsibility for the comfort of their home or office. The temperature and humidity, however, are a function of many things beyond the product, including correct sizing and operating of the unit, proper insulation and ventilation, suitable windows, and appropriate maintenance. Carrier has gone the next step to provide a service level contract for the comfort in your home or office. They will attend to all the factors to assure you of the environment you desire.

Digital Island is a web hosting company deeply engaged in a similar Total Customer Solutions objective. They host software applications for companies in well-fortified, secure, maintained, and centrally monitored data centers. Their clients can access the software via the Internet and private data circuits. The benefits from central application hosting are huge. The economies of scale of a large data center frequently make it cheaper for the customers than hosting the applications themselves. The data centers are built like Fort Knox with stability and security that an individual company could not afford, and they are maintained by professionals that most companies cannot find. As a consequence, these services are in demand and the market is growing at well over 50% a year. To distinguish themselves from entrenched competitors, such as Exodus, who are much larger, Digital Island offers a total service level agreement (SLA) aimed at guaranteeing the customer's experience. Their business model places extraordinary emphasis on an integrated, comprehensive SLA, rather than numerous individual SLAs for infrastructure components, as has been the practice of their competitors. By delivering an integrated SLA, Digital Island is able to focus on what matters most to its customers: applications availability. They have engineered their infrastructure to deliver against a comprehensive SLA. Rather than allowing customers direct physical access to the servers and permitting customers to choose from a multitude of equipment and software providers, they tightly control the component options, integration, and access, as well as manage against a well-defined process to install, maintain, and monitor applications.

The *Wall Street Journal Interactive* (WSJI) is an offshoot of the *Wall Street Journal* (*WSJ*). It set out to do more than deliver the content of the *WSJ* online. It redefined its service to deliver the total experience the customer desired from news. *WSJ* readers are focused on business, own stock portfolios, and require timely and specific information, as well as contextual news on the economy. The WSJI web format is not simply an electronic version of the newspaper. They redesigned the presentation and capability to provide the customer with a different experience. This enables close interaction and customization around each customer, to track their stock ownership, tailor news articles to their preferences, drawing on the full range of Dow Jones sources, and proactively alerts subscribers to personally relevant breaking news items. The delivery infrastructure now depends on many partners, including Microsoft, Palm, and Microstrategy, to enable delivery of timely, relevant information to customers wherever they are via wireline or wireless transmission.

Achieving Total Customer Solutions through Horizontal Breadth

Some of the most active repositioning in the telecommunications market today is by companies attempting to offer a full, integrated suite of products that fill most if not all of their customers' communications needs. The AT&T breakup in 1984 fragmented the industry into local and long distance businesses. Regulatory constraints separated TV cable from telephone businesses. Additionally, new technologies and regulations added the independent cellular mobile, paging, and online industries. In the end, consumers receive their telecommunications services from a plethora of companies – it is not atypical for a heavy user to have over five telecommunications providers with five monthly bills, and separate pricing plans.

As a result, many telecommunications companies are expanding their product scope. Figure 4.2 shows how major telecom players are jockeying for product and customer share positions. Undoubtedly, the most promi-

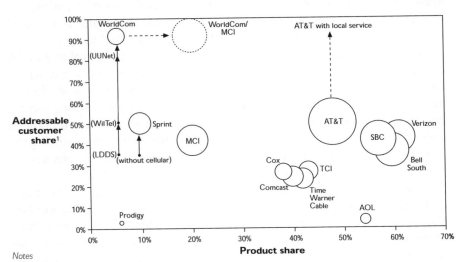

Notes

1. Weighted by target customers (Business vs. Consumers)

2. Bubble size = Total Revenue

Figure 4.2   Market positioning matrix – product share vs. customer share

Source: Dean & Company analysis, FCC, annual reports, SEC, IDC, *Datacom*, CTIA, *Statistical Abstract of the U.S.,* 1996

nent player is AT&T with roughly 50% market share in long distance services, their leading product. The horizontal axis in Figure 4.2 measures product share, which is the critical measure for Best Product positioning. The product share metric is calculated by dividing the sales of each company by the sales of the specific market they serve. Since they operate in different, but converging markets, the sum of the product market share does not add up to 100%. (For example, Bell Atlantic and Bell South today serve fundamentally different geographic territories, and both are shown with roughly 60% market share, which would be impossible if they were serving the same market.)

If we look at the horizontal axis, we detect considerable industry fragmentation. Most of the competitors today are one-product companies. This fragmentation uncovers two issues. First, there is no single dominant player across all products. Second, there are enormous opportunities to build Total Customer Solutions via acquisitions, partnerships, and alliances. Companies are not expanding their scope by themselves. In fact, even the mighty AT&T is pursuing partnerships and acquisitions, such as cable with TCI and cellular with McCaw; as well as making huge internal investments to extend its product scope to include local, state, and Internet services.

As companies expand product scope, they gain potential customer share. This is shown on the vertical axis in Figure 4.2, which measures the addressable customer share. This is calculated as the ratio of the market size of the products that each company is capable of serving to the total market of products that the company's target customer purchases.

This chart provides insight into the enormous dynamics unfolding in the telecommunications industry. If you took the conventional view, which focuses on the product share enjoyed by each company, you would come to the wrong conclusion. You would assume that there are a few strong incumbent players dominating each of their markets. However, the addition of customer share as a dimension of competitive advantage is destabilizing the industry and leading to massive shifts in market share between businesses. This has had dramatic impact on MCI WorldCom's market value.

Growing by acquisition can be an effective means of making an immediate impact. However, the value added that results is far more elusive. Bargains are hard to come by, or nonexistent, which leads to exorbitant premiums. To justify them the acquiring company is forced to create significant synergies that are understood and valued by the financial markets. MCI WorldCom is exemplary in this respect, having conducted a seemingly never-ending stream of acquisitions, the primary impact of which has been to position them as one of the leading Total Customer Solutions companies in its industry. Figure 4.3 shows the numerous acqui-

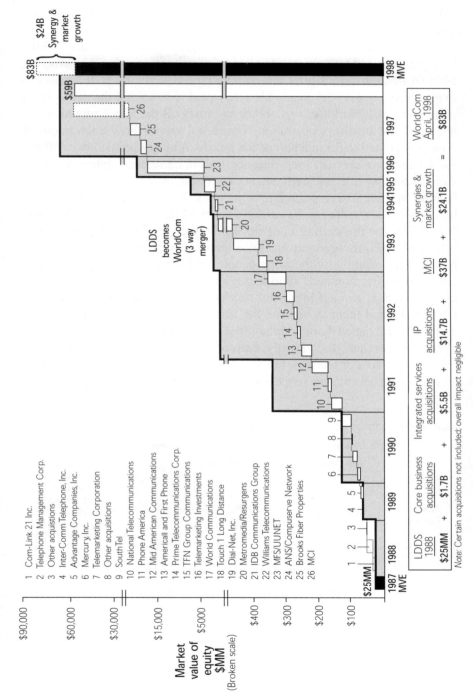

Figure 4.3 WorldCom market value enlargement

Market value of equity $MM (Broken scale)

$90,000
$60,000
$30,000
$15,000
$5000
$400
$300
$200
$100

1987 MVE — $25MM

1988 · 1989 · 1990 · 1991 · 1992 · 1993 · 1994 1995 · 1996 · 1997 · 1998 MVE

$83B

$24B Synergy & market growth

$59B

LDDS becomes WorldCom (3 way merger)

1 Com-Link 21 Inc.
2 Telephone Management Corp.
3 Other acquisitions
4 Inter-Comm Telephone, Inc.
5 Advantage Companies, Inc.
6 Mercury, Inc.
7 Telemarketing Corporation
8 Other acquisitions
9 SouthTel
10 National Telecommunications
11 Phone America
12 Mid American Communications
13 Americall and First Phone
14 Prime Telecommunications Corp.
15 TFN Group Communications
16 Telemarketing Investments
17 World Communications
18 Touch 1 Long Distance
19 Dial-Net, Inc.
20 Metromedia/Resurgens
21 IDB Communications Group
22 Williams Telecommunications
23 MFS/UUNET
24 ANS/Compuserve Network
25 Brooks Fiber Properties
26 MCI

LDDS 1988		Core business acquisitions		Integrated services acquisitions		IP acquisitions		MCI		Synergies & market growth		WorldCom April, 1998
$25MM	+	$1.7B	+	$5.5B	+	$14.7B	+	$37B	+	$24.1B	=	$83B

Note: Certain acquisitions not included; overall impact negligible sitions WorldCom has made since it started its journey in 1987 as a $25 million long distance reseller.

For each acquisition they paid substantial premiums. In the case of MFS they paid $14 billion, which was over twice its market value. Nonetheless, MCI WorldCom's stock price has outpaced these premiums so that today its market value is over 2.5 times what they paid to assemble the parts. These parts give MCI WorldCom an ability to satisfy all the telecommunications needs of the business customer. Figure 4.4 shows how each acquired company helped to fill in a part of the puzzle. A business customer will buy local telephone service, long distance telephone service, Internet access, web hosting service, and cellular service. These once distinct services now heavily overlap. The definition of what is local versus long distance varies by carrier, voice calls can be carried over the Internet, and cellular service substitutes for the calling card or 800 service, typically a part of long distance. The procurement and management of these services is being handled increasingly by the same people, and the provisioning and billing needs to be harmonized. WorldCom started as a long distance resaler, bought MFS to expand into local services; Williams added data services; UUNet allowed them to become the leading provider of Internet services; and MCI established them with facilities and customer relationships in need of bundled services. Individually, each of these companies was not distinctive in either cost or features, but as a bundle MCI WorldCom has created a service with unparalleled scope and high customer lock-in.

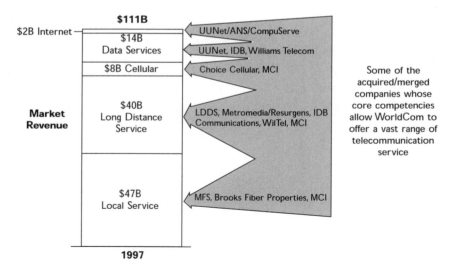

Figure 4.4   MCI WorldCom breadth of product and service

Source: Business communications services revenue – U.S. market (1997)

This bundling also yields significant economic benefits due to customer retention. This becomes apparent when one looks at the extraordinary customer churn companies struggle with today. The average Fortune 500 company reacquires its entire customer base every five years. In more dynamic industries such as telecommunications it is worse; MCI has traditionally acquired 17 million customers every year, a number equal to its base! (Obviously, some customers, normally the ones generating the highest revenue, 'spin' between competitors three or four times a year while a few stay for years.) Exacerbating this problem is the escalating cost of customer acquisition. It can cost over $5000 to acquire a small business account. Compare this to the average monthly telecommunications bill of around $1000, and an average margin of 10–15%, and one finds that acquisition costs can dominate the economics. Bundling reduces churn because customers have to confront the switching costs of multiple service or lose the benefits of a single provider. It effectively lowers the customer acquisition cost by extending the revenue-generating life of the customer associated with the one-time sales cost.

The customer benefits from MCI WorldCom's strategy through improved convenience, simplicity, and pricing. The business benefits through higher revenue per customer, higher customer retention rates, and lower cost of customer care and sales. The success of the strategy is in the company's market value. MCI WorldCom stock has generated the second highest shareholder return in the 1994 to 1999 five-year period, when compared to all other New York Stock Exchange companies. Clearly, the company is following a strategy that is changing the rules of competition in the telecommunications industry and drawing upon new sources of profitability. MCI WorldCom is attempting to shift the measure of competitive advantage from product share to customer share. Product share traditionally looks at one particular product and its sales as a percentage of the total market for that type of good. Customer share, on the other hand, is defined as the percentage of a customer's related set of needs that a single vendor can satisfy when looking across a range of related products.

Other industries have displayed the same pattern of product proliferation followed by service integration. In the financial services sector, for example, Merrill Lynch, Schwab, and Fidelity have all prospered from offering customers accounts which consolidate their brokerage, mutual funds, checking, credit cards, bill paying, and cash management services.

Defining Horizontal Breadth

The aim of Horizontal Breadth is to improve the economics of the customer and enhance customer bonding by integrating and customizing a broad scope of related products and services. It is not always necessary to own the design and manufacturing of each individual component in order to offer a customized solution. Ownership and control is a function of how the component is customized and how central it is to the overall solution. A bundle of products can create bonding opportunities. Customer preferences and usage information can be shared across services to enhance their operation around the particular needs of the customer. For example, by supplying switched and dedicated services, which can be substitutes for each other, MCI WorldCom can alter the mix depending on customer usage. When billing specifications change they need only be implemented once from the perspective of the customer.

Horizontal Breadth is more than bundling. Too often bundling is simply a means to discount prices more deeply, and customers begin to expect nothing more or less in response. Where bundling alone yields volume discounts, Horizontal Breadth enhances service by integrating and customizing a related set of products to serve the customer better than if each component were purchased and used separately.

Another Illustration of Horizontal Breadth

Amazon illustrates Horizontal Breadth in the new economy. Amazon started by selling books on the Internet, but now has extended its scope to over 18 categories ranging from music to home improvement. To further improve selection and meet the full set of needs for visiting customers, they provide the electronic storefront for a number of merchants through their Z shop program. In summarizing Amazon's primary strategic concern, CEO Jeff Bezos comes close to the very definition of a Total Customer Solutions strategy: 'To survive in e-commerce requires an obsessive, relentless focus on the customer.' Once a customer has set up an account, a customer can buy an additional item with a single click. To Amazon's 8.4 million customers (as of May 1999), this translates into convenience. Amazon views it as customer lock-in. Why would a customer switch to a competitor's site once his or her account is already up and running at Amazon?

Amazon achieves further lock-in by asking customers to input information regarding their loved ones' special occasions. It then sends its customers reminders about their inputted birthdays, graduations, and baby showers complete with recommended gifts. How does it recommend gifts? It bases recommendations on information provided by the original customer, thereby obtaining data on which to base the targeting of new customers.

Customers returning to the site are greeted with suggestions for new purchases based on the buying patterns of other customers with similar tastes. Amazon sends customers information about new releases in their favorite categories.

Tailoring and targeting customers requires obtaining and processing massive amounts of detailed and granular data. Amazon, which as of mid-March 1999 received one million hits per day, tracks purchasing behavior online and analyzes ad clicks down to the level of cost per lead. Amazon has used external help as well as building internal skills in gathering and assessing customer information. In April 1999, Amazon added Alexa Internet to its information-gathering arsenal. Alexa's technology simultaneously aids customers in navigating the World Wide Web and tracks where they choose to go and how long they spend there. Prior to its acquisition by Amazon, Alexa's primary revenue stream came from selling reports based on this captured information. Says Bezos:

> We want to get to know [our customers] the same way a small-town shop-keeper of yesteryear might have gotten to know them ... That kind of personalization is going to be extremely valuable for the customer.[1]

Amazon follows the lead of Yahoo!, another company pursuing Horizontal Breadth, which collects 400,000 megabytes of information per day about where customers go during their visits to the site. Both companies relentlessly strive to learn what products and advertisements customers like most in order to increase sales of both and the price of advertisements. And Bezos suggests that that will continue to be Amazon's focus over the next several years:

> We know 2% of what we will know 10 years from now, and most of that learning is going to revolve around personalization – making the store ideal for a particular customer, not for the mythic average customer.

Achieving Total Customer Solutions through Customer Integration

National Starch offers a good example of the Customer Integration approach. It is a premier company in the chemical industry, which was sold recently by Unilever to Imperial Chemical Industries (ICI). At first sight, National Starch appears to be a company deeply rooted in rather mundane and pedestrian products. Its origin, as its name implies, can be traced to glue and starch. The reality, however, is quite different from the first impression. It is a company that has an unsurpassed history of long-term superior performance, not only in its industry, but also compared to most other American corporations.

Its success resides in having extraordinary technological capabilities coupled with an intimate knowledge of all its key customers. The first time we conducted an audit review of the information control systems used by National Starch we were unimpressed by the quality, breadth, and detail of the information that was being collected and processed for the executives. This was not what we would have expected from a company with such exceptional performance, so we went back to the drawing board to find out what we had missed. We found an enormous amount of knowledge that was accumulated primarily by R&D personnel, technical service staff and marketing and sales managers. This knowledge covered the needs of the customers, the state of new product development, and the ability of National Starch to provide unsurpassed assistance to aid customers in the expansion of their revenues and the containment of their costs. They do not only produce adhesives and sell them by the gallon; the essence of their business is the joint working relationship with the customer.

One of the most spectacular products that emerged from this relationship was the development of a sophisticated adhesive that eliminated the need to weld the wings to the body of an aircraft. This product has two critical characteristics: it clearly contributes to the total quality of the final product, and it accounts for a negligible portion of the total cost of the airplane. These two conditions lead to a product with exceptional potential.

National Starch expertise is similarly associated with the supersonic car. In 1998, a car broke the sound barrier for the first time. Every single piece of that car was put together by National Starch adhesives. Virtually nothing is bolted or welded onto the body; it is all glued.

These accomplishments sound like technological achievements, but, taken within the context of joint development with customers, they add up to an extraordinary bonding with very important customers that creates a strong and mutually beneficial relationship. National Starch is not a Best

Product company, in spite of the fact that the chemical industry in which it resides is overwhelmingly regarded as a commodity-driven industry that epitomizes the Best Product position. The moral of the National Starch story is that by being creative in constructing a tight working relationship with the customer you can 'decommoditize' a product. The bonds that emerge are so strong because they not only provide a product, but also a unique and valuable service that enhances customer economics.

Defining Customer Integration

Businesses following Customer Integration assume some activities previously performed by the customer. They perform them more efficiently or effectively than the customer to improve the customer's economics. This typically creates a custom fit between the business and the customer that is burrowed deep into the customer's operations beyond the light of efficient markets and that cannot easily be replicated by a competitor. The customer as well as the business invest time and resources into tailoring a product and how it will be used and processed by the customer. This creates a switching cost and ties that go well beyond the investment made by the business itself and that naturally grow with use. Not all outsourcing falls into this category, for if the interface with the customer is simple and common to a broad market then the bonding is weak. For example, hosting a plain vanilla web page offers little bonding. Many data centers provide similar services, the customer interface is common, the customer needs to make little vendor specific investments, and, consequently, switching suppliers is straightforward.

Over the past 20 years, we have witnessed a prevailing trend toward outsourcing or 'virtual companies'. Nike and Dell are showcase illustrations of efficient manufacturers who hardly manufacture, given their aggressive outsourcing. Information technology – once thought too central to leave to others because it was considered the brain and neural system of a business – has moved to the point where the conventional wisdom is that you should not do it yourself. But, the real *tsunami* (tidal wave) in outsourcing is still ahead of us and is enabled by the infrastructure of the Internet. Ubiquitous and fat networks allow hardware, software, and knowledge to migrate to disparate clusters that can be remotely, spontaneously, and intimately accessed by businesses. Today virtually no venture capitalist is funding software for PCs, instead they are focusing on Application Service Providers (ASPs) that rent software and service over the Internet.

Other Illustrations of Customer Integration

Dell bypassed the traditional computer dealer distribution system altogether by providing direct telephone and then Internet distribution. Amazon used the capabilities of the World Wide Web to circumvent classic book sales channels. It is not unusual to find restructured distribution channels at the core of a redefined customer relationship. And, in restructuring these channels, Total Customer Solutions businesses can enrich the customer interface in multiple dimensions, leading to customer lock-in. Procurement and legal has to arrange contracts, finance needs to record the assets, schedule depreciation or augment leases, and IT needs to install and then maintain the equipment, and, of course, there is the end-user. For many customers Dell has streamlined and defined these interfaces using the web. When a user needs a computer, the standard software as specified by the IT department is installed, the various departments are informed, and the computer shipped ready to use. When Dell sells a computer to a customer on the web, they automatically touch the customer's financial records, inventory systems, leasing, and IT maintenance shop. It is a bond that serves both the business and the customer, and one that is not easily broken.

US Internetworking is an ASP that is a clear example of a Total Customer Solutions provider. They centrally host applications software that their clients can remotely access. Businesses that once purchased PeopleSoft software and installed it locally on their private network of servers and PCs to deal with their human resource (HR) needs can now rent the same application from US Internetworking. Furthermore, other applications specific to a client's needs, which have to interact with the HR application, can also be provided and integrated by US Internetworking. The customer benefits through lower costs, higher reliability, and less hassle. US Internetworking benefits from the customer bonding derived from a service customized to user preferences, custody of client data, and the customer's growing knowledge of how to use their systems.

Pack Online is a start-up ASP with a similar strategy. They are targeting the small business segment, starting first with dentists. The application is practice management – software to help you manage your office, for example scheduling, customer records, billing, and so on. To date, this capability has been addressed by software that works locally on a PC and is maintained by the customer. Supporting this software is getting more expensive and difficult as the software gets more sophisticated and competent IT staff become more scarce. Pack Online has designed HTML-based software that operates from a remote server that can be accessed over the

Internet. There are immediate economic benefits to the customer, such as dramatically reducing upfront capital expense (there is no software to buy and the PC can be simpler) and lowering their lifetime costs, sometimes by over 50%. This benefit is improving over time, since the cost of Internet access is declining by roughly 20–30% per annum, while the costs of IT staff are growing at 15% annually. Furthermore, a network hosted service can more easily allow the small business to connect to others in order to exchange information or transact commerce. Dentists can search for insurance eligibility, process claims, send X-rays to specialists, automatically purchase supplies, and schedule appointments with patients. These functions add tremendous utility to the small business, but also bond the business to Pack Online's service. Customers make large and ongoing investments to input their user preferences, link insurance providers, specialists and suppliers, promulgate online addresses, and to learn how to use the system. Switching providers is like moving to a new house, a huge effort not to be taken lightly.

General Electric (GE) is another company that has excelled in Customer Integration. Jack Welch, GE's legendary CEO, gets upset if someone describes GE as a conglomerate, with a set of unrelated businesses that do not add value to each other. A closer examination reveals a well-conceived Total Customer Solutions strategy. Its tremendous strength in financial services has made GE unique among its peers in its ability to provide sophisticated financing options to its customers and support to businesses in its portfolio. After all, money is the most fungible and therefore the most easily transferable resource.

Beyond financial services, GE has actively extended from selling products to providing after-market services for many of its core businesses. After years of selling CAT scanners, magnetic resonance imagers, and other medical imaging equipment to the healthcare giant Columbia/HCA Healthcare Corp., GE persuaded Columbia to let it service all the imaging equipment, including that made by GE's rivals, in each of its approximately 300 hospitals. Later, GE began to manage virtually all medical supplies as part of the deal – most of them product lines GE is not even in. Columbia has saved tens of millions of dollars, and GE has gained added revenue and a lock on a huge customer.

In the aircraft engine business, where GE effectively splits the market 50/50 with Pratt & Whitney, the commercial airlines have traditionally maintained their own engines. GE is now offering to maintain their engines, and can present a fairly compelling offer to the airlines, owing to their technical expertise and their ability to capture a higher volume of business than any one carrier. GE signed a 10-year, $2.3 billion contract with British Airways (BA) in March 2000 under which GE will carry out 85% of the engine maintenance work on BA's entire fleet – including engines made by rivals Rolls-Royce and Pratt & Whitney. Today, GE is busy transforming the carrier's maintenance practices. It is moving BA to a just-in-time inventory system for parts, and instituting self-directed teams and other advanced management practices from its own plants. David J. Kilonback, who oversees the deal for BA, says the shift saved the carrier money and management time, in addition to speedier engine turn-around. Building on the BA deal, GE inked a $1 billion, multiyear contract in September 2000 to service USAir Inc.'s GE engines.

Reflections

Customer Relationships as Strategy

The Total Customer Solutions option brings home the centrality of the customer and the need to put the customer at the heart of the enterprise. It might sound naive, but we have repeatedly encountered the admission that business organizations do not have the deep level of customer under-standing that is needed to establish a solid Total Customer Solutions strategy. This requires analysis of the customer's economics, an under-standing of what drives the customer's profitability, and a relationship structure between the business and the customer that leads to an unbreak-able bond. All executives know intuitively the value of customer relation-ships, but it is seldom the basis for a substantive strategy.

Note

1.   As quoted in Heather Green, 'The information gold mine,' *Business Week,* July 26, 1999.

CHAPTER 5

System Lock-In: Winning through Complementors

The System Lock-In position represents the strongest form of bonding and demands that the business addresses the overall architecture of the system. Instead of focusing solely on the product or the customer, we are now concerned with all the important players in the system that contribute to the creation of economic value for a particular customer. Besides the normal industry participants – buyers, suppliers, channels, and potential new entrants – we are especially concerned with nurturing, attracting, and retaining 'complementors.'[1] A complementor is not a competitor, or necessarily a supplier; it is a provider of products and services that enhance, directly or indirectly, our own offering. Examples of complementor pairings include computer manufacturers and software producers, high fidelity equipment manufacturers and CD retailers, and video cassette recorders and movie studios.

System Lock-In further expands the scope of the business relative to the previous strategic options. System Lock-In players attract, satisfy, and retain customers by attracting, satisfying, and retaining complementors. The value of the system grows with increasing participation and they enter an economic zone of increasing returns with growth. This defies conventional economic reasoning which has it roots in the behavior of the agricultural industry. As the agricultural activity expands, less fertile lands enter into production. The more you produce, the lower the incremental margins you enjoy. Network effects put an end to the universal validity of this principle. At eBay, the Internet-based auction house, the value of their service goes up with each additional buyer and seller that uses their service. But it is important to note that, while networks enable and accelerate these effects, System Lock-In has always existed. Sotheby's and Christie's are physically-based auction houses that sustained themselves for years because they were the dominant exchange point for buyers and sellers to congregate.

As with all aspects of bonding there are two necessary conditions to create System Lock-In: (i) the existence of increasing marginal returns and

(ii) external network effects. Increasing marginal returns reflect how the value of the product or service increases with increased users and usage. Network externalities reflect the fact that attractiveness of the product is not embodied in the characteristics of the product, but is external and often the function of investments by others, particularly the complementors and customers. When these conditions exist, the more a product is adopted and used the greater the benefit it confers to the customer. This translates into a virtuous cycle, where more is better, leading to even more, and so forth. This sets the stage for achieving a System Lock-In position. The increased reach and connectivity that the Internet provides has expanded the stage of opportunities. Moreover, this technology has disaggregated industries creating a network of complex interactions among fragmented and specialized participants that almost mandates the use of common standards to ensure effective exchanges.

There are three ways to achieve System Lock-In, as illustrated in Figure 5.1: Proprietary Standard, Dominant Exchange, and Restricted Access. A business successfully positioned as a Proprietary Standard draws customers because of the extensive network of complementors that are designed to work with its product. If you want to use the complementors you are compelled to use the Proprietary Standard. Microsoft, Intel, Real Networks, Palm, and Cisco are superb examples. A business positioned as a Dominant Exchange provides an interface between buyers and sellers, or between parties that wish to exchange information or goods. Once this sort of business achieves a critical mass it is very hard to displace. With eBay, sellers

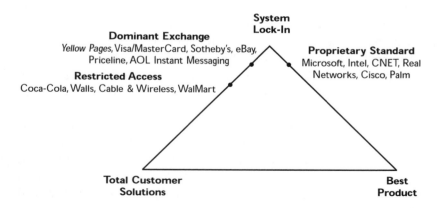

Figure 5.1   The Triangle: options for strategic planning

want to go to the site with the most buyers and buyers want to go to the site with the most sellers. Other companies with this position include the *Yellow Pages*, Visa/MasterCard, and AOL Instant Messaging. In the case of Restricted Access, the competitors are deprived of access to the customer because the channel has limited capacity to handle multiple vendors. This is the situation for the Walls ice cream cabinets that saturate small stores throughout Europe and Asia. Unilever gives these cabinets, free of charge, and keeps them fully stocked with Walls ice cream. Due to space constraints in small shops there is no room for competitive distribution.

Achieving System Lock-In through Proprietary Standards

Proprietary Standards existed before and will continue after Microsoft, but Bill Gates has definitely made it famous; perhaps because his de facto standard made him the richest man on the planet, perhaps because the Justice Department persecuted him for the alleged monopoly abuse enabled by his standard, or perhaps because his is the standard that brought IT into the hands of the everyday person. Just as Henry Ford introduced the economics of the assembly line to the lay person in the form of an automobile, Bill Gates may one day be known as the man who popularized System Lock-In as a way to compete. It is becoming more common in our new, networked economy. You will probably compete as, with, or against a Proprietary Standard business sometime in the future.

Among the strategic positions you can strive for, perhaps this is the epitome. It is the ultimate profit model, with the highest margins, greatest market share, and longest sustainability. Microsoft and Intel are the flag ships for this position. In combination, they have what is commonly referred to as the Wintel standard.

Figure 5.2 shows the complementor edge that Wintel holds. Eighty to ninety percent of the software applications are designed to work with Microsoft's PC operating systems (for example MS DOS, Windows 95, 98, 2000, and so on) and with Intel's microprocessor design (for example 286, 386, 486, Pentium, and so on).

Figure 5.2 also shows the power of complementors evident in the LAN market. This is a business that also shows the telltale characteristics of a Proprietary Standard. Novell has been the historical winner with over 5000 applications written by third parties to complement their Netware LAN operating system (OS). A LAN OS is necessary to help computers communicate, store information, and share printers and other equipment over a LAN. The applications add enhancements and functionality to the basic

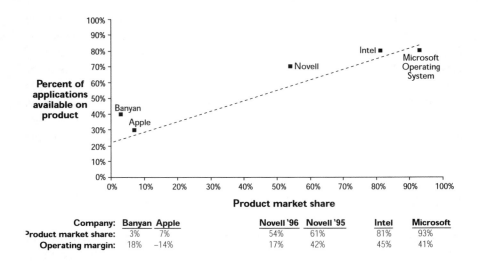

Company:	Banyan	Apple			Novell '96	Novell '95	Intel	Microsoft
Product market share:	3%	7%			54%	61%	81%	93%
Operating margin:	18%	−14%			17%	42%	45%	41%

Figure 5.2   Standards, market share and profitability

Source: Dean & Company, Value Line, SEC, Lexis-Nexis

system. Banyan, Novell, and many others were early competitors in the industry, but Novell became the dominant choice. The complementor comparison between Novell and Banyan point this out. Microsoft, with an unerring nose for de facto standards, has made a late stage push into the LAN OS market, almost giving away their Windows NT product (Microsoft's LAN OS offer) to gain share. This combined with errors by Novell, such as when they invested billions into Word Perfect in a doomed effort to be a player in PC applications, has helped Microsoft to gain significant share to a point where it may overtake Novell. There are two morals to that story. First, a Proprietary Standard is an extremely powerful position, and it is amazing how Novell has sustained itself in this market despite their gargantuan mistakes and Microsoft's investment. Second, many businesses are blissfully unaware of the nature of standards, even when they are sitting on top of them. Microsoft would appear to have a sixth sense when it comes to searching out, persistently pursuing, and then relentlessly reinforcing standards. By comparison, Novell has appeared as the person in the cliché, starving with a ham tied to their back.

The story of how Intel pursued a Proprietary Standard provides a lesson in the combination of serendipity, planning, and exertion necessary to establish this strategic position. Intel survived two amazing transformations that would kill most companies. In 1968 they were a start-up with the dream of building a business based upon what is now known as 'Moore's law.' Gordon Moore was one of the three founders of Intel, along with Andrew Grove and Robert Noyce. Moore's law is not in fact a law, but an observation that the number of transistors on a single semiconductor chip doubles every 12–18 months – and the capabilities double as well. With Moore's law in mind they thought there might be a promising business in selling memory chips to computer manufacturers. They succeeded in entering this business against six established and fortified rivals. Memory chips became an industry and Intel quickly grew to become its leader.

Then the Japanese entered the business. They entered into memory chips with the same skill, scale, and tenacity that they had used to succeed in the motorcycle, automotive, and steel industries. By 1985 Intel was facing its second great transformation, from the hemorrhaging memory business to the embryonic microprocessor business.

IBM only decided to get into the PC business after its Executive Committee had rejected the proposal over 10 times. After all, IBM's brand stood for quality and reliability honed over years as the leading supplier of computer mainframes. PCs were new, fragile, unreliable, and truly hobbyist material. The future success of PCs was highly uncertain, but their threat to the IBM brand was an absolute certainty. When IBM finally decided to enter the PC market they insisted that the business go to Boca Raton, Florida – far away from IBM headquarters. They wanted the PC business to be completely independent, not expecting to receive any support from IBM. So the fledgling IBM PC business looked to Motorola for microprocessors. Motorola was a leader in the semiconductor industry and a preferred chip provider. Motorola was prepared to take an order, but IBM wanted a partner that would send people to Boca Raton to help design the PC around the chip. Motorola was the supplier of chips to Apple Computers, which had the leadership position in the PC market, and rejected the IBM offer. So IBM also solicited help from Intel, a relatively unknown company on the West Coast who only made memory chips. Intel was glad to help, because they had such large exposure in memory chips. Privately, IBM planned to switch to Motorola after their initial introduction with the Intel chip. However, true to the bonding effects of a Proprietary Standard, IBM quickly found that they were locked into the Intel chip. Knowing that none of the other computer manufacturers would have the market clout that IBM had to develop an industry standard, Intel put a great effort on winning the account. Ultimately, the IBM PC business did generate $5.5 billion annual revenues after only four years. More importantly, IBM created the dominant design that all other PC manufacturers would copy, with Intel as a critical ingredient.

A key measure of success was the share of the Intel standard. This is not necessarily product share for Intel, and, in fact, product share can stand in the way. In the early days of the 8086 Intel had limited microprocessor fabrication capacity, but they needed broad availability so that the Intel standard could capture the highest share of PCs. Intel licensed up to 12 other companies to produce the chip, leaving themselves with only 30% of the total manufacturing revenues of the product. Beyond adding 8086 capacity, this redirected the efforts of competitors to produce an Intel standard rather than introduce alternatives. As the standard gained acceptance and Intel's capacity grew they were able to pull more production in-house. The 80286 generation was licensed to only four second sources, and the 80386 license was granted to only IBM, for use in IBM's own computers. Intel's de facto standard has now gained a 90% market share and they aggressively defend their ownership.

Profit and Intel's own product share were secondary to gaining system share for the potential Proprietary Standard. This practice of 'giveaways' is common when competitors are vying for standard ownership and when there is potential for significant bonding. Giveaways can be suicide for a 'Best Product' position, because the customers can switch suppliers when it comes time to regain the margins lost. Today, with an established Proprietary Standard, Intel charges significant price premiums. They are highest for the new generation of microprocessors. Then as competitors are able to clone the new chip, the price falls. The 80286 at launch in 1982 was priced at $360 and in 1993 was only $8. The 80486 was priced at $950 at its August 1989 launch and in 1993 was only $317.[2]

Intel managed to expand the number and diversity of complementors. The development of the 386 chip marked the transformation of the industry from dominance by IBM to a broad and growing interdependence among a number of firms in the industry. This change was encouraged by Intel and Microsoft. In 1986, IBM showed reluctance to sell any 386-based computers until they could develop an architecture that used more proprietary IBM components. Intel encouraged Compaq to be not only a leader in portables, but to lead in performance as well. Until this point Compaq had almost no experience with desktop systems. The 386 was a bet against the cheaper 286 computers and a gamble that significant 32-bit software would be developed. Compaq introduced the Deskpro 386 and it was an instant hit with consumers. The year 1986 was a watershed, helping to move the industry from a 'vertical' alignment, where a company would dominate all critical aspects of the value chain in a closed system, to a 'horizontal' alignment, with different companies operating together in an open system.

Not every product or service can be a Proprietary Standard; there are opportunities only in certain parts of the industry architecture, and only at certain times. When a company can create a Proprietary Standard it has enormous competitive advantage, which results in long-term superior financial performance. We have provided general data on the relative profits across strategies in Chapter 1. The profit distribution specific to the PC industry is shown in Figure 5.3. This chart separates the profits generated by businesses with a Proprietary Standard from the profitability of other types of business, including component suppliers and PC integrators. The lion's share of the profits has consistently gone to Proprietary Standards.

Proprietary Standards have resulted in some of the most spectacular value creation in recent history. By the end of 1998, Microsoft had created $328 billion of market value in excess of the debt and equity investment[3] in the company, and Intel had created $167 billion. In the same year, these companies were ranked 1st and 3rd in value creation among the 1000 largest, publicly owned companies in America. In contrast, IBM, while enjoying the ownership of a Proprietary Standard in the mainframe era, failed to spot and capture the emerging standards at the dawn of the PC generation, and their market value suffered accordingly. By 1995 IBM was minus $6 billion in market value creation, and it ranked 997 out of the largest 1000 companies. In 1998, after its strong recovery based on a Total Customer Solutions strategy, it ranked 11th with a value creation of $117 billion.

It should also be no surprise that the companies now rivaling Microsoft for the top spot in market value, Oracle and Cisco, are also positioned as

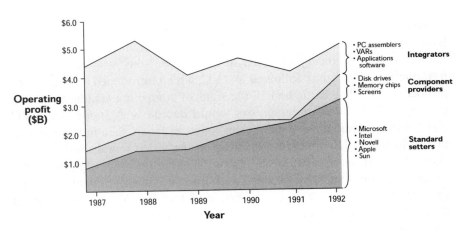

Figure 5.3   PC market evolution

Source: Moody's Annual Reports

Proprietary Standards. Oracle has a database product that is its centerpiece for its Internet software and it serves as a platform for many applications. Cisco's showcase product is the router, and, although they were not the first to sell routers nor are they the best, they dominate. Customers use Cisco routers so that they can communicate more reliably with the other Cisco routers that pervasively occupy the nodes of the Internet backbone. These customers can also avail themselves of the army of third party technicians trained to support Cisco equipment, and in this world of scarce talent that is a critically important complementor.

Defining a Proprietary Standard

An evolution in technology frequently causes an opportunity to establish a System Lock-In position. It creates new industries that offer the potential for new Proprietary Standards. As important, technology creates a network of complex interactions among fragmented and specialized participants that almost mandates the use of common standards to ensure effective interworking.

A Proprietary Standard approach requires two major achievements. First, you need to position your business as the natural locus and interface point in an open system. To integrate disparate pieces in a common system usually requires adherence to a standard that is widely recognized. This is by no means an easy task. However, it is not as difficult as the second task, which is to achieve the full proprietary ownership of the standard allowing you to appropriate the major share of value created by the system.

Not all standards are proprietary. Most, in fact, are nonproprietary and have no owner with the ability to appropriate system profits. When the video recording industry emerged in the 1970s, Sony was first with the introduction of Betamax followed by JVC, which introduced a competitive protocol, VHS. The battle had all the signs of competing standards, in that the support of the complementors would decide who succeeded. JVC chose a strategy emphasizing alliances – first in Japan, then in Europe, and finally in the U.S. – and concentrating on the video rental market. Sony chose to go it alone with an emphasis on the home recording market.[4] Despite having a superior product, and a first-to-market advantage, Sony lost the battle. However, it was a Pyrrhic victory for JVC, as the standard they designed and fought for was not one they could appropriate. VHS is a nonproprietary standard that is used by all manufacturers today, including Sony, and it gives no special advantage to JVC.

What is the lesson from this? A system with tremendous lock-in can develop around a standard, but the standard will not necessarily be proprietary. Others can imitate the standard if it has fairly simple interfaces to the complementors, and it is stable. If the standard is complex and is constantly evolving, or if it is protected by patent, then it is harder, sometimes impossible, to copy. This is not a natural outcome; companies need to work hard to achieve and then retain ownership. Advanced Micro Devices (AMD) reverse engineers the Intel Pentium microprocessor chips and sells them at a significant discount, but Intel retains effective control of the standard. Intel does this by releasing a constant stream of new products, each backwardly compatible with the earlier version, which take time for AMD to copy. When the 486 was just about to be introduced, the 586 Pentium processor development was well in hand, and the 686 design was in progress. With the knowledge that these developments are underway, customers and complementors expect Intel to continue the stewardship of the standard. If AMD were to create a renegade standard, they would have a difficult time convincing complementors to invest in it when Intel's next generation was just about to enter the market. Only Intel can introduce a new microprocessor that has the market confidence to be accepted as the new-generation Proprietary Standard. Intel, therefore, enjoys the lead time of these new products during which it commands much higher prices. Additionally, Intel has the loyalty of customers who want to maintain their Intel purchases even as the microprocessor 'clones' introduce their cheaper chips, so that they can be assured of 'first in line' status for Intel's next-generation chips. When Intel introduces a new-generation microprocessor, the new chips are typically in short supply as PC makers scramble to sell new products with the latest design. Intel's policy is to use past buying behavior as a guide to determine how many chips a customer would receive when supplies are short.

One other note, System Lock-In is specific to a segment. Even in the case of the ubiquitous PC a detailed segmentation of the market is important. While Microsoft commands most of the market, Apple has carved out some segments for itself. In desktop publishing most of the users and applications have gravitated to the Apple Mac operating system, and the reinforcing feedback effects retain Apple's position. Apple suffered from a more closed system so they were unable to meet the broad innovative investments of the entire Microsoft complementor community, but one area they did lead in was graphics. This kick-started their position which applications complementors have since sustained.

The standards around PC architecture were hotly contested over a decade ago, and it would be pointless to attempt to wrestle away the established de facto standards today. In emergent architectures, such as with the Internet, wireless, and biotech, the battles are ongoing. Real Networks exemplifies one of these battles.

Other Illustrations of Proprietary Standards

In 1995, Rob Graser, the youngest Vice President in Microsoft, launched an audio-in-demand delivery system for use on the Internet under the name of Progressive Networks. The business model, shown in Figure 5.4, goes far beyond the standard vendor-sells-to-customer structure. In this system Real Networks is a central enabler between content creators, portals or aggregators, web hosting, wireless devices, and the end-user. Real Networks supplies real player basic to end-users for free, or charges for enhanced real player plus and support. With this software installed on their computer, users can stream audio real time from the Internet, from web sites such as NPR, ABC, and CNN. Real Networks also supplies a multimedia creation tool, real producer basic, free to content providers (such as CNN and ABC), or they charge for an advanced tool, real producer plus. With this software content creators can convert their media into a format accessible by real player. Real Networks provides software for servers, real server basic for free, or (you guessed it) they charge for enhanced software, real server plus. With this software data centers are equipped to stream audio from their servers to real players, and to host new content from content creators. This same set of relationships plays out again among wireless participants, but also including handset providers and carriers who play a more influential role in that system.

Early on Real Networks aggressively pursued companies in the broadcast, entertainment and technology sectors as complementors. With complementors and free basic software they became the third most popular download product after the Internet Explorer and Netscape browser in 1997. By 1998, they had 35 million registered users and more than 300,000 hours of programming per week.

With all these different customers and complementors there is a wide array of revenue sources. In a System Lock-In position pricing strategy is no straightforward task. What participants should be charged, how much, and when leaves open many degrees of freedom and fundamentally determines the odds of success. Real Networks, for example, get roughly 60% of their revenue from software licenses, with the highest prices reserved for hosting (who may exercise the least influence on the buying process). They get 25% from services, where they provide turnkey

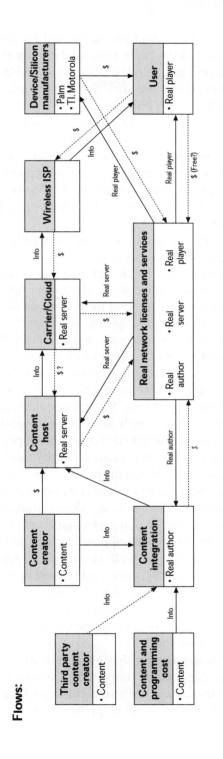

Figure 5.4 Real Networks business model

support to launch audio services for content providers, and another 15% from the advertising associated with their own real.com web sites specializing in guiding real player users to relevant content. The business still earns no income, but the prospects are such that the overall market capitalization has ranged from $2 to $10 billion.

The list could go on. Phone.com (previously known as Unwired Planet) is pursuing a de facto standard for the wireless Internet. Even Dolby is a Proprietary Standard that has continued life. We know it from audio hi-fi systems as a product used across content providers and equipment manufacturers that enhances sound quality for recorded music. But it may be renewed in wireless systems where quality is also challenged by the limited and fluctuating bandwidth.

While Proprietary Standards may be more prevalent and tightly bonded in the case of networks and technology sectors, there is similar bonding in other industries. Bessemer Securities is a leading private equity firm with over $3 billion capital for investment. Unlike many investment firms, they typically invest for the long term and are looking for businesses that yield long-term sustainable profits. Short-term flipping is not part of their strategy. This requires a focus on the business economics rather than on financial reengineering. Bob Lindsay, the CEO, looks for bonding and has found it in nontechnology as well as technology firms. Purdy manufactures paintbrushes. This basic item consisting of hog's hair bristles and wood would seem to be a hopeless commodity. Since Bessemer's acquisition of Purdy, however, they have grown both sales and profitability far faster than the industry. They have been designated by Home Depot as one of their top three suppliers. How can this be explained? Purdy has become the de facto standard paintbrush for architectural painters, and the brand most preferred by professionals. Its paintbrushes are certainly high quality, painstakingly and manually assembled to exacting dimensions, but the reason it beats competition is because of complementary assets. Purdy reaches out to schools and organizations with apprenticeships and stocks them with free or discounted brushes, as well as support. Soon-to-be professionals are weaned on Purdy brushes, grow accustomed to their feel and application, and bring them to the professional market. The professional ranks further amplify this by looking to each other to define what distinguishes a professional from the amateur. Over the years this has become a self-reinforcing position for Purdy.

Mapress is another Bessemer investment that benefits from bonding. Mapress sells stainless steel and copper tube pressfittings. When plumbers need to connect two copper pipes, they can use a fitting, which has a slightly wider diameter than the tubes, to envelope the ends of the two pipes and solder them together, or they can use a Mapress pressfitting. This is a fitting that is compressed around the two ends of the pipe to form a watertight seal. Compressing the pressfitting is much faster, and more consistent than soldering, but it requires a specific tool to do the compression. The manufacturer of the tool becomes an important complementor to Mapress. The bonding occurs with the plumber. While pressfitting is much cheaper than soldering, it requires an investment to buy or rent the tools. Plumbers will not want to buy multiple tools or carrying multiple (and heavy) tools with them, let alone stock multiple brands of pressfittings in their vehicles. Even the channels that distribute to the plumbers experience some lock-in, since plumbing supply distributors will only want to carry one manufacturer's brand to ensure that they are not carrying duplicate inventory and bearing additional customer service costs. Thus, distributors and plumbers alike find it difficult to change from an installed base. It is hard for a competitor to unseat the position of the established standard.

Achieving System Lock-In through Dominant Exchange

The *Yellow Pages* is a venerable old institution that makes money the old-fashioned way – they print it, in a manner of speaking. In fact, they print books filled with advertisements paid for by local businesses and distribute them free to households. And for this public service they earn roughly a 50% margin on sales! After the deregulation of the telephone business in 1984, hoards of new competitors crowded the field aiming to show the regulation-bound, lethargic telephone companies a thing or two. In one case the entire salesforce of one incumbent regional *Yellow Pages* organization switched to a new competitor. This occurred because the Bell Operating Company had outsourced the sales function to another company, along with most other functions including the creative, printing, and distribution work. This company enviously eyed the margins of the *Yellow Pages* and thought they could easily replicate the product. Even if the margins fell in half it would be a great business. So they hijacked the entire salesforce, and a vicious competition ensued. The analysts predicted a rapid loss of market share and declining margins. After the dust settled, the regional Bell Operating Companies held 85% of the market and retained their margins. Why? Because of System Lock-In. In this case, local businesses want to advertise in the *Yellow Pages* book that gets used by the most consumers, and consumers want to read the book with the most advertisements. As shown in Figure 5.5, this constitutes a virtuous feedback loop that is almost impossible for a competitor to break, whether with lower prices or with better

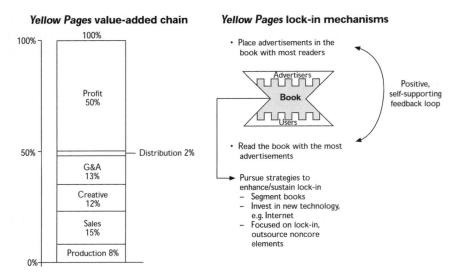

The *Yellow Pages* has achieved unrivaled profitability by establishing a positive feedback loop between consumers and advertisers

Figure 5.5   The source of profits for the *Yellow Pages*

features. When new companies entered the market they could distribute books to every household, but they could not guarantee usage. Even with steep 50–70% discounts offered by new entrants, businesses could not afford to discontinue their advertisements in the incumbent book with proven usage. Despite the enhancements of color maps and coupons, the consumers found the new books, with fewer and smaller advertisements, to have more size than utility and threw them out. The virtuous circle could not be broken and the existing books sustained their market position.

City newspapers benefit from the same phenomenon, particularly with their classified sections. Advertisers place their ads in the paper with the highest circulation and readers choose the paper with the most listings. Is it any wonder that most cities have one highly successful paper and the rest struggle to survive?

Defining a Dominant Exchange

A Dominant Exchange is business that provides a clearing house for information, money, or physical items. The value of the clearing house grows exponentially with the number of people who go there to browse, shop, or exchange items. Because the value grows with use, the leading exchange tends to dominate the market. In an ironic sense, a Dominant Exchange becomes a monopoly for a competitive market. As with all System Lock-In approaches, segmentation is again important. A business may become a Dominant Exchange for one sector, but fail in another. The *Yellow Pages* business lives or dies on segmentation. A manager needs to understand the natural trading geographies and segment the books accordingly. If the segment is too large, the book becomes ponderous and a competitor will define a book that better meets the focused needs of the market. If the segment is too small, the book will be irrelevant and a competitor will enter with a larger book that will take market share. The competitors who did succeed in taking share from the incumbents, successfully redefined the books when a better segmentation was available.

Other Illustrations of Dominant Exchange

Again, the Internet has created an explosion in businesses attempting to corner some Dominant Exchange position. A prime example is eBay, a web site where anyone can buy or sell just about anything, from Pokémon cards to entire businesses. After seeing the success of eBay, Yahoo!, Amazon and other heavyweights have offered the same service. While clearly leaders in their own right, they have not been able to dent eBay's Dominant Exchange market share. At one point eBay's servers crashed and users were unable to properly access the service for several days. Nonetheless, they retained their 85% share of the $3.3 billion market when the service was resumed. The bonding is incredible. eBay has stayed attentive to segmentation issues, offering regional as well as category segments.

Numerous bells and whistles to the online auction experience have been added by eBay to further their bonding formula. Authentication and ratings of sellers and buyers are maintained to help you to verify the pedigree of the other party you may be doing business with. This is a rating that grows with usage and consequently adds to bonding. They are providing real-time chat between buyers and sellers, electronic billing capabilities to decrease seller transaction time following the sale, and partnering with Parcel Plus and Tradesafe.

What could unseat eBay? Perhaps another technological change such as personal buying assistants. This software can scour the web looking across exchanges and retail sites for the item you want, effectively bringing buyers and sellers together without requiring a web site. On the other hand, if eBay provides these as well as the value-added bonding features of their current site, they may be able to withstand this assault.

Instinet and AOL Instant Messenger repeat this approach in different settings. Instinet is a subsidiary of Reuters that provides an electronic exchange floor for NASDAQ securities. To date this has been targeted to institutions, and they hold a commanding share of this market while maintaining extremely high margins. AOL Instant Messenger allows users to send instant e-mail messages to other users who are logged onto the system. In addition to all AOL subscribers, they have over 50 million registered users. Information is exchanged rather than money, but the lock-in is equally tight. A prospective customer is compelled to sign up to the service with the most users.

Nextel is a cellular phone company that used a variant of the Dominant Exchange position to grow in the face of tough, established competitors. The distinguishing characteristic of the Nextel phone offer was group calling. At first, industry experts considered this a lowbrow, quirky offer appealing to a minority. After all, it was reminiscent of the natural group, or 'hoot and holler,' calling that occurred with the radio handsets that cellular was meant to replace. What this conventional thinking missed is that group calling leads to bonding. Quickly a favorite of construction crews and subcontractors, they all wanted to be members of the same system so that they could form the groups that were important to each new job as it came up. Years later, the incumbent wireless carriers are now introducing group calling, but it will be difficult for them to dislodge the market segments bonded to Nextel.

Credit cards show that financial services are another industry where System Lock-In is a force in determining competitive success. The credit card industry is an exchange with a twist. In it consumers exchange money for goods with merchants using the card issued by a bank as their trading floor, so to speak. American Express was a dominant competitor in the early history of cards, albeit with a charge card rather than a credit card. Their strategy was to serve the high-end businessperson, particularly those traveling abroad. This was captured by the famous slogan, 'don't leave home without it,' and supported by a worldwide array of American Express offices. American Express provided something close to a Total Customer Solution by offering elite 'club' membership. The gold card and platinum card continue in this tradition. The bias was toward targeting the most prestigious merchants to accept the American Express card rather than securing the highest overall share of merchants.

Visa and MasterCard took a different path. They designed an open system, made their card available to all banks, and aggressively pursued ubiquitous merchant acceptance through lower merchant fees. Figure 5.6 shows the results of a strategy that culminated in a strong position as the

Cards in circulation in the U.S.

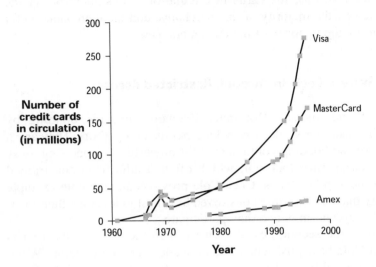

Merchants accepting credit cards

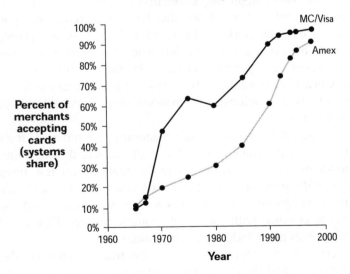

Figure 5.6   The credit card industry

Source: Dean & Company analysis, Amex Annual Report (1996), MasterCard Corp.,
Visa Corp., *The Credit Card Industry*, MasterCard Factbook (1993)

Dominant Exchange for MasterCard and Visa. Visa and MasterCard now have more than 80% of the cards in circulation. Consumers prefer the cards accepted by the majority of the merchants, and the merchants prefer the card held by the majority of the customers.

Achieving System Lock-In through Restricted Access

Proprietary Standards and Dominant Exchange provide bonding by locking in the customer while also locking out the competitors. They are at the extreme of the bonding continuum. Still powerful, but one step away from this is competitor lock-out, which often results from constrained distribution and supply chains. Coca-Cola provides an elaborate example of a company that has carefully considered how best to leverage their position in the full system in which they participate.

Coca-Cola is the second best-known *word* in the world – the first is 'okay.' Coca-Cola has consistently been a leader in value creation. When Coca-Cola went public in 1919 – 33 years after pharmacist John Styth produced the first batch of the beverage in a three-legged brass kettle in his backyard – its first offering of stock cost $40 per share. If you had a visionary grandfather who bought one share in 1919, then at the end of 2000 with all of the splits and dividends that have occurred since, you would own shares with a total market value of $5 million. This remarkable performance cannot be explained by the intrinsic characteristics of the product alone, however satisfying the taste, or by the careful customer targeting efforts. Coca-Cola is neither a Best Product nor a Total Customer Solutions company. It has achieved insurmountable System Lock-In through Restricted Access.

The initial temptation is to ascribe Coke's position to the power of their brand, since Coke owns the number one brand in the world. There are, however, a number of well-known brands in the market, yet few have demonstrated the profit-generating potential of Coca-Cola. Coca-Cola's franchise is built upon System Lock-In. This lock-in is a function of the relationship it has established with each of its complementors. Figure 5.7 is a schematic of the soft drink industry in the United States.

The key players are the suppliers, the concentrate producers, the bottlers, the distributors, and the consumers. The two leading concentrate manufacturers are Coca-Cola and Pepsi, which together accounted for 73% market share of the $50 billion U.S. retail market in 1996.[5] The next four producers, which include Dr. Pepper/Seven-Up, Schweppes, Royal Crown, and A&W, have less than 15% of the market. The remaining

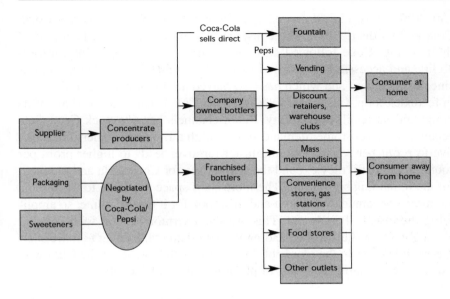

Figure 5.7 The soft drink industry structure

Source: Adapted from the Cola Wars Continue: Coke vs. Pepsi
in the 1990s, Harvard Business School Case 9-794-055

market share belongs to local and regional producers. While Coca-Cola and Pepsi exhibit extraordinary financial returns,[6] the remaining players have had continuing losses and changes of ownership. This pattern is common in a system that has been locked in, where one or two players appropriate most of the economic value created by the industry and the rest struggle.

One can quickly gain an understanding of Coke and Pepsi's grip on the industry by looking at the sources of competitive lock-out. Let us take the perspective of Coca-Cola. Purchasing from all the suppliers is negotiated and controlled by Coke, not by the bottler. This allows Coke to provide the bottler with huge economies of scale. Correspondingly, the huge volumes make the suppliers dependent upon Coke. Coke also provides the bottler with the complete know-how necessary to run their business, including marketing, research, technology, new products, advertising, and logistics support. In return for exclusive territorial rights, the bottler commits to efficient operations according to Coke's policies and practices, including 'door–store delivery' of the products to the distribution channels. This practice enhances the economics of the channels. Due to the physical limitations of shelf space and fountains, the draw of the brand, and the fact that soft drinks have high turnover, there is a natural lock-in between Coca-Cola and its distributors. The consumer end-user is also a critical part of the bonding. Coke followed an explicit strategy of acceptability, affordability, and accessibility (referred to as AAA) which has guided its actions since its inception and which has also played an important role in the lock-in feedback loop. Customers look for Coca-Cola because of the draw of its brand and its retail accessibility. Retail channels heavily stock Coca-Cola because of this customer demand and the high turnover. Retailers are sensitive to profit per square foot and faster turnover leads to higher profit per square foot. Thus, they expand the shelf space for Coca-Cola and reduce it for the remaining soft drinks. The more shelf space available to Coca-Cola the more consumers will find it and then look for it the next time, so amplifying the effect of its brand. This creates a virtuous cycle, with demand leading to more shelf space, leading to more demand, leading to more shelf space, and so on. In the words of the late Roberto Goizueta,[7] the CEO who led Coca-Cola during its years of phenomenal profit growth:

> People always ask me, 'What's your strategy for growth?' I always say it's simple. I tell people do not make it too complicated. Each day we must make Coca-Cola more acceptable, more available, more affordable to more people in more situations than the day before. Put another way, success largely depends on our ability to make it impossible for the consumer to escape Coca-Cola.

Of all the sports stadiums in the U.S., only two do not serve Coke. Roberto Goizueta told us that there are only 3 inns out of 300 in the Swiss Alps that do not carry Coca-Cola. This is only because the families that own them have a vested interest in one of Coke's competitors. Every year during the winter he gets 30 letters from people complaining that they have been to one of these 3 inns and they couldn't get a Coca-Cola. Goizueta continued, complaining, 'I have yet to receive one letter from one person who has been staying in one of the other 300 inns saying, "I was surprised to find Coca-Cola at this inn and it was great!"' Coca-Cola has become so ubiquitous that people expect to find it everywhere. It is this expectation that compels distributors and retailers to stock the product and further propels its dominance.

There are two almost unbelievable statistics that point to this success. Consumption of Coca-Cola in the U.S. typically exceeds that of any other beverage, including tap water, and in 1996 consumption was 363 eight-ounce cans per capita, the equivalent of everyone in the United States drinking one can a day. When you consider that Coke makes more than 80% of its income outside the U.S.A., it makes it all the more impressive.

A final comment on the relationship between Coca-Cola and Pepsi: although these companies are bitter competitors, in the conventional sense, they also complement one another. In 1975, Pepsi launched the now famous national blind test that showed that the majority of Americans preferred Pepsi to Coca-Cola when the brands were not disclosed. This was just another flash point for a legendary rivalry in the U.S. However, we have seen a steady increase in market share for both Coca-Cola and Pepsi from that time until now and a concurrent increase in the total market. According to Roger Enrico,[8] CEO of Pepsi:

> The warfare must be perceived as continuing battle without blood. Without Coke, Pepsi would have a tough time being an original and lively competitor. The more successful they are, the sharper we have to be. If the Coca-Cola Company didn't exist, we'd pray for someone to invent them. And on the other side of the fence, I'm sure the folks at Coke would say that nothing contributes as much to the present-day success of the Coca-Cola Company than ... Pepsi.

What lesson can we draw from the case of Coke and Pepsi? Brands are almost always meaningful tools to improve competitive position. When coupled with Restricted Access, however, brands can lead to bonding. Based upon our experience and research, brands without Restricted Access lead to several points in increased margin or share, and this sometimes pays for the advertising and promotion that created the brand. However, with Restricted Access, brands can have huge economic impact of the type created by Coca-Cola. It may not be too surprising that we find that the most widely recognized brands are typically owned by consumer product companies vying for distribution through constrained retail channels.

To achieve Restricted Access you need to diagnose the overall delivery system, identify the most constrained points, and then position the business to dominate these points. Distribution channels are an apparent and common control point, but there are others. The cornerstone of WalMart's success was based upon opening stores that would satisfy *all* the retailing needs of a rural area within a 15–20 mile radius. Sam Walton discovered (or created) a less than obvious bottleneck in distribution to rural communities, and filled it so completely with a large-scale, low-cost channel that existing competitors could not afford to compete and potential new entrants were preempted. WalMart created a de facto monopoly for each rural location. To some extent this advantage was absent as WalMart began to grow into larger metropolitan areas where the bottlenecks could not be created. Not surpisingly, their performance began to fall off.

In the new economy, constraints are beginning to arise in bandwidth or devices. For some time to come the local cable company may be the sole provider of high bandwidth transport access to homes, to the extent that open access is not legally required (and perhaps even if it is) this may lock out some broadband applications. Correspondingly, wireless services put a premium on small, portable devices. There are growing space constraints on these devices. Applications that require a special chip or massive memory may only be able to get market share on a first come, first served basis. The first application to get reasonable share may lock out alternatives and become the dominant provider.

Using Direct Channels to Achieve System Lock-In and Total Customer Solutions – The Case of Unilever in India and Mexico

Typically a Best Product strategy depends on generic mass channels for distribution, such as supermarkets, food stores, drug stores, and so on. There are two issues associated with this channel selection. First and foremost, the channel is going to block the firm from the final consumer which will limit the intimate understanding that is so essential for development of a customer-oriented strategy. Second, mass channels are only good for mass consumers, excluding the two extremes from receiving proper treatment. Those extremes are the very poor and the very rich.

That is why consumer product giants, such as Unilever, have to concentrate effort in creating direct channels to satisfy those segments. Take the case of Unilever and the very poor market segment (Figure 5.8). One of the best businesses in Unilever is its Indian company, Hindustan Lever. The mass market in India is large, consisting of about 800 million people living under extremely poor conditions. It would be unthinkable for Unilever to dismiss this market simply because its existing products and distribution channels are inappropriate to deal with it. This demographic segment is normally referred to as the D & E segment, the lowest level of income and consumption power, at the other end of the spectrum from the richer A, B, and C segments. People in this segment do not have steady income. They cannot afford to buy a full box of detergent or a bottle of shampoo. They do not go to the mass distribution channels. What does Hindustan Lever do? That is when creativity and technology play a fundamental role. Hindustan Lever used its best technology to produce very inexpensive products to serve the D & E market. It developed a new kind of detergent sold in a package with a dose sufficient for only one wash load, and a shampoo with a quantity enough for one hair wash. Moreover,

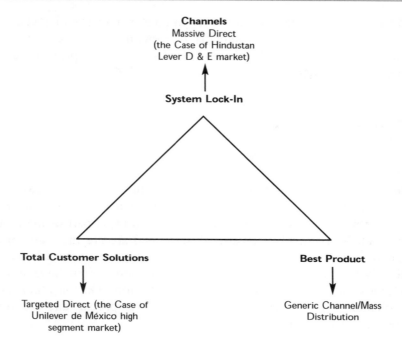

Figure 5.8   The role of distribution channels
in the three strategic options

it channels those products through four million outlets throughout India, one million managed directly by Hindustan Lever, the remaining three million covered by exclusive distributors. All of them are connected via IT capabilities managed centrally by Hindustan Lever. They are also exploring opportunities to use banks as complementors to provide credit to both distributors and consumers. This massive direct and *exclusive* distribution channel, in combination with an assortment of complementors designed to work only with Unilever distribution, establishes a clear System Lock-In with highly profitable margins. Unilever is rolling out this approach to cover other important D & E markets, such as Brazil.

On the rich market segment we look to Unilever de México as an example. Its newly appointed chairman, Tom Stephens, is developing a Total Customer Solutions strategy targeting the most important and richest customers, such as the five-star hotels in Mexican resorts. The idea is to produce a customized package of all the products and services available to Unilever, expanded by other key complementors such as Kimberly Clark, and then to deliver them directly through their own distribution channels. Again IT provides critical support by tracking customer inventory, automating replenishment, fulfilling orders, invoicing, profiling usage, and so on.

Reflections

Seek and Support Complementors

While many businesses fail to build successful customer relationships, few managers need to be reminded of the importance of the customer. On the other hand, the notion of complementors is not a part of the typical manager's lexicon. Alliances are old news and are not the focus of our discussion of complementors. Alliances are highly structured, contractual, and select affairs of resource powerhouses, and often have a short lifespan as a contest between bargaining powers. On the other hand, complementor relationships are natural and reciprocal, and are at the center of network economics.

Notes

1. The concept of complementors has been introduced by Adam M. Brandenburger and Barry J. Nalebuff, *Co-opetition* (New York: Doubleday, 1996).
2. Dan Steere, 'Intel Corporation (D): Microprocessors at the Crossroads', Graduate School of Business, Stanford University Case BP-256D, Exhibit 8, p. 24. May 1993.
3. *Fortune*, November 22, 1999.
4. Patricia Sellers, 'How Coke is Kicking Pepsi's Can', *Fortune*, October 28, 1996.
5. Michael Cusumano, Y. Mylonadis, and R. Rosenbloom, 'Strategic maneuvering and mass-market dynamics: the triumph of VHS over Beta', *Business History Review*, vol. 66, Spring 1992, pp. 51–94.
6. Coca-Cola's 1996 return on equity was 60%, in 1995 the ROE was 56.2% and 36% in 1999 – 5-year average ROE (1994 to 1999): Coca-Cola 55%, Industry Average 44% .
7. *Beverage Digest* interview, 1991.
8. Roger Enrico, *The Other Guy Blinked and Other Dispatches from the Cola Wars* (New York: Bantam Books, 1988).

CHAPTER 6

Creating a Strategic Agenda: The Case of Motorola Semiconductor

In the previous chapters we have explained the centrality of the Triangle in making the critical strategic choices for a business and a firm as a whole. We will now put these valuable concepts into a practical setting, by discussing how to develop a comprehensive Strategic Agenda, anchored in the foundations of the Triangle. We will do this within the context of a very exciting case: the repositioning of the semiconductor business of Motorola.

The Delta Model in Practice: The Semiconductor Product Sector of Motorola

The case of the Semiconductor Product Sector (SPS) of Motorola is an ideal illustration of some of the elements of the Delta Model in practice. First, this is a young industry that has experienced a fast evolution and significant increase in competitive intensity. Intel has dominated the personal computer segment of the market, which accounts for about one third of the total industry. The remaining segments still do not have dominant players. In this respect, there are enormous opportunities for filling the leadership void. Second, industry evolution is following the trends of the new economy – technology that generates innovations combined with the globalization of business to boost productivity. These are conditions particularly suitable for the application of the Delta Model. Third, Motorola had just appointed, in March 1997, Hector Ruiz to be the President of SPS. He came from a successful tenure as the head of the paging business of Motorola, promoting it to a position of widely acclaimed global leadership. In a presentation at MIT, Hector characterized the changing nature of the semiconductor business as follows:

Old World		New World
Cost-based decision making	➡	Value-based decision making
Life cycles measured in years	➡	Life cycles measured in months
Technology push	➡	Market pull
Technology centric	➡	Application specific
Wait for evolution	➡	Drive standards
Buyer–supplier relationships	➡	Partnerships
Quality product focus	➡	Quality of all business processes
'Socket' wins	➡	System wins

This transition forcefully describes why Best Product strategies, which had been the predominant strategic position in the past, might not be the desired option in the future. In fact, there are clear indications that the industry is ripe for a Total Customer Solutions approach and it might even offer potential to secure Proprietary Standards, which could lead to the type of System Lock-In that is enjoyed by Intel in the PC segment of the industry.

In 1983, according to Dataquest, Motorola ranked number one in the world with 11% market share; in 1997, it had dropped to number five with a mere 6% of the market. Hector Ruiz was given the challenge to turn around the performance of Motorola in the semiconductor industry. It was Hector's role to reestablish a global leadership position. One of his first decisions was to appoint a core team to help him in defining a new strategy and structure of the SPS. One of us had the privilege of being a member of his team and brought in the Delta Model to assist in this task.

Strategy

The Triangle is the starting point for strategy formulation, because it allows us to consider the critical choices of positioning. When we are working with a corporation that is engaged in a portfolio of business activities, as with Motorola Semiconductor, the first step in the application of the Triangle is to define the businesses of the firm. This initial task, referred to as business segmentation, is of critical importance in strategy. The way we define the businesses – usually designated as Strategic Business Units (SBUs) – has enormous implications, because it establishes the focus of strategic attention. Most of the strategic analysis is centered on the business units and their proper interactions. When using the Triangle at the firm level, we want to recognize the existing and desired strategic positioning of each business unit within the Triangle and reflect on the implications for action resulting from the strategic evolution of the businesses.

Historically, SPS was managed with a product-centric organization, which best served the 'old world' ways of doing business. The products were vertically integrated and managed in a fairly autonomous fashion. This created two undesirable outcomes. First, it contributed to the development of a 'silo' mentality that created barriers to sharing resources across businesses. This was particularly dysfunctional in an industry where technology benefits in one area have to be passed quickly into other areas, and common manufacturing platforms and uniform design represent enormous sources of competitive advantage. Paradoxically, SPS has the widest portfolio of state-of-the-art technologies of any company in the world. The fragmentation of these capabilities, however, was handicapping Motorola's potential leadership. A similar statement applies to manufacturing facilities. Given the short product life cycles, it is economically important to share fabrication facilities across products. Second, unique needs began to emerge from different market segments, including transportation, consumer products, wireless, and networking and computing industries. At the same time, there were important global accounts that covered a wide array of industrial segments that needed to receive consistent, coordinated support.

Business Segmentation

The industry trends, as well as the inefficiencies from a product-driven organization, led the management team to conclude that a market-driven segmentation was a more appropriate perspective to capture the future opportunities in the industry. It was therefore decided to define four market-focused businesses. This was a bold move because it shifted the orientation from products to markets, and drastically reduced the number of business units, thus leading to a concentration in the markets with the highest potential. Let us explain the segments:

- *Transportation systems:* Address systems that help people work, play, and travel. This includes semiconductors for body electronics, powertrains, safety, engine management, intelligent transportation systems, telematics, motor controls, and other new products and markets to be determined. Motorola is facing tremendous opportunities in the world's automotive and strategic industrial markets. SPS is the leader in the automotive industry, being number one in the United States and with a very strong showing in Europe. SPS growth is not restricted to the automobile industry, but its charter includes the creation of total semiconductor systems and software solutions for the strategic industrial market.

- *Consumer systems:* Address systems that help people to be productive and have fun. This includes semiconductors for imaging, displays and modems, storage, digital cameras, entertainment, set top boxes, smart cards, consumer media, and other new areas as they develop. There are great growth opportunities in entertainment technologies such as electronic games, video discs and cameras, audio equipment and digital displays. Personal and home electronics are also exciting areas. The PC peripheral market, including keyboards, sounds cards, imaging and printing technologies are required market focuses.

- *Wireless subscriber systems:* Address systems that help people and machines on the move. This includes semiconductors for analog cellular, cordless, digital cellular, messaging, wireless data, and so on. The goal is for SPS to achieve global leadership in wireless subscriber system solutions. Additionally, it will become Motorola's center for expertise in digital and signal-processing technology solutions.

- *Networking and computing systems:* Address the infrastructure for people to communicate, play, and work. This includes semiconductors for subscriber modems, central office switching, routers, handsets, cellular base stations, PC value-added technologies, networking products, customer premises equipment, mobile switching centers, and other new products and markets as determined. The market for networking and computing is exploding. New technologies are being developed at a very fast pace and there are great opportunities for growth, especially within emerging and developing nations, as well as Japan.

These four business units do not exhaust the realm of activities for SPS. A fifth business unit, Semiconductor Components, was added to encompass the large amount of commodity components that are an inherent part of the semiconductor industry. It is a product-driven segment that also serves the purpose of filling the pipeline for the distributors of SPS who would find their needs largely unmet by the market-driven business units. In addition, from a strategic point of view, the Semiconductor Components business is intended to include highly critical and unique components that could be essential for the market-driven business to achieve superior competitive advantage.

At this point, SPS has selected the critical focus of analysis that would greatly influence the strategic management process. Although one could dismiss it simply as an act of segmentation, in fact, the impact of this *decision* will turn out to be much more pervasive. The business segmentation often determines the way the businesses are positioned, strategies developed, resources allocated, metrics collected – in a broader sense, how the company is going to manage itself. Implicit in this initial segmentation is a set of hypotheses that somehow tell us that this is the 'right' way to manage the firm. These hypotheses will be tested, repeatedly, both in the strategy formulation and implementation process. If, after this inquiry, the segmentation still prevails, the decision embedded in the business segmentation will prove to be the one having the highest strategic significance. Segmentation is not only an act of reflection, it is a source of action.

The Triangle

Motorola's SPS Triangle is depicted in Figure 6.1. The statement of strategic position is both clear and powerful. The Semiconductor Components business is anchored in the Best Product position, as it should be. The way to win in that business is through volume that allows for the exploitation of economies of scale and experience curves to achieve Low Cost. The purpose of the four market-driven business units is to move from Best Product into a Total Customer Solutions position, with the expectation that they might achieve a System Lock-In position based upon Proprietary Standards.

The clarity of the Triangle is its ability to communicate in a simple form the distinct, hard, and complex choices made by Motorola. Yet implicit in this Triangle lies a powerful and rich understanding of the radically different ways a business needs to be managed in order to achieve these choices.

The Mission

The next task is to produce a mission statement that describes verbally the challenge implicit in the strategic position reflected in the Triangle. We believe that these two instruments – the Triangle and the mission – play an important and yet different role in communicating the essence of the desired competitive position of the firm. The two combined are better than either one alone.

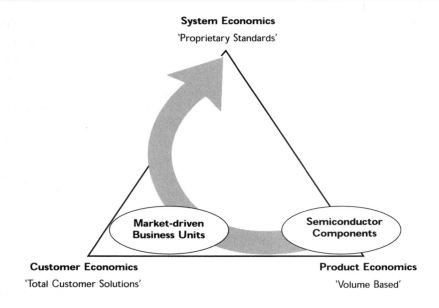

System Economics
'Proprietary Standards'

Market-driven
Business Units

Semiconductor
Components

Customer Economics
'Total Customer Solutions'

Product Economics
'Volume Based'

Figure 6.1   Motorola SPS Triangle

Mission statements take many forms. We prefer those that communicate, both to the internal organization as well as to the relevant external constituencies, the central purpose of the organization and the challenge implicit in its achievement. The mission is primarily articulated by the CEO of the firm. What it says the organization will not do is as important as what it says it will do. This defines how well the organization is focused.

The mission statement that was reached by the SPS executives reads as follows:

The Future We Will Create

Regain our leadership position in the semiconductor global businesses:

...developing, manufacturing, marketing, and distributing semiconductor products and software that offer total system solutions

...with architectural standards, that we own...

...focusing on
    ⇨ networking and computing,
    ⇨ wireless subscriber,

⇨ consumer, and

⇨ transportation

...markets.

Objectives:

- Overwhelmingly wanted by customers.
- #1 or #2 in those markets we serve.
- Consistent 15–20% return on net assets.

There are various elements of this mission statement that need to be emphasized:

1. The SPS mission starts by clearly stating its commitment to regain global leadership in the semiconductor industry. This is, in itself, a most demanding and challenging task. It was not stated lightly by Motorola executives. Nothing could be more damaging to the internal culture of the organization, as well as its external image, than to use the mission to express a bravado that will not be achieved. This was not the case with Motorola, a company that once was the undisputed leader of the semiconductor industry and now is pledged to regain that position.

2. It emphasizes the necessary functional capabilities required to accomplish this objective: development, manufacturing, marketing, and distribution of semiconductor products and software. This statement makes clear the need to excel at the key back-end functions of the firm – development and manufacturing – as well as those which are in the front end – marketing and distribution. These functions play a key role in achieving the necessary core competencies that are needed to succeed. Notice also the requirements for excellence attached to software, which is critical for SPS businesses.

3. It conveys the desired competitive position centered in offering Total Customer Solutions and subsequently developing Proprietary Standards that could generate large systems value for their customers and lead to a System Lock-In position. This part of the mission is what encompasses the greatest transformation: moving away from a product-focused organization into the other relevant vertices of the Triangle.

4. It targets the four markets that have been selected as the key industrial segments in which to seek leadership. The four market segments, and the business units centered on their definition are the managerial driving forces of SPS.

5. It concludes by expressing how to measure the intended accomplishments of the mission. The stated ultimate objectives again represent a
formidable challenge, which are drawn in quantitative as well as quali-
tative terms.

Strategic Agenda

The mission statement has to be expanded into a full Strategic Agenda in
order to become an explicit charge to the whole organization. The
mission alone is not enough to identify the key tasks that the organization has to undertake, and the responsibilities that have to be assigned
to its key executives.

In our methodology, this is accomplished by the Strategic Agenda.
There are four components in a complete Strategic Agenda, as illustrated
in Figure 6.2, each one of them having a fairly specific role. When taken as
a whole, they provide a rich definition of the key strategic tasks and their
implementation domain. The components are:

- *Strategic thrusts:* These are action-oriented issues that collectively
capture the totality of the tasks needed to implement the mission and the
desired strategic positioning of the businesses.

- *Organizational structure:* Each strategic thrust is mapped into the
existing organization structure to determine the proper allocation of
responsibilities and authorities associated with the key executives of
the firm.

- *Business processes:* Whenever a strategic thrust cannot be assigned to a
single organizational unit for its implementation, it means that it generates a business process. This is a set of activities that cuts across several
organizational units within the firm's organizational structure. It is
important to recognize the nature of these business processes because
they require careful horizontal coordination among lateral organizational units.

- *Performance:* The progress of each individual strategic thrust has to be
properly monitored. This is accomplished by defining adequate indicators of performance, as well as time-driven events that follow its proper
execution. Collectively these performance metrics play a central role in
assuring a high quality of implementation in the Strategic Agenda.

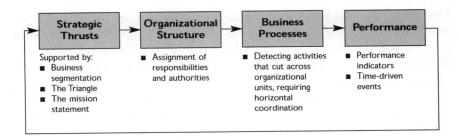

Figure 6.2   The components of the Strategic Agenda

Although these four components of the Strategic Agenda are intrinsically interrelated, we prefer to deal with them in the sequence described above. First, we determine the strategic thrusts because they provide the foundations in which the remaining elements rest. Next comes structure, because we need to organize ourselves in a way that is most suitable for the implementation of the Strategic Agenda. Subsequently, we identify the key business processes, which are heavily dependent upon the strategy and the structure of the firm. Fourth, we indicate the necessary metrics and reward mechanisms, which are going to be the key determinants of personal behaviors that will allow us to extract the best of our strategy in the given organizational context.

It should now become apparent where the Delta Model fits within this framework. The Triangle is an important part of the formulation of the strategic thrusts. It expands the strategic options of a business and gives us the basis to articulate its vision, which then must be translated into a concrete and pragmatic Strategic Agenda.

The selected strategic position that emerges from the Triangle has obvious implications for the definition of the organizational structure. The Best Product, Total Customer Solutions, and System Lock-In strategies call for a very different type of supporting organizational structure. A business that modifies its strategic position invariably calls for a reexamination of the previous organization; it is unlikely that it will serve well the newly adopted strategy. No longer can organizations be regarded as permanent and enduring because the strategies that they support change in response to environmental changes.

The Strategic Agenda and organizational structure both define the nature of the critical business processes of the firm. The Delta Model recognizes three Adaptive Processes – Operational Effectiveness (the production and delivery of products and services to the customer),

Customer Targeting (the management of the customer interface), and Innovation (the process of product renewal) – which are pervasive, in the sense that we will encounter them in every possible strategy or structure. The Strategic Agenda, however, will enrich the content of the processes, transforming them from generic processes to business specific and tailored tasks. This subject will be dealt with extensively in Chapter 7.

The concepts of Aggregate and Granular Metrics are a central part of the Delta Model performance component of the Strategic Agenda. Chapters 9 and 10 examine these issues.

The Strategic Agenda of Motorola Semiconductor Product Sector

The process of producing the Strategic Agenda is based on a rich interaction among the top executives of the firm. We believe that the process of strategy formation is as important as the final output. A properly coordinated process leads toward an enthusiastic consensus among top executives, with a strong personal commitment toward the agenda.

The full Strategic Agenda – including its four components – can be neatly expressed in one single chart. Table 6.1 represents the Strategic Agenda for Motorola SPS in which the four components – strategic thrusts, organizational structure, business processes, and performance measurements – can be easily traced. Each component is now discussed in more detail.

- *Strategic thrusts*: The first column of the chart lists, in order of priority, the strategic thrusts that are part of the Strategic Agenda. It is important that, in the opinion of the decision makers, the list addresses all the key relevant strategic issues, and provides a managerial environment which is stimulating and challenging. The first two thrusts were particularly impacting. Motorola, after many years in the memory business, decided to exit dynamic random access memory semiconductors (DRAMS) – a segment characterized by enormous competitive rivalry and very low profitability – and discontinue its support for the power PC chip for the Apple computer. These were tough decisions that will have enormous implications both internally and externally. Motorola decided, de facto, to concede the PC computer business to Intel and concentrate their efforts in four markets. The rest of the thrusts are very much in line with moving out of Best Product positioning – except for the components business – and seeking a Total Customer Solutions strategy with potential for System Lock-In based on technology proprietary standardization. Each one of the thrusts should be described in more detail, for

Table 6.1 Motorola SPS Strategic Agenda

Strategic thrusts	CEO	Transportation	Network and computing	Wireless	Consumer	Semiconductor components	Technology	Manufacturing	Human resources	Finance	Marketing	Information systems	Communications	Europe, Middle East, Africa	Asia, Pacific and Japan	America	Business Processes	Performance measurements (examples)
1. Exit DRAMs	①	2	2	2	2	2	1	1	2	2	2	2	2	2	2	2	B	■ Time to exit ■ Cost/gain ■ Customer impact
2. Shift power PC capabilities to win in market-driven units	①					2	2						2				1	■ Time to product introduction ■ Number of products
3. Create semiconductor components group		2	2	2	2	①	2	1	2	1	2		2	2	2	2	B	■ Time to implementation
4. Create market-driven groups	①	1	1	1	1	2	2	1	2	1	2	2	2	2	2	2	B	■ Time to implementation
5. Define architectural strategy and potential standards	1	1	1	1	1		①	1			1			2	2	2	CT	■ Percent common platform ■ Complementor share
6. Create marketing capabilities responsive to each business unit	1	1	①	①	①	1					1		2	1	1	1	CT	■ Customer share ■ Customer retention ■ Resources by unit
7. Attract and retain best talent	1	1	1	1	1	2	1	1	①	1	1	1	1	1	1	1	B	■ Number of recruits ■ Source ■ Performance
8. Technology acceleration and deployment	1	1	2	1	2		①	1		1		2		2	1		1	■ Time to market ■ Percent of sales from new products
9. Procurement and outsourcing strategy	2	2	2	2	2	1		①	2				2				OE	■ Number of suppliers ■ Unit cost
10. Understand SPS factors affecting customer's cost and revenues	①	①	①	①	①	2	2	1			1			1	1	1	CT	■ Customer profitability ■ Customer benefits ■ Customer investments
11. World-class performance programs	2	2	2	2	2	①	1	①	2					2	2	2	OE	■ Unit cost relative to competitors

Key

1 Key role in formulation and implementation
2 Important role of support and concurrence
① Identifies the 'Champion', who takes leadership for the strategic thrust execution

B Business model
OE Operational Effectiveness
CT Customer Targeting
I Innovation

purposes of communication and implementation. Figure 6.3 shows an illustration of the type of format we use for that purpose.

- *Organizational structure:* This is identified by the key organizational units that are displayed in the columns of the chart. We can immediately visualize how each strategic thrust is embedded into the organization. We used the convention of assigning a '1' to that organizational unit which has a key role in the implementation of the action programs implicit in the corresponding strategic thrust, and a '2' to the unit that plays a significant support role. Whenever there are several '1s' along a row, implying that there are many key players, a circled '1' – 'Ⓛ' – identifies who is going to play the role as champion of that thrust. This technique is effective at providing a straightforward mapping between the Strategic Agenda and the allocation of responsibilities within the organizational structure. It is easy for us to identify clearly the role being played by each of the top executives of Motorola. We simply have to follow each organizational unit and look vertically at the participation the executive has in the pursuit of the overall agenda. For instance, we see that the CEO is directly in charge of the three thrusts – given their sensitivity and significance – and also plays a key role in three additional thrusts. The role of each player is very useful information to communicate throughout the organization.

- *Business process:* A process is a set of activities that cuts across various organizational units of the firm. The chart identifies whether a strategic thrust originates a process (when there are several '1s' and/or '2s' along the strategic thrust row), and the nature of the resulting process. It conveys an immediate sense of the degree of interconnectedness along the various organizational units in the execution of the Strategic Agenda. From the point of view of the Delta Model, we can also classify them according to the three Adaptive Processes: Operational Effectiveness (OE), Customer Targeting (CT), and Innovation (I). The processes that carry a broad managerial connotation are identified as pertaining to the business model (B). Now we can look both at the horizontal and vertical responsibilities in the chart to visualize both the individual roles of each executive (the vertical lines), and the need for horizontal coordination required by each thrust (the horizontal lines). It is very telling that in the case of Motorola Semiconductor each of the thrusts generates a process that cannot be executed solely by a single organizational unit, but requires participation of several other entities. In our experience, this is the rule rather than the exception. That is why, in today's complex business environments, teams are so critical, and

Name	Understanding Customer Profitability
Description	Identify the top 20% customers of Motorola SPS and perform an in-depth analysis of their cost and revenue structures, leading toward the development of customized value propositions
Responsible Manager	Chief Financial Officer – in this stage of the thrust
Other Key Participants	All Business VPs and Required VPs
Other Important Contributors	Semiconductor Component VP, Technology VP
Key Indicators for Management Control and Targets	Customer profitability Customer benefits Customer investments in SPS-related businesses Other industries should be identified as part of this thrust
First Major Milestone Description	Presentation to the Executive Committee of preliminary findings
First Major Milestone Date	March 1, 1998
Resources Required	Added project resources with relevant expertise
Statement of Benefits	Clear understanding of customer profitability potentials. Firm assessment of benefits should be part of this thrust output

Figure 6.3   An illustration of the definition of strategic thrust

horizontal integration is more significant than the vertical hierarchy to ensure proper execution of the strategic thrusts.

- *Performance*: The metrics that support each strategic thrust combine to create a critical set of performance indicators. Since the thrusts represent crucial issues in the Strategic Agenda of the firm, it is logical to conclude that the metrics associated with the monitoring of the thrusts' performance should constitute the basis for the executive information system of the firm. As seen in Figure 6.3, the metrics typically involve two different concerns: the monitoring of performance against a specific thrust, and the timing of the realization of critical events in the form of specific dates as progress milestones.

For all the reasons already explained, we believe that the strategic agenda is a central foundation for proper strategy development. The one chart, in Table 6.1, is remarkable in that it serves as a one-page (often a large single page) road map for the business. The strategic thrusts are prioritized, responsibilities are assigned, processes are identified for effective collaboration, and, finally, metrics are specified.

SPS is a rich example on the exercise of leadership in an organization in need of redirection. Rather than falling back on the common practices of restructuring and reengineering, that often demoralize management as well as the rank and file, Hector Ruiz chose to embrace another form of leadership. He and his team embarked on a journey of renewal by bringing an inspiring new vision to fruition. At the heart of the architecture in this new vision resided the Triangle, the mission statement, and the SPS Strategic Agenda. Together these were the pillars of a new strategy that led to a totally new organizational structure, more appropriate to the new challenges of the semiconductor industry.

The Process of Defining the Strategic Agenda

We now can briefly summarize the process we recommend to define the Strategic Agenda of the firm, as presented in Figure 6.4. The business segmentation is the first step that decides the way in which the organization will focus its managerial attention. The Triangle helps in making the critical choices for the strategic positioning of each business. The mission statement articulates the resulting purpose and top objectives of the firm. Finally the Strategic Agenda, with its four components – strategic thrusts, managerial accountability, business processes, and performance – completes the process with a highly pragmatic and concrete statement of the strategic tasks of the firm.

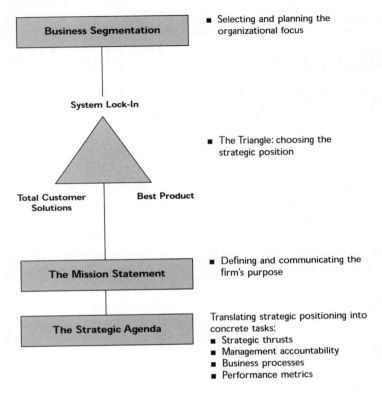

Business Segmentation
■ Selecting and planning the organizational focus

System Lock-In

■ The Triangle: choosing the strategic position

Total Customer Solutions   **Best Product**

The Mission Statement
■ Defining and communicating the firm's purpose

The Strategic Agenda
Translating strategic positioning into concrete tasks:
■ Strategic thrusts
■ Management accountability
■ Business processes
■ Performance metrics

Figure 6.4   Defining the Strategic Agenda

CHAPTER 7

Execution is not the Problem: Aligning Execution with Strategy Is!

Here is the paradox. People are working harder and more productively than ever before, but executives are worrying more and more about execution. CEOs believe that their organizations cannot effectively carry out new programs. Various pundits have responded to these concerns with a flurry of so-called panaceas. Managers have been bombarded by fad upon fad addressing the perceived need for improved execution. These include total quality management, time-based management, business reengineering, and the seven habits of highly effective managers. We will argue in this chapter that managers are misguided in focusing solely on project execution, instead, they must carefully address the alignment of execution to strategy.

Is execution the major problem for most companies? It certainly can be one problem. There are, however, two major fallacies inherent in the sole, or primary, pursuit of perfect execution. First, a pure focus on execution leads to similar practices across companies – they strive for similar rather than distinctive strategic positions. This similarity creates a field of commodities that drives down margins and limits market growth. This exclusive focus on operational excellence is the ultimate manifestation of the Best Product (BP) strategy. This implicit adoption of the Best Product option naturally leads to an inwardly focused, cost-cutting mindset, often supported by restructuring and reengineering. By embarking on draconian cost cutting, executives create a predisposition toward subtraction, rather than addition. While this brings with it more efficiency, it also results in the potential loss of capabilities to pursue other strategies such as Total Customer Solutions (TCS) or System Lock-In (SLI).

Second, businesses operate in a dynamic environment where decentralization is required for survival. The only way to decentralize effectively is to share a common purpose. An overriding focus on operational improvement precludes the development of a strategy that can provide this purpose. When an organization operates with a cost-cutting mentality, but no strategy, individuals may be efficient in their execution, but work at cross-purposes to one another. Their organization often finds itself in disarray. Leadership is nonexistent, confusion reigns, and frustration becomes the prevailing mood. The cost-cutting mentality is a trap because it can prevent managers from thinking about how to achieve leadership and a strategic position that yields sustained competitive advantage and superior long-term financial returns.

Unfortunately, this implicit strategic choice is self-fulfilling. If a business focuses on being faster and cheaper, then the only way for it to excel is to get ever faster and cheaper. It is no surprise that execution is of paramount concern to executives. Our conclusion is that while execution is critical, the alignment of execution to strategy is of overriding importance.

In previous chapters, we proposed a framework to allow a company's executives to create a vision of the business and to define its strategic position. The purpose of this chapter is to show how that strategic position should be aligned with execution, with the intent of better defining the strategy and better executing against it. Since business conditions always change, a core aspect of this approach is the feedback necessary to adapt to a dynamic environment.

The Delta Model accomplishes this critical mission by:

- defining the key business processes
- aligning their role with the desired strategic position
- providing the necessary feedback in each process
- defining the metrics that allow for coherent integration across these processes to produce a unifying sense of action and ensure results.

The Adaptive Processes: Linking Strategy with Execution

Just as the business unit is the focus of attention when selecting a strategy, the business process is the focus when executing against that strategy. A process is a structured and measured set of activities designed to produce a specified output of value to a particular customer or market. This definition places a strong emphasis on how work is executed.

Business processes are defined in terms of outputs; functions, on the other hand, are defined in terms of inputs. Functions – such as research and development, manufacturing, and marketing – are the inputs required to generate products or services. If an organization is structured according to functions, as is often the case, the business processes will cut across these units. That is why it is imperative to view processes as the means to implement strategy. Using processes in this way avoids the fragmentation that is inherent in a functional approach by providing coordination across functional entities. This is central to effective execution.

Through its business processes, a company must not only identify and organize the tasks critical to the realization of its Strategic Agenda, it must also develop flexibility and responsiveness to the ever-changing business environment. Properly defined business processes supported by effective feedback mechanisms are the ideal foci for adaptation. Without this integrated view, the firm is fragmented into isolated silos that obstruct cooperation, exude parochialism, and foster rigidity. When we ask executives today what mechanisms they have to administer the daily routines of business, they describe reports, committees, budgets, line responsibilities, and so on. When we ask what mechanisms they have in place to sense the need for change and create it when necessary, there is often a lengthy silence. To fill this need, a company's processes need to be adaptive. To address this duality of roles – the alignment of execution to a distinctive strategy and the need for adaptation to change – our framework relies upon three critical Adaptive Processes: Operational Effectiveness, Customer Targeting, and Innovation.

A great deal of controversy surrounds the definition and even the number of appropriate business processes for a firm. Based on our research, we have identified three common business outputs – delivering products to customers, managing customer relationships, and developing new products. These correspond to three fundamental adaptive processes that are always present and that align with key strategic tasks:

- *Operational Effectiveness:* This process is responsible for the delivery of products and services to the customer. In a traditional sense, this includes all the elements of the internal supply chain. Its primary focus is on producing the most effective cost and asset infrastructure to support the desired strategic position of the business. In a more comprehensive sense, operational effectiveness should expand its external scope to include suppliers, customer, and key complementors, thus establishing an extended supply chain. This process is the heart of a company's productive engine as well as its source of capacity and efficiency.

- *Customer Targeting:* This process addresses the business-to-customer interface. It encompasses the activities intended to attract, satisfy, and retain customers, and ensures that customer relationships are managed effectively. Its primary objectives are to identify and select attractive customers and to enhance their financial performance, either by helping to reduce their costs or increase their revenues. The ultimate goal of this process is to establish the best revenue infrastructure for the business.

■ *Innovation:* This process ensures a continuous stream of new products and services to maintain the future viability of the business. It mobilizes all the creative resources of the firm – including its technical, production, and marketing capabilities – to develop an innovative infrastructure for the business. It should not limit itself to the pursuit of internal product development, but should extend the sources of Innovation to include suppliers, customers, and key complementors. The heart of this process is the renewal of the business in order to sustain its competitive advantage and its superior financial performance.

While an individual firm's circumstances and strategy affect the specific character and content of these processes, they are almost always present in some form. Through observation of the ways in which businesses actually carry out these processes, we have identified the necessary elements of each. In this chapter we explore the fundamental roles that each process must play to consistently support a distinct strategic position.

The Alignment of Adaptive Processes with the Chosen Strategic Position

Structure *and* processes should follow strategy. We have observed repeatedly that most successful companies do things differently from their competitors, and that their actions demonstrate a strong alignment to a distinctive strategy. Nonetheless, as we mentioned earlier, most businesses carry out their processes in pursuit of the Best Product position by default. They view Operational Effectiveness as the singular pursuit of a low-cost service or product; Customer Targeting as the pursuit of maximum product volume; and Innovation as the attempt to be first to market with new products. Regardless of their stated strategies, most companies today occupy the same Best Product position.

In the Delta Model, the Triangle is the engine that drives the selection of a strategic position, which in turn defines the role of each of the Adaptive Processes (Figure 7.1). There must be a direct link between the strategy and the business processes. This linkage is critical because the role and priority level of each process depends on the chosen strategic position.

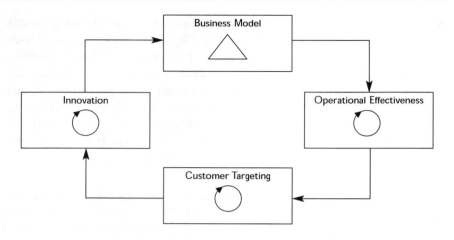

Figure 7.1   The Delta Model: linking strategy with execution

The Role of Operational Effectiveness as an Adaptive Process

Operational Effectiveness is fundamentally concerned with providing the lowest possible cost infrastructure, but its specific objective depends on the strategy of the business. When it supports a Best Product strategy, its objective is to reduce the stand-alone product costs based on a thorough understanding of the product cost drivers. One cannot presume that the value of the same cost element for the same product or service will be similar for different competitors – typically the variations in cost are significant. We have studied costs across dozens of industries, from financial services to consumer goods, and the same pattern often emerges: the difference between a low-cost competitor and a high-cost competitor is a multiple of two or three for any given cost element. Cost drivers are the factors that explain this variation – some are controllable and others are not. These can include items such as the scale of the operations (for example measured in volume produced per month in a facility), the experience level (measured in the accumulated volume produced by the facility or worker), the density of the service area (measured by the customers or sites serviced in a given geographic region), the customer mix (measured by the percentage of new vs. mature customers, or small vs. large customers), or the product mix (measured by the relative complexity to produce or service products within a family), to name but a few relevant drivers. Furthermore, the drivers a company selects must be specific to that

Table 7.1   The changing role of Operational Effectiveness
in supporting the chosen strategic position

		DESCRIPTION OF THE ROLE		
		Focus of attention	**Output**	**Objective**
STRATEGIC POSITION	Best Product	Internal value	Internal cost infrastructure	Best product cost
	Total Customer Solutions	Internal and customer value chain	Combined internal and customer infrastructure	Maximum customer value
	System Lock-In	Internal, customer, and complementor value chain	System infrastructure	Enhance system performance

company. In our experience, however, two to four factors can generally explain 80% of the variation in costs for any element.

The role of Operational Effectiveness in supporting the strategic positioning of a business is described in Table 7.1. It shows how the focus of attention, the output, and the objectives change when a company aims to achieve a Total Customer Solutions or a System Lock-In rather than a Best Product position. The change is profound. In a Best Product position the focus of attention is on the internal value chain, the objective is to have the 'best' product costs (that is, the lowest cost for the specified product whether commoditized or differentiated), and the necessary output to achieve this objective is the internal cost infrastructure.

In the case of Total Customer Solutions, Operational Effectiveness switches from focusing on the value chain and cost infrastructure of the business itself to focusing on the value chains and cost infrastructures of its customers. The objective is to maximize each customer's net income by increasing their revenue or reducing their costs. The implications of this change are significant. It affects organizational structure, administrative systems, the way R&D is conducted, alternatives used for outsourcing (including the use of alliances), configuration of plants, use of distribution channels, design of marketing plans and deployment of salesforces. In other words, when a company moves from the BP position to the TCS position, it should modify every single activity of the value chain.

Sometimes, companies that occupy the TCS position will carry out initiatives that have a negative impact on stand-alone internal costs because they have a greater positive impact on customers' net incomes. For example, National Starch stations its R&D teams at customer sites, although, from a pure product cost perspective, it is more rational to consolidate this function geographically. They also have customers without National Starch R&D teams onsite who visit their facilities regularly and interact with researchers and technicians who might otherwise be concentrating on more efficient production. The focus on the customer at National Starch is evident even among executive board members, who can be excused from board meetings, but would never think of skipping their monthly meetings with customers and the National Starch R&D, manufacturing, and marketing executives.

There is a final point to be made concerning the role of Operational Effectiveness in support of the Total Customer Solutions strategy. Because the focus of attention is on the bundle of integrated products that together address the full scope of customer needs, the infrastructure should address the potential synergies and horizontal linkages among these products. This is made more complicated when the bundle needs to include products from other suppliers.

The need to implement efficient billing and customer care systems adds to the magnitude of this task. You cannot talk to managers in the telecommunications or energy industries today without hearing about problems related to billing or customer care. These systems are critical to allow for a single bill for multiple services, cross-service discounts, and integrated single-point-of-contact help desks. They cost billions of dollars to install, and billions more to maintain. For some phone companies, customer care is a greater expense than the network itself. The problem can be particularly vexing for established players who are tied to legacy systems they find expensive to leave and impossible to improve.

Operational Effectiveness and System Lock-In

In the case of a System Lock-In strategy, Operational Effectiveness must address the infrastructure of the complete economic system with the objective of enhancing its performance. This goes beyond the internal costs and the customers' economics to include the complementors' value chains. System Lock-In players set out to obtain bonding by developing the most valuable set of complementors with which to attract customers. By cultivating a large number of valuable complementors and encouraging them to invest in the system, while making sure that they remain financially healthy, a company can reinforce the attractiveness of its system and the strength of its lock-in position.

In the 1980s, Novell established its NetWare product as a Proprietary Standard for Local Area Networks (LANs). Essential to their System Lock-In position are the 5000 applications designed to run on the NetWare LAN Operating System (OS). Novell did not write these applications. In fact, neither Novell nor any company acting alone could hope to invent all the creative and valuable programs developed by the thousands of software houses operating independently and inspired by a diverse range of customer experiences. However, Novell could, and did, make considerable investments intended to make it easy for these software houses to act as they have. Novell has a complete infrastructure of activities to support its complementors, including starter packages, discount programs, training sessions, and traveling workshops. They segment their complementors into groups, the way other companies segment their customers. They do so to target them with specific programs geared toward supporting their economic needs and their contribution to the overall system. Novell stopped manufacturing hardware to reduce conflict with independent hardware providers, and thus encourage them to endorse Novell as the dominant standard. The success of these actions is evident in Novell's rapid growth in the late 1980s and early 1990s, from the edge of bankruptcy to over $2 billion in revenue with 40% net margins.

Product costs are less relevant to the System Lock-In position than they are to the other strategic options. However, Operational Effectiveness as a business process plays an important role for System Lock-In players because it contributes to the definition of the system's overall configuration. With a valuable system in hand, the key question is how to identify the leverage points in the system architecture where System Lock-In is possible and the degree to which the system's economic value can be appropriated. For the firm that owns or hopes to obtain System Lock-In there is a strategic choice to be made regarding how profits are distributed across the system. Excessive greed can discourage investments by complementors and even generate concerted efforts to break the 'lock.' In the case of Microsoft, for example, there is an active consortium of companies, including Sun and Oracle, that invested in the demise of Microsoft's lock-in.

MasterCard and Visa provide a strong contrasting example. They have structured themselves as associations owned by the banks that distribute their credit cards. The banks are key complementors in the system because they bring to MasterCard and Visa a critical mass of customers seeking credit cards. The banks, together with the retailers that accept the cards, help sustain the lock-in.

The Role of Customer Targeting as an Adaptive Process

Customer Targeting is aimed at attracting, satisfying, and retaining desirable customers, and is therefore key to generating a company's revenue streams. When combined with Operational Effectiveness, which defines the cost structure, Customer Targeting shapes the company's profits. The defining element of Customer Targeting is the customer, and the nature of the customer relationship depends on the chosen strategic position. By contrast, we often hear that a firm should be customer-focused or customer-intimate, without any qualifications or conditions. The changing requirements of Customer Targeting across strategic positions point out how ambiguous that statement is.

Table 7.2 shows how the role of Customer Targeting varies along three dimensions depending on the chosen strategic position. Whereas the objectives for Operational Effectiveness referred to cost drivers, in the case of Customer Targeting, the focus is on profit drivers. We will show how profit drivers are significantly different for different strategies. Finally, we will comment on the outputs necessary to achieve the objectives. The outputs revolve around customer interfaces, which also differ from strategy to strategy.

In the case of Best Product, the customer is the generic recipient of a volume-driven, standardized product. In the case of Total Customer Solutions, the customer is a segmented and specifically targeted end-user with

Table 7.2   The changing role of Customer Targeting in supporting the chosen strategic position

	DESCRIPTION OF THE ROLE		
	Focus of attention	Output	Objective
Best Product	Distribution channel, 'generic customer'	Channel mix	Maximize product volume and product market share, minimize distribution cost
Total Customer Solutions	Targeted customer	Target market intelligence, Customer interface	Maximize share of each customer
System Lock-In	Relevant business system	Network of complementors, Complementor interfaces	Maximize share of complementors

individualized requirements. The TCS player meets the customer's needs via a customized and/or bundled set of products. In the case of System Lock-In, the definition of the customer has the broadest scope and, importantly, includes the system complementors. In our experience, the system can have blurred boundaries when the industry is emerging and standards are being formed. Also, the definitions 'customer,' 'channel,' and 'complementor' are dynamic and subject to continuous reassessment and resegmentation.

The drivers of profitability also depend on the chosen strategic position. The Best Product company has a product perspective and seeks to maximize volume through a portfolio of channels that can access the widest range of customers. It prioritizes the customers who are heavy users and the channels that draw them. In the case of Total Customer Solutions, profits are concentrated more by customer than by product. In other words, the variation in profitability by customer is greater than the variation in profit by product. Therefore, it is important to select the most profitable customers and vertical markets in which to expand one's market share. There is a resulting focus on increasing customer share rather than product share, on expanding the range of products offered, and on extending the reach of our value-added chain to enhance our customers' economics. We illustrate this focus on vertical market slices for Total Customer Solutions businesses and the contrasting focus on horizontal market slices by Best Product businesses seeking product coverage across segments in Figure 7.2.

When would profitability be determined more by the customer than by the product? This happens when the costs of acquiring and retaining the customer are high, due to the characteristics of the service, the customer, or the industry, or any combination of these. As one example, consider the changing characteristics of the credit card industry. In the early 1980s the credit card industry was booming because the penetration of cards was low, there were compelling values to attract customers, and relatively few competitors pursuing customers. The cost of acquiring a customer was less than $50; today, efficient marketers spend over $200 to acquire each customer. This increase is directly proportional to the number of solicitations, because a promotion's 'hit rate' is inversely proportional to the number of competitive solicitations that a prospective customer receives. An increase in costs, however, does create an opportunity for bundling financial services. A single, expensive customer acquisition can generate revenue across a range of products.

This example does not suggest that industry characteristics alone determine the viability of a Total Customer Solutions position or any other

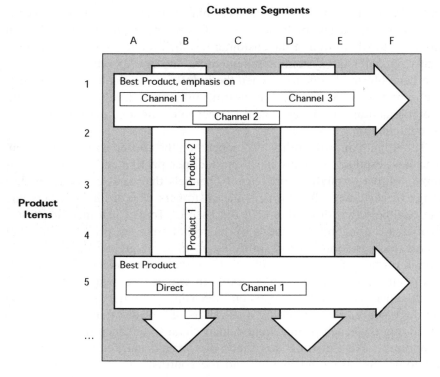

Figure 7.2   Best Product companies take a horizontal market cut, Total
Customer Solutions businesses take a vertical market cut

strategic position. Industry sets the stage, but there may be successful businesses in all three corners of the Triangle at the same time in the same
industry. The Internet access industry has participants like Erol selling a
Best Product, while AT&T positions its WorldNet service within a bundle
of telecommunications services. The character of the service is different
for each and the value proposition of each appeals to different customer
segments. In fact, a Best Product business may wholesale its product to a
Total Customer Solutions provider that then repackages it within a bundle.

Whereas the Best Product business focuses on product coverage and the
Total Customer Solutions business emphasizes vertical markets, the
System Lock-In business must address the full range of products and
customers since its goal is to serve as a core element in the system architecture. Relationships with the full range of complementors are required to
fill this need. Complementors should include businesses that distribute to
the largest and leading vertical markets as well as businesses that provide

related products that are core to the system. We will return to the Novell example to illustrate the point. Novell targets and serves the software developers, computer/server companies, and printer manufacturers whose products are essential to the LAN system, but they also shower attention and service on the 35,000 value-added resellers (VARs) that sell LANs to vertical markets. No potential complementor was left unaddressed in Novell's effort to secure the high market share they needed to become a dominant Proprietary Standard.

The customer interface is the last dimension upon which we will comment where we find contrasts in the way the Customer Targeting process supports the strategic positions. In the Best Product strategy the customer interfaces are often restricted and narrow. Frequently, the only connection between a Best Product company and its customers is the relationship between a sales representative and a buyer. While there might be contact between other people within the customer organization and the vendor's billing and customer care teams, these are generally transactional in nature. Typically, the dialogue that takes place is specific to the matter in hand, such as pricing, inventory replenishment, shelf space utilization, merchandising displays, and promotional activities. Again, the primary concern is to move a volume-driven product intended for mass consumption at the lowest possible cost as quickly as possible.

Total Customer Solutions players require much more robust customer interfaces. The interactions between the firm and its customers are not restricted to salespersons and buyers. Rather, they extend to an array of professionals on each side of each interaction. Ideally, all the major business and functional interests are represented, involving personnel from line management, R&D, manufacturing, distribution, marketing, sales, services, and so on. The Total Customer Solutions player must develop an intimate knowledge of each customer's business, its organization, the markets it is serving, the products and services required to satisfy its customers' needs, the capabilities residing in its organization, and its financial positioning. In brief, it must develop a complete understanding of all aspects of its customers' businesses in order to establish solid and mutually rewarding partnerships.

Figure 7.3 illustrates the limited type of customer interface common to Best Product players. In contrast, Figure 7.4 illustrates the complex set of interrelationships of the Total Customer Solutions interface.

The limited interface of the Best Product position can induce myopia. A company that only communicates with its customers' buyers will know nothing of its customers' plans for the future. This presents a clear danger for Best Product players. Choosing the right channel mix, which is key to

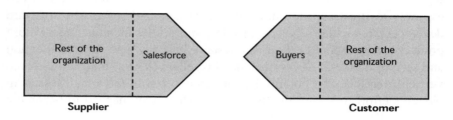

Supplier   Customer

Figure 7.3   The traditional customer interface in the Best Product strategy

Source: Patrick Preux, 'Customer Targeting, Sustainable Competitive Advantage, and the
Competencies', unpublished MA thesis, Sloan School of Management, MIT 1998

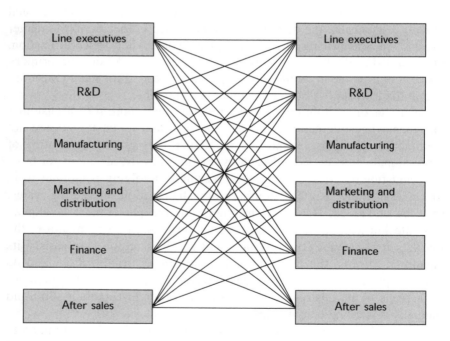

Figure 7.4   The typical customer interface in
the Total Customer Solutions strategy

Source: Patrick Preux, 'Customer Targeting, Sustainable Competitive Advantage,
and the Competencies', unpublished MA thesis, Sloan School
of Management, MIT 1998

sustaining a company's competitive position, is not simply a question of finding the market access points that have the most volume today and selling to them, it is also a question of anticipating and taking advantage of the frequent changes in the distribution landscape. The choice can have fundamental and irreversible consequence.

The strategies of two 'Best Product' businesses in the PC industry illustrate this point. Compaq Computer received an early boost in sales at a critical time in its development by leveraging an existing broad computer dealer network. The local dealer presence was important at that stage in the development of the PC industry, when consumers had to see and touch the product to understand what it did. About six years later, Dell Computer entered the industry. Although dealer channels were still the predominant route to the customer, Michael Dell understood the evolution of the industry and realized that customers no longer required the physical hand-holding of the local computer dealer. He also understood that PCs were becoming a price-sensitive commodity, and that dealer channels added an unnecessary cost. Dell went directly to the customer via phone, mail, and now the Internet. Compaq and other established PC providers have found direct sales difficult to imitate because of the conflict with their legacy dealer networks. In the past five years, Dell has surpassed every other U.S. company in stock price appreciation. It has the lowest-cost channel, the lowest inventory levels in the industry, and the ability to deploy the latest technology the quickest – not a bad formula for a Best Product position. Every business today should worry about the 10X force that could change the channel landscape and disrupt their efficient access to the market. Furthermore, having conquered the Best Product positioning and being wary of the long-term commodity consequences, Dell then used their networking knowledge and interactive customer interfaces to establish a Total Customer Solutions position to tightly bond with customers.

The System Lock-In position, as we have said previously, requires the broadest and most complex set of activities. Sizing the overall system in which the business operates and identifying the potential key complementors is an arduous task requiring strong involvement from the most talented executives with a deep and broad knowledge base of the industry. If an industry is suited to the establishment of a Proprietary Standard, a Dominant Exchange, or Restricted Access, the player that identifies, effectively positions themselves, and quickly locks in the key complementors will be the most likely to gain System Lock-In.

The Role of Innovation as an Adaptive Process

Innovation is concerned with preserving the viability of the business through the continuous renewal of it product base. In that sense, innovation is the central instrument for product development activities. What we have encountered in our work with a wide range of executives is that the conventional view of innovation is implicitly linked with the Best Product strategy. Excellence in innovation is associated with the ability to introduce a continuous stream of new products of superior quality with great efficiency in timing and execution. Typically, innovation leadership is understood as being first to market, and the creation of a dominant design that gives the innovator the chance to establish the standard set of product attributes that customers will come to expect and complementors will come to support. The infrastructure that supports the effective delivery of the stream of products is based on a common platform for the delivery of an entire family of products. This platform permits the realization of economies of scale by merging the delivery processes of a set of related products and the flexibility to customize each member of the product family.

The common platform is believed to be the most effective way to deliver new products to market. Examples include the PDP series of DEC, the J cars of GM, the 360 series of IBM mainframe computers, and the long line of Honda motorcycles.

This is end of the story for the conventional view of innovation. However, while being first to market and gaining the dominant design is important and challenging, it is always not the end goal of a proper innovation process. In order to make clear the potentially broader charge and richer requirements of the innovation process, we will examine how its role changes when it is intended to support the two other strategic options: Total Customer Solutions and System Lock-In. For a visual description of the role of Innovation, see Table 7.3.

For Total Customer Solutions players, the role of Innovation is turned upside down relative to its role for Best Product players. Instead of deploying internal competencies to generate standardized, high-volume products that satisfy the needs of a faceless generic customer, they focus on a targeted set of customers whose businesses they try to enhance. They tie their product platform to those of their customers to facilitate joint development of new products. Their goal is to respond to the full set of customer needs by providing a customized bundle of products. This close association with customers generates an extremely strong form of customer bonding.

Prior to its acquisition by Unilever about 12 years ago, National Starch's most important customer was Proctor & Gamble (P&G). P&G and

Table 7.3   The changing role of Innovation in
supporting the chosen strategic position

		DESCRIPTION OF THE ROLE		
		Focus of attention	Output	Objective
STRATEGIC POSITION	Best Product	Common product platform	Family of products	First to market, dominant design
	Total Customer Solutions	Customer's platform	Joint development	■ Enhance customer's results ■ Customized bundle of products ■ Integrate into customer's activities
	System Lock-In	Open platform	■ Manage proliferation of complementors ■ Breadth/range of applications ■ Application interfaces	Harmonized system architecture

Unilever are fierce rivals that compete against each other throughout the world. Immediately after the Unilever acquisition, National Starch (NSI) lost the P&G account. This led to a huge loss in revenues, and a tremendous amount of grief. In 1997, Unilever sold NSI to Imperial Chemical Industries (ICI). In his first press conference after the acquisition, ICI's CEO asserted that NSI's business would improve dramatically because it had been freed of all constraints on selling products and services to Unilever's competitors. Following this announcement, representatives of the Kimberly Clarke company called to express their disbelief. Kimberly Clarke had competed head to head with P&G in the lucrative disposable diapers business. Kimberly Clarke had developed a strong and productive relationship with NSI once P&G had ceased to be an NSI customer, which led to innovative new products and technology. NSI and Kimberly Clarke had established mutual lock-in and dependence that was part of Kimberly Clarke's competitive arsenal against P&G.

There are enormous implications to be drawn from this story. In pursuing a Total Customer Solutions strategy, companies select customers with whom they want to establish deep and trusting relationships. By forming relationships of this type with certain customers, Total Customer Solutions players must necessarily avoid relationships with other potential customers. In other words, locking in some customers may cause you to exclude others. Penetrating vertical markets presents specific challenges. Unlike the Best Product strategic position, the Total Customer Solutions position tends not to allow companies to work with all the players (or with all players in a similar fashion) in a given product area.

Conventional wisdom holds that R&D laboratories are the primary source of innovation. This is evident in the widespread use of the ratio of R&D spending to sales to measure the strength of a product pipeline. Companies with ratios of the order of 8% are often said to be building streams of products for the future, while those with ratios in the 2% range are said to be 'milking their businesses.' These ideas are misleading.

MIT Professor Eric Von Hippel conducted one of the most objective and thorough studies of innovation. He looked at 253 specific cases and arrived at a profound conclusion: customers are the primary source of innovation in industries where customers are the immediate beneficiaries of innovation, in other words, look to customers for Innovation when pursuing a Total Customer Solutions strategy. Given the specialized technical abilities required for successful product development today, this seems crazy. But in fact, the detailed discussions regarding products and needs that successful Total Customers Solutions players tend to initiate with their customers often yield their most inspiring ideas.

Innovation and System Lock-In

The role of Innovation in supporting a System Lock-In position is the most decisive and the most encompassing. Innovation is the centerpiece of a successful lock-in strategy. Here again, however, the role has little to do with the conventional view of new product development. Instead of just capturing the benefits of its own innovations, a System Lock-In player seeks to benefit from the innovations of all the complementors in its industry. To be successful here, it cannot keep its technological capabilities a secret, it must make them widely available, and encourage as many parties as possible to access its open architecture and develop their own products, applications, and services in ways that make use of and support that architecture. It sets out to make its technologies and products the common denominator of an entire economic system.

Many argue that the turning point in Microsoft's development was when IBM contracted with the company to provide the operating system for all IBM PCs. We think that in fact the turning point was when Compaq approached Microsoft to buy the same PC operating system that IBM used. Until then, every PC manufacturer had its own unique or customized operating system. Compaq wanted to sell IBM compatible computers so that a customer could switch to Compaq comfortable in the knowledge that the software applications he or she had bought, written, or customized for the IBM would work on a newly acquired Compaq. For most customers, the investment in software, processes, and training is many multiples greater than the investment in the PC hardware itself. Bill Gates had the wisdom to agree to Compaq's request. A less insightful executive might have insisted on customizing Compaq's operating system in hopes of generating higher margins. As a result of his decision, Microsoft's DOS became the common denominator for a large and growing PC industry.

Near universality is a typical trait for a System Lock-In business. Intel's Andy Grove dreams of one billion computers on the Internet. Bill Gates wants a computer in every home (today the penetration is almost 50%, by comparison cable TV's penetration is 60%). The phone company delivers a copy of the *Yellow Pages* to every house. Coca-Cola prides itself in offering universal accessibility.

Whereas classic product R&D is the source of innovation for a Best Product business and customers are the source for a Total Customer Solutions business, complementors are the primary source of Innovation for a System Lock-In business. It harnesses the benefits of that Innovation and can assist in an explosion in creativity by assuming some of the common functions in the system, making business simpler and less costly for complementors. For example, they may not need as many resources as previously or the scale to deploy them efficiently. Visa and MasterCard provide retail support, brand advertising, rewards programs, and merchant settlements that allow their member banks to focus on acquiring and maintaining end-users. This promotes product fragmentation and proliferation which accelerate creativity in the market via trial and error on the part of new participants in the market. (A successful standard requires thousands of complementors, not a handful.) System Lock-In players may in the end build into their standard platforms some of the functionality once provided only by complementors that have gained widespread popularity. When the Internet was an obscure network, for example, Microsoft was happy to let others provide the browsers. When it looked as though PC users would use the Internet in significant numbers, Microsoft started to develop a browser of its own and to integrate it into the common operating system platform. A company that takes over functions from one complementor must be sure to preserve its relationships with other complementors and thereby maintain the integrity of its system. The more successful a standard becomes, however, the more freedom its owner has to compromise any one complementor relationship for the sake of dramatically improving its own competitive position, as Microsoft sought to do.

Just as the customer interface takes on a critical role for a Total Customer Solutions business, the application interface – which links the Proprietary Standard to complementors' products – takes on a critical role for a System Lock-In business. The interface must be sufficiently complex and everchanging to prevent complementors from easily imitating it. At the same time, it is essential to maintain backward compatibility to preserve the legacy infrastructure that represents the core value of the standard itself.

At some point, dramatic changes in technology will force a change in the standard platform that eliminates backward compatibility. IBM led the database software industry when the architecture and technology was based on flat files. There were, and still are, a large number of applications using this technology. But today, the technology of relational databases is far superior in functionality and ease of use – by a factor of 10 or more. Oracle captured the Proprietary Standard for this new database architecture. It has achieved System Lock-In, but, like IBM before it, Oracle is vulnerable to the next killer technology. Some think that the next killer technology will be object-oriented databases. While Oracle may dread this development, it can be assured that because of the value generated by the complementors in its system, any new technology cannot be simply twice as good as the old one – it has to be 10 times better.

The semiconductor industry serves as an example of how the role of innovation depends on a company's chosen strategic position. Hitachi and NEC are among the leading producers of DRAMS. This segment has been characterized by short product life cycles and declining prices. To succeed, these companies develop new chips every one to two years that employ technology four times better than the previous generation in facilities that now cost over $1 billion to construct. These two companies occupy the Best Product position and pursue a breakneck stream of internally sourced innovation to support their competitive advantage. In contrast, Motorola's semiconductor business occupies the Total Customer Solutions position. The automobile industry is an important vertical market for Motorola. A car can have as many as 100 chips to control many of its functions. These chips are critical to Differentiation. Motorola works closely with car manufacturers to develop customized chips; the innovations are jointly developed. Finally, System Lock-In provider Intel has depended on the rapid development of a complex standard. They developed five generations of microprocessors between 1978 and 1996. The speed of development and the complexity of the chip keep them well ahead of AMD, which is the leading producer of Intel clones. At the same time, they are not simply making faster chips, they are also expanding the scope of their chips to include functionality previously found on neighboring chips or in software, while religiously maintaining backward compatibility.

Arriving at a Strategic Position: Critical Success Factors

The essence of each strategic position is represented by the objectives of the Adaptive Processes. It is important now to summarize the net effect of combining the processes to create a strategy as shown in Figure 7.5. Most companies implicitly or explicitly strive to have the lowest product cost, achieve maximum volume, and to be the first to market with new products. These activities – whether deliberately planned or not – lead to a Best Product position. A Total Customer Solutions company must combine an altogether different set of objectives: superior customer value, tight customer bonding, and customized, bundled products. A company seeking System Lock-In depends on superior system performance and a prolific but integrated system architecture organized around their product standard that defines the gateway that complementors and customers must use to access the market.

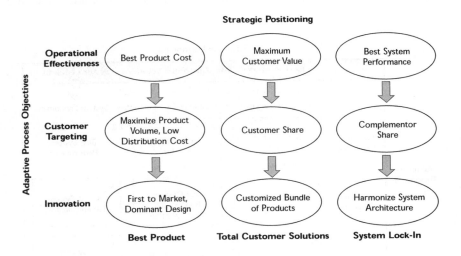

Figure 7.5   The role of Adaptive Processes in supporting the strategic positioning of the business

Prioritizing the Adaptive Processes

Just as the roles played by the Adaptive Processes depend on the chosen strategic position, their relative importance changes as well. The assignment of priorities to the Adaptive Processes is controversial. There are some who would assign equal importance to each process. They would argue that companies must simultaneously pursue Low Cost, excellent Customer Targeting, and superior Innovation. We believe that prioritization is key. The goal of this prioritization is not to render certain processes insignificant, rather, it is to recognize the intrinsic differences among the strategic positions and their attendant tradeoffs.

Figure 7.6 illustrates the prioritization of the Adaptive Processes associated with each strategic option. The top left to bottom right diagonal, which we refer to as 'the consistency corridor,' links the top priorities for each strategic position.

The Best Product position requires a low-cost infrastructure, which originates with Operational Effectiveness. Next, it requires the support of a stream of new products to extend its current vitality into the future, which Innovation provides. Finally, Customer Targeting is intended to provide mass access to distribution channels.

The first priority of the Total Customer Solutions position is effective Customer Targeting that identifies the required product bundles and the

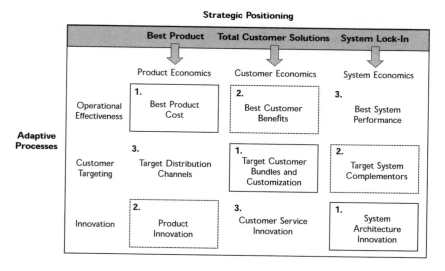

Figure 7.6   The priorities of Adaptive Processes in each strategic position

need for customization. Operational Effectiveness ensures the efficient delivery of the products and services that enhance the customer economics. Innovation is given lowest priority because companies aspiring to the Total Customer Solution position do not require the type of leadership in new products, services and features that companies aspiring to the other strategic positions do. Often the new product capabilities required to support this strategy come from strategic alliances and close collaboration with customers.

Innovation is the highest priority for companies aiming for the System Lock-In position. For System Lock-In players, Innovation is often geared toward the development of a system architecture that allows for the creation of a Proprietary Standard or dominant exchange. The next level of support comes from targeting complementors. The goal is to lock these complementors in and to lock competitors out. Operational Effectiveness, geared toward improving system performance, is of lowest priority to System Lock-In players. Again, the priorities we have assigned indicate the importance of the processes relative to one another, although the process assigned lowest priority for a given strategic position is not unimportant in an absolute sense.

Reflections

Processes are not Strategy

During the last two decades there has been a passionate emphasis on restructuring, reengineering, cost cutting, lean manufacturing, and other similar paradigms. In the face of that fervent exhortation many companies have explicitly, or implicitly, assumed that operational effectiveness in itself is a strategy. This is an incorrect and dangerous presumption. While a lean infrastructure may be appropriate to pursue a Best Product strategy, it may do this by eliminating functionality superfluous to being low cost but essential to establishing the relationships necessary in a Total Customer Solutions or System Lock-In. What emerges is a company unable to differentiate itself other than by efficiency. As these practices become more prevalent among competitors, the industry becomes commoditized, and customers are reduced to choices only based upon price.

This is a particularly dangerous siren for incumbent firms, where there is little precedent in converting an established organization to the clear low-cost leader. As mentioned in Chapter 3, the remarkable low-cost players have typically been new to the industry – Nucor, Southwest Airlines,

WalMart, and so on. Their success lies in having new processes with zero legacies, and some industry gurus might have even said they had a certain naiveté about how the business traditionally works. There are more examples of established players succeeding at Total Customer Solutions positions – IBM, GE, National Starch – than at becoming low-cost players. The established players are able to use their inherited breadth in product scope and deep customer relationships to forge extensive bonds.

Not only has Operational Effectiveness been confused with strategy, so too has Customer Targeting and Innovation. Every new practice or technology brings such new exhilaration that some companies endorse them to the detriment of the overall strategy. Even Capital One has become so intrigued with its Customer Targeting aptitude that it has felt compelled to follow a strategy of applying this competence template to other industries, including cellular and insurance. But to no avail, these diversions have met with little success and, moreover, have served as a distraction from its credit business.

Processes are not strategies for the same reason that a human is not simply an amalgamation of protoplasm, amino acids, calcium, and other minerals. Life is an emergent property, more than the straightforward sum of its parts. Strategy is also an emergent property, not fully evident in its pieces and truly greater than the sum of its parts. It is important to consider a business at two levels: its strategy and its activities. The objective and its means. Exclusive attention to activities evokes reality, but loses meaning. It adds precision, but loses the point.

We are strong advocates of a granular perspective, as we will explain fully in Chapter 10, and of processes. As stand-alone items they are potent techniques. Their power to reshape a business, however, lies in their alignment with strategy.

CHAPTER 8

Delta.com: Reinterpreting the Internet Industry

If we were to be faithful to history, the Soviet Union should receive credit for the invention of the Internet. The U.S. Defense Department responded to President Eisenhower's concern over the surprisingly early launch of *Sputnik* in 1957 by founding the Advanced Research Project Agency (ARPA) in 1958. Their intent was to push American researchers to catch up with and ultimately surpass their Soviet counterparts. And, while the Americans were not as far behind as they had feared, ARPA was successful in moving them forward. In eighteen months, ARPA's scientists had collaborated to develop the first successful U.S. satellite. About six years later, under the direction of Dr. J.C.R. Licklider, ARPA[1] turned its attention to the U.S. military's use of computers and networks.

In 1969, the Defense Department commissioned ARPAnet, a packet-switched network with which to conduct networking research. It was used to link together universities and laboratories with defense contracts, allowing them to communicate freely with one another and collaborate on projects. Designed as a secure network capable of withstanding a nuclear attack by the Soviets, ARPAnet initially comprised computers with 12 kbytes of memory each. This closed network of computers, less powerful than today's pocket calculators, is the direct ancestor of today's all knowing, universally accessible Internet.

Between 1971 and 1984, with the advent of e-mail, Usenet newsgroups, and international connections, the number of computers on ARPAnet climbed from 23 to over 1,000. By 1987, owing to the arrival of NSFnet, which opened a part of ARPAnet to nongovernment traffic, the number of connected computers rose tenfold, to over ten thousand. In 1989, the year that the first e-mail relay between a commercial online service (CompuServe) and ARPAnet went live, there were over 100,000 ARPAnet-connected computers. In 1992, two years after the network officially became the Internet, a Swiss research facility called CERN[2] created the World Wide Web and the number of connected computers passed 1 million. By 1994, the year the first florist began taking orders on the

Internet, there were almost 3 million connected computers and over 14 million Internet users – and businesses started to take serious interest.

As at the end of 2000, there are over 200 million Internet users. Internet pioneer Vinton Cerf had a remarkably clear vision of the future when, in 1993, he said that:

> it seems likely that the Internet will continue to be the environment of choice for the deployment of new protocols and for the linking of diverse systems in the academic, government, and business sectors for the remainder of this decade and well into the next.[3]

In 1984, just prior to the divestiture of AT&T, the U.S. telecommunications industry had a market value of around $300 billion. Today, the telecommunications industry has a market value of approximately 2 trillion dollars, and over half of this is oriented to the Internet. This is 15% of the total market value of all publicly traded companies. This represents the infrastructure alone, the carriers, switches, fiber, routers, and manufacturers of this equipment and software. It does not include the values derived from the Amazon or eBay dot.coms, or the e-business investments made by incumbents. It is a massive infrastructure, greater than that in electric utilities ($300 billion) or airlines ($30 billion). It is an infrastructure around which many other businesses have designed their products, services, and internal processes. Even if there is a better system out there, the investments to date assure us that the TCP/IP (Transport Control Protocol/Internet Protocol) architecture is here to stay.

While there can be no question about the network becoming a central facet of business, questions remain about how businesses will profit from the Internet. Many analysts publicly state that they do not know whether or how most companies in the Internet industry will make money. The success of even the largest and most established Internet business, such as Amazon, is in doubt. Along with these ventures come unconventional business practices that until recently were unheard of. Netscape gave away their browser product for free. Internet access providers, such as Mindspring and AOL, charge customers the same monthly rate regardless of how much time they consume on the network. Publishers such as the *Washington Post* make massive investments in information services that have marginal usage relative to their traditional paper assets.

In the search for a profit engine in this mysterious economy, venture capitalists and market analysts alike have chased after each new business model, only to drop it when the next exciting variation rises on the horizon. First, Internet access is popular, then content, followed by B2C e-commerce, which is trumped by B2B. Failing each of these, infrastructure (such as fiber, optoelectronics, and routers) is deemed the only way to make money, and now even that is becoming a dimmer light against the electromagnetic radiance of wireless. Are all these models ultimately doomed? Or, is Warren Buffet right when he says that just because the Internet succeeds does not mean that anyone will make money in it. Look at the erratic and depressed profitability of airlines, despite the continued popularity of air travel.

The Delta Model leads to a different perspective. Whether a business is engaged in content, B2C, B2B, or infrastructure is not so important. Eventual and sustainable success is more influenced by the strategy the business adopts. In other words, whether a business is in the content sector or the e-commerce sector says less about their viability than the position they achieve in the Triangle. Let us examine several of these sectors in turn through the lens of the Delta Model.

Content

Content providers supply information to users. However, not all content is the same. This is apparent when looking at three content providers: sports site ESPN.com, web portal Go, and the technology news and information destination CNET (Figure 8.1).

ESPN.com has made itself the primary Internet destination for enthusiasts seeking news, commentary, and statistics about every major spectator sport. It has done so by being 'first to market' among sports sites and by focusing on the quality of its product. ESPN was in fact one of the first

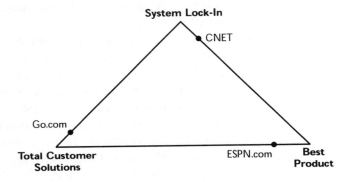

Figure 8.1   Content positioning in the Triangle

major 'traditional' media outlets of any sort (news, sports, entertainment, and so on) to develop an online presence. And those that followed – including sports-focused competitors CNNSI.com (a joint venture between CNN and Sports Illustrated) and CBSsportsline.com – copied its design. Each of the sites can be viewed as the online component of a broader based media business (television in the case of ESPN, CBS, and CNN; a magazine in the case of *Sports Illustrated*). All three sites have headline sports news on their opening pages along with links to news and information on each major sport, direct links to statistics for all sports, and links to stores selling branded merchandise online. All three offer search tools, free e-mail and fantasy sports. And all three advertise their own material at the tops of their primary pages and the products and services of other companies further down. Each competes for customers based on the quality and timeliness of their information and the appeal of their format. The Best Product wins the most customers, Differentiation has been diffi-cult to sustain because it is easy to imitate competitors and it is hard to bond with customers.

ESPN is also part of an exclusively Internet-based customer solution called Go.com. Launched in January 1999 by the Infoseek and Disney corporations, Go.com was among the top five sites in user traffic within half a year. The 'network' brings together the content of ESPN, Disney, and ABC; the search capabilities of Infoseek; free web-based e-mail, site development tools and hosting services; a branded adult content filter (called GoGuardian); and a specialized Go version of the Microsoft Explorer web browser. Go's primary intended market is users new to the Internet. It aims to gather together trusted, familiar content and all the key Internet tools in one well-organized place.

Go's focus is clearly on its customers. It offers customized content capabilities to users to give them the specific information they want each time they return to the site – and it tracks users' movements through the site to offer them still more content that they are *likely* to want. Go locks in customers by hosting their personal web pages, pages that they cannot take with them to other sites. Similarly, the 'username@go.com' e-mail addresses that users can register for free are not portable to other mail providers. The site also offers a suite of services – including bulletin boards and chat rooms – that gives users opportunities to create content of their own. Once users become part of Go-sponsored online communi-ties and return expressly to view content created by fellow community members, they are locked in in yet another way. Finally, Go aggregates links to online merchants in a way that allows users to search for specific products or services irrespective of the merchant offering them. In doing so, it further builds customer relationships by serving as a channel for the merchant.

In building Go, Infoseek and Disney are looking to serve as a channel to more than just online merchants. They are also looking to be the channel for their customers to all other Internet sites. Their publicly stated aim is to organize all the Internet content that a user might want to view or create. They have taken the 'web portal' model – whereby sites like Yahoo! and Excite vie to become the jumping off points for web users – to a new level. Instead of sending users off to content providers or merchants with whom they have no formal affiliation, Go has brought under its umbrella content and services of every major type. Through its Infoseek search engine, it will send users to unaffiliated sites if they choose to search for such sites, but it highlights its own offerings in all areas in its attempt to keep customers on 'the network' for as long as possible.

While the Go Network and many of its fellow web portals are building effective customer solutions, few web content producers have gone beyond customer solutions to achieve System Lock-In. One that has this potential is CNET, number 15 on the list of most valuable Internet companies with almost $3 billion in market capitalization. CNET has multiple Internet sites and a television station, but the focus here will be on its flagship site, CNET.com. The site is best known for its editors' detailed evaluations and comparisons of every type of technology device and service. It also provides technology news, Internet search capabilities, job search services and software downloads.

The company's description thus far does not seem to make for a business plan meriting $3 billion of market capitalization. What is so special about CNET? The answer is simple: complementors. Well over 50% of CNET's press releases in a given month are about deals signed with complementors. The *New York Times*, NBC, Compaq, Dell, Gateway, and many other big names in media and computing, as well as thousands of merchant and web site affiliates have deals of some kind with CNET. Not only are users seeking technology shopping advice or news at countless affiliated sites directed to CNET, but once they arrive, they find comparisons of all the major products or services in the category that interests them. Sellers are drawn to CNET because it is a magnet for users and because CNET allows users to click through directly to the 'buy now' pages of a seller's site once they have settled on a product or service. Users are drawn to the site because CNET gathers together all potentially desirable sellers. The sustained positive feedback loop, much like that belonging to the *Yellow Pages* described in an earlier chapter, creates a difficult-to-assail position and results in a very valuable company. CNET goes one further step toward lock-in. Users are able to write and post product reviews. Shoppers looking for product information can access these reviews. As a consequence, buyers are partly drawn to CNET for the user reviews, and then leave behind additional reviews creating yet more value for the site. CNET becomes more valuable with usage because of the investment by users, not just by CNET. The power of this feedback loop will be tested over time, but it adds to the sustainability of the business because of factors external to CNET's own product investments.

In the terminology of the Delta Model, ESPN.com is aiming for a Differentiated Best Product strategy, Go.com is pursuing Horizontal Breadth, and CNET is aspiring to a Proprietary Standard. They are all content providers and their success is still in question, but their strategies are strikingly different. They should follow different pricing and processes. For example, CNET can argue that making the site free will build the complementor adherence that they can later use to extract rents when they are tightly bound to the market. ESPN.com has no means of long-term bonding, and needs to cautiously consider early giveaways. Free products may win many customers, but they can easily switch to a comparable sports site when prices are imposed. For ESPN the money is better spent on a better product that makes them incomparable to other sports sites, and, in fact, that is the tactic they have employed.

E-commerce

E-commerce is to retailing what web content is to media. As seen above, while all content businesses get advertising revenue, how they earn it varies according to their strategy. Similarly, all e-commerce largely gets revenue from transactions, just as retailing has done for centuries. How e-commerce earns this transaction revenue varies considerably. Earlier in this book we described three companies that highlight these differences: SureTrade, Amazon and eBay (Figure 8.2).

All are deeply entrenched in e-commerce. Amazon and eBay are the third and fourth most valuable Internet companies with market capitalizations that have each exceeded $30 billion. Amazon is following a Total Customer Solutions strategy via Horizontal Breadth. They provide the broadest scope of products to consumers on the Internet including books, videos, art, electronics, healthcare, hardware, kitchen, lawn and patio, and toys. Most importantly, they personalize these offers to each customer using the past behavior of each customer as a guide.

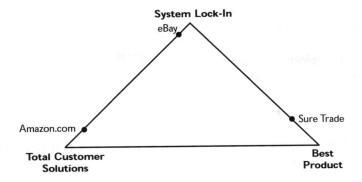

Figure 8.2   E-commerce positioning in the Triangle

Amazon is not the only dotcom pursuing a Total Customer Solutions strategy. Office.com is a joint venture of CBS and Winstar and is positioned to bring a wide range of information, products, and services relevant to operating a small business. Schwab and Fidelity have built empires by bringing a broad, yet integrated set of financial products to consumers. In fact, after years of being out in front with this e-business strategy, now virtually all their institutional competitors are following suit. Whether the incumbent financial institutions have the technical skills is one question, whether they can learn the trade of customer bonding quickly enough to stem their decline in market share is the bigger question.

eBay has achieved System Lock-In as a Dominant Exchange. They also have breadth in their offer, but it falls out of the huge number of sellers posting items for sale. The huge number of sellers is the source of competitive positioning. Sellers seeking the most buyers, who in turn want to find the most sellers creates the feedback that sustains the business. They have segmented the trading zones around multiple markets, whether defined by geographies, industries, consumers, or products types, and have gained the critical mass to make their service the Dominant Exchange in each. It is not the only exchange, even Amazon and Yahoo! have created auctions to compete head-to-head. Amazingly, even these Internet powerhouses have been unable to dislodge the grip of eBay, testifying to the power of bonding once achieved.

Priceline and FreeMarkets are also attempting a System Lock-In strategy, again in the mold of a Dominant Exchange. Priceline allows travelers to bid on air travel and hotels. FreeMarkets allows reverse exchanges where buyers can request bids for industrial parts. In fact, a number of the

B2B ventures have had a strong Dominant Exchange bias. The challenge has been to identify markets sufficiently big and structured so that lock-in can develop. For example, there is not a lot of lock-in inherent in 20 participant networks. Priceline is facing a challenge from the airlines themselves who are ganging up to provide a similar service. A Dominant Exchange is stronger when there are many buyers and many sellers; concentration among the sellers is a vulnerability that Priceline is suffering from.

None of these companies is following one pure play strategy. While Amazon is best characterized by Horizontal Breadth, they add capabilities that add System Lock-In types of bonding. For example, Amazon enables customers to post reviews of books and other products. This creates the sort of bonding we described earlier with CNET. Shoppers value the reviews, and in using Amazon leave reviews of their own thus adding to its general appeal. Amazon also provides recommendations to shoppers based upon the buying behavior of others who were interested in the same book or music CD. These recommendations grow more robust as more people visit Amazon's site. Amazon's Z Shop program allows independent retailers to showcase their products. Amazon allows visitors searching for products to find Z Shop, the merchant is responsible for shipping the product, and Amazon collects a fee. As important as the fees is the added bonding Amazon gains. They are able to capture more of the customer's spending and better understand their buying patterns. This draws yet more customers to their site and locks in more Z Shop merchants. This illustrates how bonding is built feature by feature. Product development is normally hotly debated and prioritization is usually based on incremental profits, customer preferences, and cost. To this list should be added bonding. It should be a key factor used in prioritizing business development projects.

Finally, SureTrade demonstrates that the Best Product approach is alive and well on the Internet. It provides trading services that compete against industry leaders E*TRADE and Schwab by beating their prices. Streamlined processes and a low-cost channel allow for a viable competitive position, but there is always the threat of a lower priced alternative.

SureTrade is joined by other companies pursuing Best Product strategies on the Web. Victoria Secret, Land's End, and Egghead have turned to the Internet as an alternative distribution channel. Incumbents all too frequently maintain their Best Product positioning even while moving to the new technology. Egghead has had outstanding success in almost completely converting to a web-based operation. As a national retail chain selling software, they have closed nearly 160 brick and mortar stores, reduced their salesforce by almost 800 people, and eliminated over 80% of their inventory, while expanding sales from $380 million in 1997 to $500 million in 1999. They target 3.8 million small business customers with a weekly circulation of over 10 million e-mail pieces. With a virtual presence, consolidated operations, and a patented automatic e-mail-based notification and customer service system, they have achieved low-cost distribution and high customer satisfaction – for now. While a great success story, there remains vulnerability to either imitation, or more aggressive pricing.

One Vertical Market: Multiple Strategies

We can further clarify the distinct nature of the strategies in the Delta Model by looking at three Internet companies pursuing the same vertical market with a blend of e-commerce and content. DrPaula.com, iVillage, and Parent-Watch all engage in content delivery, community development, and commerce related to children and childcare. But they do so in markedly different ways. In a clear Best Product play, DrPaula.com's staff physicians try to generate the best answers to questions relating to pediatric healthcare. iVillage tries to satisfy every online need of its target audience, women, and ParentWatch is trying to establish System Lock-In (Figure 8.3).

DrPaula.com – Differentiation

DrPaula.com is an online source for free pediatric advice. A host of other child-related sites offer health advice along with advice of every other sort

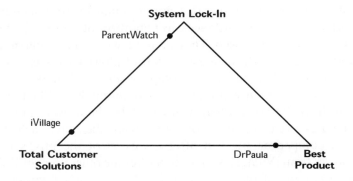

Figure 8.3   Strategic positions for one vertical market

and a variety of other features. But the health advice at many of them is either licensed from another provider or private label generic content. DrPaula.com, on the other hand, is staffed by a team of eight pediatricians and a breastfeeding expert who answer users' questions. The company's primary focus is on producing the clearest, most effective online pediatric advice available.

Customers are urged to return to the site based on the quality of the advice they have received. And they can be assured that DrPaula.com will be 'first to market' with the information they seek because it is information generated expressly on the questions they ask. At other sites, where pediatric advice in the form of magazine-type articles is one of dozens of generic features, they would have to hope that their particular experience is common enough to have been addressed.

iVillage – Horizontal Breadth

iVillage is an Internet destination for women. It bills itself as the place where women can 'talk about everything.' It offers free e-mail, chat rooms, expert advice, games, stock quotes, news and weather, a mortgage calculator, a recipe finder, a career shift quiz, and a good deal more. On the subject of children and childcare alone, it offers the following: Parents' Place, the 'parent-helping-parent community site'; Parent Soup, a collection of parenting communities and information; iBaby, a baby products store; iMaternity, a store selling maternity wear; a kids' résumé maker; a due date calculator; and articles of all sorts.

iVillage clearly positions itself as the one-stop shop for all a woman's information needs – those that are specific to her role as woman professional or mother, but also those that are common to all consumers of online information as well. They seek to minimize their users' interest in going anywhere else on the web. They do not have the best content available in every category – DrPaula.com's staff of physicians is hard to beat for pediatric advice – but they have a complete set of offerings.

Their offering is not only complete – it is inimitable. When iVillage describes itself as the place where you can 'talk about everything,' they mean that their users can join their communities and then have each other as resources. A competitor site can offer a variety of incentives to woo customers away from iVillage, but it cannot offer the other users of iVillage.

iVillage uses most of the same tactics as Go, discussed earlier in the chapter – customized content based on user profiles, nonportable e-mail addresses and personal web pages, and so on – and it has used them to develop an unassailable position in the child-related community and commerce space. Unlike Go, which followed strong competitors Yahoo!, Netscape, and America Online to market, iVillage was the first site of its kind to successfully implement a more focused Total Customer Solution. And its strategy is serving it well: it had one of the most successful IPOs (Initial Public Offers) in Internet history and it has purchased a number of its high quality competitors, such as Parent Soup and Parents' Place.

To beat iVillage at its own game, a new entrant would have to innovate to develop a Proprietary Standard, and then leverage that standard to create System Lock-In. That is exactly what ParentWatch is attempting to do.

ParentWatch – Restricted Access

ParentWatch is in the business of delivering streaming video images of children in childcare centers to their parents over the Internet. It does so using a network of complementors. While its end-users are parents, ParentWatch treats its relationships with childcare centers with the sort of care and thought that Total Customer Solutions players tend to reserve for their customers.

In a single year, ParentWatch has built an embedded base of centers larger than any other provider – including some that have been in business for more than four years. The key to its approach is that the service is entirely cost-free to the centers. ParentWatch makes the initial capital expenditure to procure and install the onsite cameras, video servers, and CPUs. It then covers all operating costs as well – monthly phone line and ISP charges, maintenance costs, and customer support.

While this approach provides an economic value proposition for child-care centers, there are still centers that hesitate to accept the system – generally either because they feel that the new system will take staff time away from other efforts or they are uncomfortable with some aspect of a video service. In response to this, ParentWatch offers the center an alternative: a free computer workstation and an easy-to-manage customized web site for the center. Center directors can populate the site templates with information about special events at the center, lunch menus, curricular changes, calendars, and a host of other information. In exchange for the free computer and site, the center must agree that, if at any time during the following ten years they choose to install a video system, it must be a ParentWatch system.

In implementing this strategy, ParentWatch effectively locks out competitors during the crucial 'land grab' phase of this new market development. There are approximately 100,000 childcare centers in the United States, of which only about 150 offer Internet viewing services. Whichever competitor develops partnerships with the most centers at the beginning of the 'land grab' is most likely to survive the eventual shakeout.

ParentWatch lock-in extends beyond childcare centers to the parents themselves. By becoming the exclusive provider at a given center, they establish themselves as the only choice for parents at that center interested in the service, short of switching centers. This is the basis for a number of ancillary revenue streams. At maturity, revenue from e-commerce and advertising should comprise a substantial portion of overall revenue. ParentWatch is targeting an extremely focused population (from an advertiser's viewpoint) with a service that should generate heavy usage. In fact, the average ParentWatch user spends three times more time at the Parent-Watch site in an average month than an average eBay user spends at eBay – and eBay, according to MediaMetrix, is the stickiest site on the web.

Network Infrastructure

To many analysts infrastructure is the last refuge in the search for profit in the Internet. Even if it is not clear how companies can make money using the Internet, there is money to be made in selling them the network infrastructure. However, we would argue that the amount of profit available over time is largely a function of the strategic positioning of the participants rather than the sector they are participating in. Infrastructure is a large segment encompassing carriers, ISPs, and equipment manufacturers. Let us look at two of the most promising sectors of infrastructure, broadband and wireless, to see how businesses are being positioned.

Today roughly 60% of homes and businesses in the U.S. have access to the Internet. This number drops to something like 30% for the developed countries in Europe and the Far East. Penetration will continue to increase, but at a slower rate. The first wave of the Internet has reached a mature phase. Over 95% of this Internet access is over dial-up modems. Modems connect a computer to the Internet backbone using standard telephone lines by converting the digital signals needed by the computer into analog signals that can travel along a network designed to carry analog voice communications. Speeds are constrained to less than 56 kbits per second. There are two Internet waves to come, broadband and wireless. Broadband raises the bandwidth speed for the end-user to over 1 megabit per second using digital subscriber loop (DSL) technology, fiber, cable modems, or fixed wireless. Existing trends suggest that over 80% of all Internet traffic will travel over local broadband connections within five years. Wireless is a third wave, untethering network access allowing PCs, personal digital assistants like Palm, and mobile phones to reach the Internet while on the go. Consequently, there are a number of businesses contesting for attractive strategic positions in these two markets.

Broadband Infrastructure

In the broadband market we find companies pursuing a broad range of strategies from Proprietary Standard to Low Cost (Figure 8.4). Our review starts with Akamai, perhaps the most sensational business in this sector. When Akamai went public in 1999, its stock price jumped over 450% on the first day of trading and its market value exceeded $20 billion. What was behind this enthusiasm? Akamai is in the business of helping content providers (for example Yahoo!, Martha Stewart Living) to more reliably stream rich media to their customers. The Internet backbone is expanding exponentially each year, but as it gets more far flung and congested it presents troublesome bottlenecks to broadband content that interfere with fast and dependable delivery to the end-user. Akamai allows businesses to store their content in servers located in data centers closer to the customer, and then deliver it over the least congested route as determined by complex algorithms and network traffic information they frequently update. They ensure quick and reliable broadband content delivery. This is invaluable to content providers because added seconds to download a page or conduct a transaction dramatically raises the likelihood that customers will leave and possibly not return.

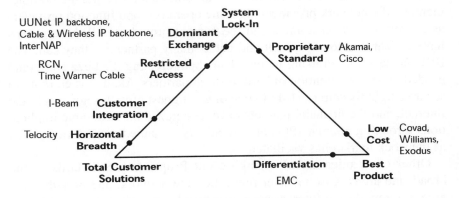

Figure 8.4   Broadband positioning in the Triangle

Akamai has a powerful business model because they have all the elements of a Proprietary Standard. Their customers are the content providers. Their complementors are their network partners, ISPs and data centers that host their servers. Content providers want to use the broadband content delivery enabler with the most network partners, and network partners want the enabler with the most content providers. This creates a sustaining feedback that could lock-in Akamai's position. Speed and share are essential to their success in order to gain the ubiquitous deployment of network servers and the critical mass of content providers. In the words of their CEO George Conrades:[4]

> We think of our business model as a virtuous circle that has three components. First is our technology. Second is our customers, the content providers. Third is our network partners, the ISPs that host our servers. The technology attracts the content providers because it enhances the experience they can deliver to end-users. As we attract more customers, our servers come to contain more and more of the Web's most popular content. That makes our servers attractive to the ISPs, for two reasons: by hosting our servers, they're able to deliver the content more quickly to their own customers; and they save on transit costs because the content travels much shorter distances. And finally, as our servers are incorporated into more networks, our technology becomes more attractive to the content providers because we're able to deliver their content even more quickly to users.
>
> That's the virtuous circle: Better technology attracts more content. More content attracts more networks. More networks mean better technology. And around we go.

Akamai structured its organization to simultaneously pursue complementors, the network providers, data site operators, and function providers as aggressively as customers and the content providers. All these groups have a clear mission to go out and get as many partners as they can. The IPO was less about raising money than about creating the buzz and brand needed to get the attention of hard to reach partners. Akamai is en route to secure a tight System Lock-In in one of the highest growth segments in the Internet, and the financial markets have recognized the economic implications through a popular IPO and a relatively sustained market value even as the stock market has vacillated.

Other companies are also staking out Proprietary Standards in the broadband arena. Cisco is ever present on the network, and broadband is no exception. As the Internet goes broadband the likely congestion points will be at the router and server nodes, rather than along the fiber transmission routes. So a strong position here will lead to high demand and margin leverage. Cisco has an 80% share of all routers. While competitors such as Foundry have chipped away at the high margin, high-end router segment where broadband resides, Cisco continues to maintain a 75% share. Cisco's complementors include other Cisco routers already embedded in the network, with which enterprises and networks want to ensure compatibility. They also include the technicians and design consultants, who are scarce assets primarily trained to work with Cisco because of its popularity.

The IP backbone itself may prove to be another source of System Lock-In, due to Dominant Exchange. ARPAnet, which evolved into NSFnet, was the original, government-subsidized IP backbone. Today, the backbone has multiplied into a collection of hundreds of private networks. To provide retail customers with Internet access, an ISP needs to establish some interconnection, or 'peering' relationship, with other networks. In the early days of the Internet, this was done via a select number of designated public Network Access Points (NAPs) located across the country, such as at MAE East in Tyson's Corner, Virginia or MAE West in Mountain View, California. As the Internet outgrew these access points, networks negotiated private peering relationships between themselves. Peering is a source of Dominant Exchange.

IP backbones are fungible commodities when thought of in terms of their fiber route miles or gigabit capacity. Networks are constantly exerting 'one-upmanship' on cost or capacity. In the U.S., Qwest outbuilds AT&T, Level 3 outbuilds Qwest, Williams outbuilds Level 3, and so on. In Europe the pattern is the same, KPNQwest outbuilds the local telephone companies, Viatel outbuilds KPNQwest, and so on. Nevertheless, IP backbones are not necessarily destined to become commodities. They differ enormously in their peering relationships.

From the clutter of a thousand networks, a natural tiering of IP backbones has emerged which is growing stronger over time. UUNet (a part of WorldCom), Sprint, Cable & Wireless, ebone (in Europe), and select others have emerged as Tier 1 IP backbones (Table 8.1) that have the majority of the private peering arrangements with other networks and ISPs. Peering relationships are expensive and difficult to set up; so naturally, ISPs and networks want to establish a peering relationship with the IP backbone that has the most peering relationships. This improves the odds that their traffic will move across the Internet more quickly and reliably with the fewest hops. IP backbones therefore can aspire to achieve some of the economics of Dominant Exchange. Their network customers want to be connected to the IP backbone that has most of the network interconnections.

Table 8.1 The tiering of North American IP backbones

Level		Customers		Network				
		Business customers	Consumers	Dial-up ports	POPs (points of presence)	Private peering arrangements[2]	Public peering arrangements[2]	Backbone connections with ISPs
Tier 1	MCI WorldCom	73,300	–	IMM (UUNET)	1,100	105	199	2,952[3]
	Sprint	2,800	130,00	N/A	500	58	79	867
	Intermedia (Digex)	90,000	N/A	N/A	N/A	5	22	687
	Cable & Wireless	34,500	–	N/A	300	41	29	569
	GTE Internetworking	3,400	700,000	600	375	68	43	313
	AT&T	N/A	1.5MM	670	630	57	65	382
	PSInet	50,000	–		500	11	99	246
	Verio	260,000	–	–	180	4	31	346
Tier 2	Concentric	20,000	–	–	350	15	6	<82
	Epoch	1,500	24,000	–	208	5	10	<82
	CAIS	400	3,000	480	10	N/A	N/A	<82
	e.spire	20,000	50,000	8,900	48	6	4	85
	ICG	N/A	N/A	4,900	236	N/A	N/A	<82
	CRL (Applied Theory)	5,000	15,000	N/A	36	N/A	N/A	107
Tier 3[1]	BRAVO Net	2,100		304	–	–	–	–
	Netrax	6,000		850	–	–	–	–
	Inreach	30,000		4,500	–	–	–	–
	Jetlink	15,000		1,803	–	–	–	–
	Lightspeed	35,000		4,903	–	–	–	–
	Approx. 5,000 other smaller ISPs							

Notes:
1. No distinction has been made between business customers and consumers.
2. With 25 Top ISPs.
3. Certain connections may get transferred to Cable & Wireless.

Cable illustrates the value of Restricted Access in the broadband infrastructure. There are a variety of affordable broadband access technologies to the home including DSL, direct broadcast satellite, wireless, as well as cable. Cable, however, may well prove to have the broadest and lowest cost pipe over the next ten years. This capacity can be used to deliver video, Internet data, and telephony services, multiplying by threefold the current revenue stream cable companies have received thus far. Hence, we have seen the advent of cable overbuilders, such as RCN, Knology, and Altera, that are adding new cable systems to compete with the incumbents, AT&T Broadband (which includes TCI and Media One), Cox, and Comcast. The value these companies will capture is from being one of two broadband, integrated service providers to the home. This value would be fleeting if the number of cable providers could easily expand, but the costs of building cable access directly into the home is so overwhelming there may well be sufficient demand to profitably serve only two cable companies. The strategy mimics that of WalMart, who build stores with the capacity to fulfil all the needs of a particular rural community, and with the scale to be lowest cost. As long as no one else is foolish enough to add a similar scale store and add excess capacity with the risk of endless price wars, Walmart retains a near monopoly.

I-Beam is an example of Customer Integration. I-Beam is in the business of providing systems integration for broadband content delivery systems integration. As mentioned above, while Internet capacity is expanding at 100% annually, there are bottlenecks to broadband delivery. Video transmission can hit a roadblock because of a constraint on a particular backbone route, an overloaded peering node, router congestion, or server capacity limitations. There are ways around these bottlenecks, but they require special skills and tools for navigation. I-Beam, Intervu (a part of Akamai), and Activate harmonize all the pieces of the network to allow effective broadband delivery. They work closely with the customer to arrange special interactive events or provide regular broadcasts. Companies can do this more reliably and inexpensively by outsourcing the task to specialists.

Telocity offers a broad range of services and products along with broadband transmission, and thus pursues a position of Horizontal Breadth. Telocity began life as a DSL provider, in the manner of Covad, Northpoint, or Rhythms. These companies use the Local Exchange Companies copper loop to provide high-speed DSL access lines to businesses and consumers. They do this by installing their own digital subscriber line access multiplexing (DSLAM) equipment in rented space in the central offices where the copper loops converge for the incumbent local exchange companies. Telocity realized that while DSL might become a commodity business, customers would still face obstacles in using DSL service. So they altered their business model to become a full end-to-end service provider. They outsource the DSL line itself from Rhythm or a similar competitor. Telocity provides the residential user with a box, which serves as their gateway to the Internet as well as a hub for data connectivity throughout the home. Because of this stand-alone gateway, the user does not need DSL modem cards in their computer, they have continuous Internet access, and they can connect it directly to other appliances (such as the TV). Beyond this Telocity provides an integrated array of broadband services including firewall protection, digital voice, home security, computer support and software delivery, video telephony, and home networking. They facilitate easy installation and enable users to access the applications that make broadband so compelling. Their goal is to be the Total Customer Solutions provider for residential broadband.

Finally, we do see a number of companies that compete on Differentiation and Low Cost. Williams provides low-cost bandwidth. Exodus is a large-scale, low-cost provider of colocation and hosting services. EMC offers differentiated storage services. EMC shows that a Best Product position can still generate huge value, growing to a market capitalization of over $200 billion, exceeding that of IBM. They are the market leader in high performance data storage, which has been growing at over 100% per annum over the past three years as companies rely more and more on remote data centers. While disk drives themselves are a commodity, the software that manages data storage is not, and EMC has a strong reputation and commands price premiums. EMC has a 50% share in established market for external, multinode RAID storage. The question is how will EMC sustain this position. Without some transition to gain customer bonding, the challenge for EMC will be to devise equally differentiated products in the newer emerging segments of network attached storage and storage area networks. Thus far, their share in these segments is only around 30%.

This review shows the gamut of positioning within the infrastructure sector. It does not cover all the companies, or products, but it does demonstrate that all infrastructure companies do not have the same prospects. It is as important to understand the bonding elements of their business model, as it is to understand the growth and structure of the sector they participate in.

Wireless Infrastructure

Wireless penetration ranges anywhere from 25 to 60% across the developed economies. This is expected to rise to over 80% over the next 10 years. Wireless voice, and wireless Internet access will reach the same ubiquity as television and telephony have today. As with the Internet in general, the profitability of wireless ventures is spotty. Nokia, Ericsson, and Qualcom have healthy returns, yet most wireless carriers show growth but no profits. For most companies in this sector high growth is likely, whereas profits and sustainability are the question. The Delta Model provides insights into the likely outcome and reveals a dramatic variation in positioning across businesses (Figure 8.5).

NTT DoCoMo may be the flag ship for System Lock-In in this sector. Japan, which has lagged behind in many developments in the Internet, may be the leader in wireless Internet access because of DoCoMo's success. NTT DoCoMo provides wireless service to Japan. Their i-mode service is a proprietary platform that allows users to exchange short messages and access web sites, which has gained over 13 million subscribers within two years. The service is so popular that over 80% of new cellular customers choose NTT DoCoMo over competitive offers. This has reversed an otherwise general decline in market share held by DoCoMo as new wireless competitors have entered the market. DoCoMo's Instant Messaging service is a Dominant Exchange, which mirrors AOL's Instant Messaging service. Users prefer the DoCoMo Instant Messaging service because they can gain access to the most users. In fact, AOL now partners DoCoMo Instant Messaging to further amplify the lock-in.

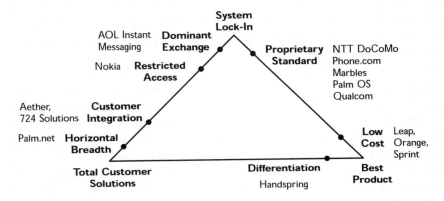

Figure 8.5   Wireless positioning in the Triangle

Over 18 million websites are registered on i-mode. These complementors need to conform to i-mode's platform, but there is no charge unless they wish to become 'premier' information providers that are featured on the DoCoMo home page and search engine. With such a large and growing base of sites, they are rivaling other standards, such as WAP (Wireless Application Protocol), for dominance on the wireless web. If consumers want to access these i-mode sites, they need to subscribe to the DoCoMo service.

Other companies could adopt the i-mode standards. This raises the question of whether wireless standards such as WAP or i-mode will represent Proprietary Standards, or whether they will become standards that cannot be appropriated. WAP is an alternative standard and was introduced by phone.com to deal with the constraints of wireless networks, which have limited bandwidth and processing power. To get around these problems engineers at Phone.com created Wireless Markup Language (WML), which is an open programming specification derived from the Internet standard Hypertext Markup Language (HTML). Handheld Device Markup Language (HDML) allows applications to run on existing Internet web servers and infrastructure without modification. Correspondingly, Phone.com's Handheld Device Transport Protocol (HDTP) is designed to exchange data. The Internet's Hypertext Transmission Protocol (HTTP) does not perform as quickly or as efficiently for wireless networks as does HDTP. Phone.com founded the WAP forum to promote the new standards, and now has over 500 members including Motorola, Nokia, and Ericsson.

WAP and i-mode may more closely resemble the standards fought over during the introduction of VCRs, rather than the de facto Proprietary Standard of Microsoft Windows or Intel. As mentioned earlier in Chapter 5, Proprietary Standards should have open interfaces to the complementors, but the platform itself should be hard to imitate by competitors. While it is still not clear whether i-mode's wireless Internet platform will lead to lock-in, it is more likely that the instant messaging service could sustain its Dominant Exchange position.

Palm, on the other hand, may be able to obtain a Proprietary Standard with its operating system (OS). Palm is the leading supplier of personal digital assistants (PDAs) with 80% of the market, despite their intense competition from Microsoft's Windows CE platform. Over 100,000 software developers write applications to work with the Palm OS. Palm has licensed the OS to third party manufacturers such as Handspring and Sony. Omnisky has developed a wireless modem that allows the Palm OS to access the Internet. While they started as a simple tool for individuals to use as calendars, address books, and memos, it is now a mobile device capable of wireless voice, data, and soon video communications and processing.

Users prefer Palm in order to access the full range of complementors working with Palm OS, and to access other Palm users directly since the device is able to exchange information with an infrared beam. Beyond Microsoft, phone makers and some carriers may ultimately vie for this market, including Nokia, Motorola, and DoCoMo. Palm, however, has established a formidable lead in complementors that will be difficult for a competitor to match.

Marbles is a complementor to Palm, but it is also a potential standard in its own right. Marbles has developed software that allows the Palm to be used as a 'dumb terminal.' With it users can run applications that are too complex to run on a small PDA, or too bandwidth intensive to communicate on narrow wireless connections. Marbles can do this by using a remote server to host the application and then send only the minimal instruction set necessary to fill the screen on the Palm. Software resident on the Palm helps to further reduce the instruction set making even better use of the limited bandwidth available. As a result, a user can access almost any application, interact complex databases, and be presented with a rich graphical interface. Marbles provides a standard set of tools that enterprises or content providers can use to make their applications go wireless. If it achieves a critical mass, Marbles could become a standard platform. Users would prefer it because it works with many applications, and enterprises prefer it because it would be resident on many PDAs.

One application available on Palm using the Omnisky wireless connection is from Fidelity. Using it a customer can access their Fidelity account balances, stock portfolio, and even trade stocks. This application was created for Fidelity by Aether. Aether's strategy is to deliver a completely integrated wireless system tailored to meet the individual needs of its customers. They do this by combining their engineering and software skills with their own proprietary tools as well as with standard products in the industry. They are clearly pursuing a Total Customer Solutions position. Aether's annualized revenues are only $36 million, but their market capitalization is $3.6 billion. Their customers include Reuters, Bear Stearns, and Charles Schwab.

The wireless carriers are largely positioned as Best Product businesses. Orange, AT&T Wireless, Verizon, and others are in a mad race to gain as many customers as they can in order to get the scale necessary to below cost and earn a margin. The hurdle for scale will grow even more with the advent of 3G digital networks. These are the higher bandwidth wireless data networks that are anticipated in the next generation of services. Over $30 billion was raised in auctions in the UK for the spectrum to be used for 3G. Similar auctions or beauty contests are underway in other countries.

This investment combined with the new radios and cells sites necessary for 3G make it even more important to have high market shares and high revenues per subscriber. The real dilemma for carriers is how to create and then sustain profits in a high fixed cost business with multiple competitors that is increasingly undifferentiated. This problem will be exacerbated by slower subscriber growth. It can cost a carrier over $500 to acquire a subscriber so it will be critical to find ways to bond with customers in order to limit the high cost of churn and the potential for price wars.

Again, wireless infrastructure is one sector, but it contains many different strategic positions. Creating and sustaining profits will be a function of bonding.

Incumbent Strategies

The observations thus far show that the Delta Model is an effective tool for describing Internet strategies. Bonding is the new force unleashed by the networked economy, and since bonding is the highlighted dimension in the Delta Model it is tailor-made for diagnosing Internet strategies. Where descriptions of content, e-commerce, B2B, or infrastructure may fail to predict success, Proprietary Standard, Dominant Exchange, Customer Integration, or Horizontal Breadth are good indicators of sustainability.

This brings us back to the incumbents who are facing the venture-funded dot.com hoards. As mentioned earlier in the book, the majority of incumbent companies have deliberately or inadvertently been pursuing a Best Product strategy. This positioning limits their ability to harness the Internet and can put them at a disadvantage relative to the dot.coms. It is this positioning that allows E*TRADE to grow its brokerage business at the expense of Merrill Lynch. It allows MCI WorldCom's UUNet to take data communications share from AT&T. It allowed Amazon to dominate the book market while Barnes & Noble struggles with its online presence.

At the same time incumbents eager to reposition themselves for bonding have excelled. Charles Schwab moved from a discount broker position competing on costs to a premium Total Customer Solutions provider enabled by the Internet. Schwab's market capitalization has grown to $40 billion since redirecting its strategy toward more bonding.

Enron has established Enron Online to secure a Dominant Exchange position for its electricity and natural gas trading operations. After launching Enron Online the number of transactions has increased 2.5 times in the first month alone. They have the largest web site for trading electricity by a factor of ten relative to the next largest competitor. After only two years, web-based trading accounts for 30% of their transactions. Trading is now their core operation, accounting for 70% of their $2 billion in annual earnings before taxes.

Sotheby's continues to control about 20% of the $3 billion high-end art auction market. In this market buyers typically are present at the auction because the items have such high value. Sotheby's was the first of the high-end auction houses to move online for the mid-range market. They aggressively locked in 4700 professional dealers that they were able to carry over due to their commanding presence in the high-end market. Sotheby's has averaged 10,000 new registered bidders per month, as compared to the 5–10,000 new customers per year that has been the norm for them in live auctions.

Kodak has had less success in the transition to digital and Internet technologies. It has attempted to transfer their brand and position in the photographic film industry to digital photography. They have consistently captured 40 and 50% of the global consumer color film and photo paper market, respectively. While close to number one in the digital camera market, they have only 25% share. The loss in share may be explained by Kodak's Best Product positioning. There is little bonding with customers and complementors that can be transferred over to a new technology.

Clayton Christenson has recently written an insightful book[5] about the challenges that incumbents face when confronting disruptive technologies. He contrasts Sustaining from Disruptive technologies. Sustaining technologies are new technologies that lead to immediate and incremental improvement in performance, whereas disruptive technologies are those which initially have worse performance than the established technology, but also have a different value proposition altogether because of different features, form, or functionality. One example is transistors as a disruptive technology to tubes. Transistors had worse performance when used in the same application as tubes, but over time the cost performance improved, and ultimately their unique features such as size and power consumption made them a dominant technology. For example, pocket radios are impossible with tube technology, regardless of the price. Christenson shows how disruptive technologies almost always unseat the leading incumbent firms, for a number of reasons. First, incumbents feel compelled to follow the needs of their mainstream customers, and these customers have no immediate need for disruptive technologies that diminish performance. Second, incumbents cannot find the growth they need in the small emerging markets characteristic of disruptive technologies. And finally, incumbents are skilled and drawn to market research-based initiatives, whereas disruptive technologies have customer demand that appears to be unknowable at the outset. Of course, any distillation of a profound book down to a single paragraph is bound to be shallow and miss the subtleties of the research, so we would refer you to the book itself for further clarification. With this understanding, however, it is important to point out how bonding and the Delta Model relate to this work and the often fatal impact of disruptive technologies on incumbents.

The virtue of bonding is that it sustains a business independent of the product (or service) being sold. It does this by creating externalities in the form of customer and complementor investments around the specific product. While this cannot permanently sustain a business with significantly underperforming products, there is evidence that bonding grants additional time for the bonded incumbent to adopt and learn disruptive technologies. Furthermore, the investments of the complementors and customers can leverage the adoption of the new technology. The most abrupt market share discontinuities due to disruptive technology occur with businesses in a Best Product position. It is not surprising that the dramatic cases of disruptive share loss cited by Christenson involve Best Product companies in industries such as computer disk drives, mechanical excavators, steel manufacturing, and electric motors. The leading companies in these industries were classic product-oriented businesses. They gained their dominance by features or Low Cost and the bonding was minimal. They could monitor and absorb sustaining technologies, but were always vulnerable to the introduction of a better product.

Bonding reduces this vulnerability. It is not a guarantee of survival, but it gives the time and tools to cope with drastic change. Intel provides one of the more telling illustrations.

Earlier in the book, we told of Intel's achievement of its microprocessor standard and its ascent to industry leadership. The success of the IBM PC and PC-compatible systems, complemented by the System Lock-In of Microsoft's DOS, solidified Intel's position as the dominant supplier of microprocessors, the central processing units of the PC and other electronic computing and control systems. By 1985, the Intel x86 microprocessor architecture was firmly entrenched in the design of these products.

But future success was much less certain. In the mid-1980s, a rival chip architecture developed at the University of California at Berkeley and Stanford University seriously threatened Intel's dominance of the microprocessor market. Dubbed RISC (Reduced Instruction Set Computing), the new design offered a simpler and much higher performance processor architecture, predicated largely on the 80/20 rule. The core objective of RISC was straightforward: to develop a processor chip that optimized the execution of the most frequently used microcode instructions in a single processor clock cycle, as against the multiple clock cycles required to execute the more numerous and complex instructions of so-called CISC (Complex Instruction Set Computing) chips such as the x86. RISC designs performed more complex operations by combining their smaller set of more basic instructions in ways that executed the identical functions as their CISC cousins – akin to the way in which the multiplication of numbers can be accomplished through a series of simple additions. Using smaller and simpler instruction sets, RISC promised lower cost, faster performance, shorter design cycles, and efficient scalability, and was poised to be a major disruptive force in the microprocessor world.

The major challenge for Intel was that the instruction sets for RISC chips were totally incompatible with those of its own CISC-based architecture. Intel's leading-edge microprocessor at the time, the 386, had been meticulously engineered to execute all the instruction code of its predecessors (the 8086 and 286), ensuring backward compatibility with the plethora of existing software applications, while extending its functionality and performance through the introduction of still more complex instructions. If RISC proved to be truly superior in cost and performance, Intel's hegemony in the market was in great jeopardy.

By 1988, RISC chips from MIPS, IBM/Motorola, Hewlett-Packard, and most notably, Sun Microsystems, with its popular SPARC processor, began hitting the market and made significant headway into the emerging high-performance UNIX workstation market. Buoyed by this success at the high end, competitors began to take aim at the lucrative mainstream PC market. Sun aggressively licensed the SPARC design to other integrated circuit manufacturers and championed an extensive Open Systems standards movement to win broad market acceptance.

The installed base of the x86, however, proved to be a formidable asset for Intel in weathering the RISC storm. The System Lock-In secured via the swelling network of x86 customers, complementors, applications, and distribution channels buffered the immediate impact of RISC competition and afforded Intel the time to respond to this significant market disruption. Compatibility with existing applications and systems proved to be a major barrier to new entrants, even at this relatively early stage of PC market evolution. Intel capitalized on this advantage in two ways. First, it accelerated development of its next-generation processor architecture, the 486, which was designed to greatly streamline execution of instruction code – negating many of the performance advantages of RISC – while maintaining 100% software compatibility with the current-generation design. Second, it embarked on an aggressive parallel development effort for a RISC processor of its own, which would preclude compatibility but would realize performance advantages inherent to RISC designs. The second processor could potentially be utilized as a coprocessor to the 486, and if the RISC threat proved to be real, Intel had hedged its bet on the 486 itself. The two design teams competed with one another while sharing details of their respective efforts. In the end, many of the innovations of the RISC design were incorporated into the 486 as designers cleverly figured how to engineer them with no loss of backward compatibility. The resulting processor, introduced in 1989, was a fully compatible, hybrid CISC/RISC design that thwarted the competitive RISC threat and extended Intel's dominance in the PC market.

RISC processors did manage to ride the wave of robust growth in the market for UNIX engineering and graphics workstations and, more recently, LAN and web servers. But ultimately, the only major PC design win by RISC was the IBM/Motorola PowerPC chip, which found its way into the Apple Macintosh – not displacing the dominant Intel x86, but rather cannibalizing the incumbent 68000 CISC processor of the distant market runner-up, Motorola.

Oracle is a similar example of a business that has used bonding to sustain and even leverage its position as technologies change. Oracle's first claim to System Lock-In was established with its database software. Oracle's relational database software became a Proprietary Standard. The complementors are the thousands of enterprises and software firms that write applications that manage data housed in Oracle's software. Oracle initially created a market value of over $10 billion by winning this title in a contest with IBM, Informix, and others.

The software industry has continued to evolve and Oracle has adroitly adapted with it. The next seismic shift to hit the high end of the Richter scale in software was in Enterprise Resource Planning (ERP). SAP, PeopleSoft, and AG Edwards ushered in enterprise-wide software that helps companies to manage consistently data across all their various activities. Previously, businesses would use different software for each operation and each had its own unique database. As work flowed across each operation inconsistencies could crop up in the fragmented databases. ERP software would better integrate data and software leading in many cases to huge improvements in efficiency and understanding. The market expanded quickly. Oracle used its System Lock-In bonds to establish a strong ERP position. They developed ERP solutions for financial management, human resources, manufacturing, salesforce management, supply chain management, among others. Rather than fading away against the emergence of new ERP technology, Oracle's growth surged, more than doubling their market capitalization. Figure 8.6 shows how Oracle climbed to yet a higher plateau in valuation as it adapted to ERP capabilities.

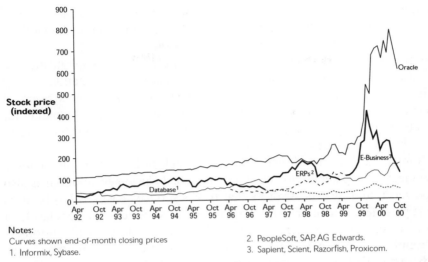

Notes:
Curves shown end-of-month closing prices
1. Informix, Sybase.

2. PeopleSoft, SAP, AG Edwards.
3. Sapient, Scient, Razorfish, Proxicom.

Figure 8.6   Oracle climbed to new heights with each new technology

The next transformation to hit the software industry was e-business. Companies were using the Internet and its associated protocols to extend their information management and exchange beyond their corporate boundaries to include suppliers and customers. The classic ERP businesses had focused on internal company information flows, used non-Internet mechanisms, and had the wind knocked out of their sails. Their stock prices plummeted. Oracle continued to ascend along with the other e-business proponents, such as Sapient and Scient. Again, Oracle had been able to use the bonding it had established in an earlier life to position itself with the Internet-centric crowd. Oracle expanded into e-commerce based upon its database engine. They promoted ASPs and thin clients that were dependent upon Internet access and central data centers that operated servers using the scalable and sophisticated Oracle databases. As Figure 8.6 shows, Oracle has not only weathered the storms of change, but they piloted their organization to the safe harbors of each new technical hurricane. Bonding has given them the stability and capability to do so.

Auctions provide another example of bonding providing sustainability as technology changes. In the autumn of 2000, eBay laid off 15% of the staff at its Butterfield's auction house, signaling problems at its high-end online auction. eBay acquired San-Francisco-based Butterfield & Butterfield auctioneers in April 1999 for $260 million. Butterfield was a 2nd-tier player relative to Sotheby's and Christie's, but eBay saw the deal as a way to gain expertise and credibility in the high-end art and collectables markets. This expertise combined with eBay's Dominant Exchange position was expected to beat the incumbents. Two lessons can be drawn from this outcome. First, the incumbent with bonding can prevail against even the most intimidating new entrant, if they employ their complementors in a reasonably responsive strategy. Second, granular segmentation is very relevant to bonding. eBay's Dominant Exchange position is segment specific, for example, eBay can command the consumer auction market for baseball cards (plus hundreds of other granular segments), but lose to Sotheby's in the high- to medium-end art market.

Similar stories exist elsewhere. System Lock-In is not the only bonding that creates the potential for sustainability, Total Customer Solutions is also a powerful tool. It is noteworthy that IBM's services business has been its most persistent source of growth and profit. This services business has long been engaged in Customer Integration, by working closely with customers to jointly develop their computing and communications solutions. Similarly, while DEC's minicomputer business crashed, its customer solutions business was sustained and eventually sold to Compaq. This group also pursues a Customer Integration strategy by working closely with customers to design and maintain their computer systems and LANs.

How can Incumbents Gain Bonding?

Given the importance of bonding in our networked economy, it needs to be a top priority for the CEO. To do this executives need to look systematically across the business to:

- Identify all potential customers and complementors.
- Consider how to restructure the interfaces with these groups.
- Find ways to enable and encourage them to invest in utilizing your products and services.

Not all Internet or networking investments lead to bonding. E-commerce supply chain management is a networking investment that may enhance the product-oriented goals of efficiency and effectiveness, but often does little to effect bonding. This can do more to bond you to your supplier than to your customers and complementors.

In this search for bonding, the first stop for many companies is with customer relationship management (CRM). This extends beyond sales to include all aspects of customer care including provisioning or delivery, maintenance, account inquiry, billing and collections. It is not uncommon to find that a customer is contacted for some customer care activity 35 times for every single sales contact. So clearly there is an extensive customer interface to begin working with, and for many Best Product businesses addressing customer care is a practical first step to progress to a Total Customer Solutions position.

The conventional view of customer care is one of a cost center. It is an auxiliary obligation incurred as part of selling a product, and the goal is to minimize costs. The technicians who designed the product define the information used. Availability is set by the standard business day and it operates within the product silo that it serves. Overall the effort is on cost management as long as customer complaints are not excessive.

USAA, Schwab, and Mindspring take a very different approach to CRM. This is reflected in their alignment of tasks, as well as in their technology. Their Total Customer Solutions orientation is contrasted to the conventional cost-centric approach in Figure 8.7. In this new alignment, customer care solves unmet needs by the customer. The goal is to enhance the customer economics, and the business' overall profitability. Content includes that generated by product technicians, but is supplemented by user contributions. Availability is molded to the convenience of the customer, by utilizing a broad mix of interactive channels at all times of the day. Since the objective is to provide a solution, customer care often integrates a broad portfolio of products, both internal and external to the business. Finally, the overall effort is to enhance the customer economics regardless of the obligations within the confines of any one product.

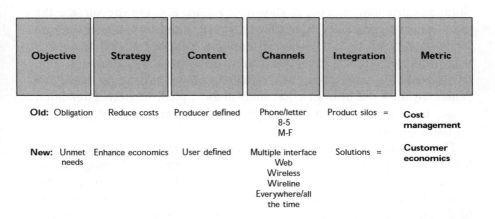

Figure 8.7   Comparing old and new paradigms for customer relationship management

These are good conceptual guidelines, but they have little effect unless translated into specific activities. Table 8.2 outlines the change in alignment that is implicit in moving from cost-centric CRM to a Total Customer Solutions strategy. This realignment goes well beyond injecting new web technology into the system. The technology simply enables a change in strategy, which, as noted earlier in the chapter on process alignment, necessitates a holistic recalibration of many tasks. In shifting from a strategy centered on costs to a Total Customer Solutions orientation, the primary metrics change from cost per call minute to profit per customer. Incentives to reduce call duration change to increase the calls fully answered on the first try. Compensation that is salary based changes to base salaries with high incentives. Channels that are available during business hours and broadcast static information change to a mix of dynamic web, wireless, and wireline channels that are available to customers anytime and anywhere. Content that is defined by technicians is extended to include content contributed by customers, as they use and describe their experiences. This user-defined information can be shared via message boards, chat groups, and other community messaging.

Value to the customer improves as they get more meaningful help. Value to the business improves as customers bond to the business. Bonding results from customers learning how to use a more sophisticated system. Switching vendors requires relearning. Additionally, bonding improves with the number of customers since each new customer contributes to the content and the community of users.

We can measure the full economic impact by looking at one ISP who transitioned their CRM from a cost-centric approach to a Total Customer Solutions orientation. This is shown in Figure 8.8. On the surface the costs appear significantly higher. Cost per call minute was higher because of the quality of the staff. The call duration was longer. Call frequency was initially higher because the improved service was drawing upon latent needs. Faster response time resulted in lower utilization of the call center. In total the upfront costs more than tripled. Customer retention alone, however, more than offset this cost leading to a very profitable initiative overall.

The challenge here is to fully recognize the benefits. There is a lag between the upfront investment relative to the economic advantage due to longer customer tenure. Furthermore, the cost of customer churn is not normally recognized economically, let alone as a line item in the business profit and loss statement, despite the huge impact it has on value. The benefits also varied enormously by customer type, requiring Granular Metrics to help to detect and calibrate the system over time.

Table 8.2 Realigning customer relationship management activities: from cost-centric to solutions-based

	Low cost	High quality	Upsell	Total Customer Solutions
Customer segmentation	■ Limited use of segmentation to differentiate customer care	■ Segmentation based on quality – driven off customer metrics	■ Segmentation to target sales potential	■ Segment customers by profit level and apply differential customer care based on profitability
Metrics	■ Focused on cost minimization – $/call minute	■ Cost and quality metrics – $/call minute – customer satisfaction	■ Cost and revenue metrics – $/call minute – revenue/call	■ Profitability measures – by customer/segment – by product – by time period to differentiate service
Incentives	■ Focused on achieving minimum service levels – call duration – # of calls	■ Based on cost and quality – call duration – customer satisfaction	■ Mix of cost and revenue – call duration – customer satisfaction – revenue/call	■ Focused on customer problem solving – right first time – account growth ($)
Customer feedback	■ Limited – contact with customer not viewed as an opportunity for information gathering or dissemination	■ Limited – customer interaction may be used to gather data on call quality	■ Moderate – primary attention to information acquisition	■ Extensive use of real time and ex-post surveys to gather information on services, products, processes, policies, pricing and competition
Content	■ Defined by technical experts	■ Technical experts	■ Technical and marketing	■ Technical/marketing experts ■ Information tailored to each customer ■ Customer-defined content, customer contributions
Career/ promotion path	■ If any, limited to customer care organization – high staff turnover	■ Potential opportunities within customer care organization	■ Opportunities beyond customer care possible	■ Well-defined path available within and beyond customer care
Skill set	■ Reactive, focused on programmed response to questions	■ Empathy and technical capabilities	■ Mix of care sales	■ Proactive problem solving with a mix of capabilities – care, sales, research and so on
Compensation	■ Low-salary based	■ Low, limited bonus	■ Medium, salary and some bonus	■ Medium–high, salary upside, e.g. options and various nonmonetary awards (recognition, trips and so on)
Customer care channels	■ Phone, letter to broadcast 'static' information – 8 to 5 – Monday to Friday	■ Phone, letter, web browser availability – 24 hours – 7 days	■ Proactive use of channels to push information to customers – 24 hours – 7 days	■ Bias toward dynamic channels, interactive web, messaging, phone, wireless – anytime – anywhere
Communication	■ Care rep to customer	■ Rep to customer, supervisor coaching and education	■ Rep to customer attuned to marketing programs	■ Access to expert community – customer rep – technical – other customers, chat rooms
Customer acquisition	■ None	■ None	■ Emerging responsibility – specific programs/ products	■ Explicit value creation responsibility across entire product range
Organizational integration	■ Influence limited to customer care organization	■ Influence limited to customer care organization	■ Some involvement with marketing	■ Consistent source of change ideas across business – driven by customer contact – supported by organization
Pricing innovation	■ No role	■ No role	■ Limited opportunities role based on programs/ products	■ Used as ongoing source of competitive information – driven by customer contact
Product innovation	■ Limited impact	■ Limited impact	■ Role based on relevant program involvement	■ Important source of customer and competitor ideas – direct information link to product management
Customer retention	■ Indirect impact	■ Direct impact through high-quality care	■ Important role through upselling responsibility	■ Explicit responsibility through quality care and problem solving

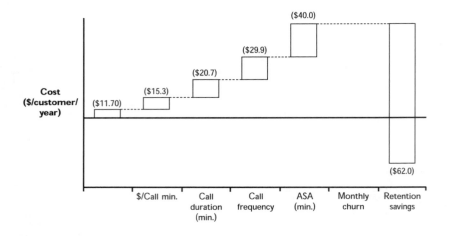

Figure 8.8 Customer care economics with a Total
Customer Solutions orientation

Reflections

The Internet is all about bonding. The dot.coms with the greatest success have incorporated bonding as the central theme of their strategy, whether in content, e-commerce, B2B, infrastructure, wireless, or whatever category. The incumbents without bonding are most vulnerable to disruptive technologies, whether in the form of the Internet or another killer technology. Fortunately, the Internet is a tool for incumbents and dot.coms alike, so there can be a level playing field for those prepared to employ the strategies of bonding.

Notes

1. Later renamed DARPA, Defense Advanced Research Project Agency.
2. Conseil Européen pour le Recherche Nucleaire (European Laboratory for Particle Physics).
3. Bernard Aboba *The Online User's Encyclopedia* (Addison-Wesley) November 1993.
4. *Harvard Business Review*, May–June 2000, pp. 118–25.
5. James M. Utterback, *Mastering the Dynamics of Innovation* (Harvard Business School Press, 1998).

CHAPTER 9

Measuring Success: Aligning Strategy, Processes and Metrics

Strategy without measurement is like poetry; it is wonderful but not a very practical way to communicate. Thus far we have concentrated on the big issues of strategy: generating a vision by selecting a creative strategic position using the Triangle; developing a Strategic Agenda that supports that vision; and properly aligning the key tasks of execution through the Adaptive Processes. Now we turn our attention to the overall issue of metrics as a critical element to measure the success of the business. Metrics are required to define performance, delineate accountability, monitor progress, and establish the feedback mechanisms necessary to change the course of action whenever this is needed. As we will show in this chapter and the next, metrics have to be defined in the large and in the small – what we refer to as Aggregate and Granular Metrics.

Some Reflections on Metrics

Brilliant strategies are often dependent upon the creative and inspiring genius of those who are in charge of their formulation. Brilliant execution, however, has to be based on objective, factual, and often detailed metrics that permit the appropriate follow-up of the strategic tasks throughout the whole organization. From this perspective, the strategy formulation process is often fluid, unstructured, intense, and relatively short. It could also be a lot of fun! Having a group of executives involved in the development of a shared strategic vision leading toward the explicit definition of the mission of a business and its Strategic Agenda can be quite exciting. The tasks of execution that are left behind have a completely different character. They involve a much larger group of people, in fact the complete personnel roster should be part of it. They require detailed and vast amounts of work. The operational side of the business can be plagued with what might seem to be trivial minutia, but it is the unavoidable collective work that makes an organization really successful. And at the heart of all of this challenge is the development of a comprehensive set of metrics, whose primary purpose is to ensure that strategy and execution are properly aligned.

Richard Fairbanks, the successful CEO of Capital One, used to say: 'At Capital One we measure everything.' He really means it and he attributes that level of commitment to implementation as the key driver to his success. But what is 'to measure everything'? How do we go about using an orderly method of addressing the enormity of this challenge? We believe that one of the greatest strengths of the Delta Model is that it is indeed capable of guiding the gigantic task of metric development in a consistent and systematic way. But prior to reviewing the implications of the Delta Model and metrics, we need to reflect on some critical issues regarding the design of an effective metrics system.

Avoid Excessive Dependency on Financial Metrics

Financial and accounting-driven measures of performance are widely used in most corporations. This is to be expected since the creation of economic value is the central imperative for business success. However, there are severe problems that result from an exclusive dependence on financial metrics. First, these metrics report on past performance, but they have little to say about how well prepared you are to face the future challenges impacting the business. Sometimes, because of its inherent historical reporting nature, accounting data can give you a distorted view of the business situation.

Take the case of the president of a prominent American company who asked us to assist in a consulting assignment. In our initial conversation he expressed his deep concern about the nature of his business. He told us, commiserating about his performance system, that he had been relying entirely on financial data as the sole indicator of the business' success. Indeed, last year's financial results were outstanding. The business profitability, its balance sheet, and the quality of its financial statements were all record-breaking. In reality, however, the business situation could not be more gloomy. This was a high-tech company whose future was dictated by the strength of the new product offering coming from the R&D pipeline. The company had had a very good record of product development in the past, which was the cause for its current success. However, the patents of most of its blockbuster products were about to expire and all the emerging new products failed the last feasibility tests. The product development pipeline, therefore, was empty. Since the usual new product cycle was about seven to eight years, there was little to do to achieve a quick reversal of the awful situation. Even worse, the metrics used by the company had prevented a full understanding of this situation well in advance of the existing catastrophic conditions, when there would have been enough time to take corrective actions.

Financial metrics alone are not enough. They need to be complemented by other relevant performance indicators which are more future oriented. We need to understand the future drivers of cost, revenue, profit, and innovation to achieve a full, comprehensive, and well-balanced view of the business performance.

Establishing the Proper Degree of 'Stretch'

Metrics alone do not convey the intensity of the challenge they impose on the business organization. This materializes when we attach to the metric a specific *target* and a *deadline* for its implicit execution. Take as an example 'customer market share,' as an appropriate metric to use in many cases. When expressed in a vacuum, we do not know what the true managerial implications are of this performance indicator. However, if we say 'increase WalMart customer share in detergents from 18 to 25% during a one-year period,' we have a definite picture of the challenge involved. These two components of the metrics – target and deadline – are absolutely critical and should be specified for every indicator. Their composite effect defines the degree of 'stretch' that is passed on to the organization. If the stretch is exceedingly high, we will discourage the key employees since they will be condemned to self-defeat. If stretch is too low, it will create an environment of sloppiness and complacency. If the degree of stretch is the right one, we will develop the invigorating, exciting, and entrepreneurial climate that is so essential for a successful organization. The quality of leadership is truly at stake when defining the proper stretch that the firm can bear.

Metrics as the Source of Learning

The whole metrics system has to be designed with the purpose of learning in mind. We live in a changing environment. The Strategic Agenda we develop has to be continuously monitored in order to address potential changes in the direction we are following. Thus, we should embed in the metric system appropriate feedback mechanisms that will educate us on which aspects of our strategic actions are working and which need to be modified. This is particularly the case when dealing with Granular Metrics which capture the full variability of our outcomes. The metrics should be able not only to detect the sources of those variabilities, but also to identify its sources, and then produce the necessary intelligence that allows us to innovate, learn, and improve.

Metrics and the Delta Model

Figure 9.1 provides a summary of the key stages that are part of the implementation of the Delta Model. If followed through to completion, a full set of metrics is produced, totally aligned with the Strategic Agenda, that guarantees the proper definition of business performance, the assignment of managerial responsibilities, the monitoring of the desired progress, and the feedback mechanism which brings about learning and change, whenever needed.

There are three different types of metrics that emerge from the Delta Model. Each has a distinctive role to play but together they provide the overall coherence that is required from the full set of performance indicators. The three types are: task-driven metrics, Aggregate Metrics, and Granular Metrics.

We will illustrate how this set of metrics is derived from an application of the Delta Model to the Singapore Post. We will briefly examine the Singapore Post as a whole, but concentrate on the analysis of a single business – the vPOST – which is a new electronic initiative.

The Case of Singapore Post[1]

Post offices all over the world are facing tremendous challenges in the areas of electronic substitution, competition from both the private couriers as well as foreign postal administrations, deregulation of the postal market in developed countries, and increasingly demanding customers.

In the context of Singapore Post, these threats are compounded by the growing number of households equipped with personal computers, and high Internet subscription rates. The Singapore government's thrust into IT and the deployment of Singapore ONE (One Network for Everyone) will further intensify the level of competitiveness in the mail industry in Singapore. These infrastructure initiatives, coupled with an already high and ever-growing computer literacy rate, will boost the government's objectives of moving Singapore toward a cashless and paperless society.

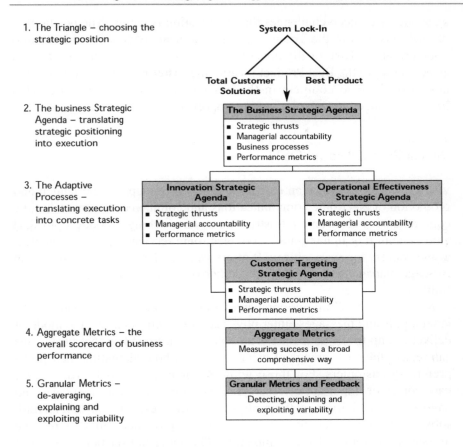

1. The Triangle – choosing the strategic position

2. The business Strategic Agenda – translating strategic positioning into execution

3. The Adaptive Processes – translating execution into concrete tasks

4. Aggregate Metrics – the overall scorecard of business performance

5. Granular Metrics – de-averaging, explaining and exploiting variability

Figure 9.1   The Delta Model – the complete framework

Thus it is critical that Singapore Post seeks a cohesive corporate strategy in order to meet the challenges of a highly dynamic environment in Singapore. The Delta Model provided unique insights on how to analyze the critical situation of Singapore Post, and helped to develop a coherent Strategic Agenda and the supporting metric system.

Singapore Post Business Segmentation

Singapore Post identified six SBUs, five being existing businesses in search of a clear redefinition and transformation; the sixth – vPOST (virtual post office) – is a new business unit that might be a significant response to the deep challenges the organization is facing. The positioning of each business in the Triangle provides a clear roadmap to this desired transformation. Historically, most businesses have been implicitly treated as belonging to the Best Product positioning. After reflection, all five businesses decided to compete in the other vertices of the Triangle. This implies a collective task of gigantic proportions.

Virtual Post Office (vPOST)

vPOST service provides an electronic platform to support the launch and promotion of electronic communications and commerce. It aims to build a comprehensive electronic infrastructure as far-reaching as today's physical mail system. It is an integrated set of electronic services, providing an electronic address for every citizen. It offers value-added services such as total message management, certification authority service, and e-commerce and fulfillment services.

Basically, vPOST allows companies and individuals to send and receive letters, bills and messages either physically or electronically – the mode of delivery is up to the consumer. The service is designed so that businesses can realize the cost savings of using e-mail, without alienating their print-preferring customers. For those without e-mail accounts or who prefer hard copies of important correspondence, vPOST will print messages and have postmen deliver to their physical addresses. On the other hand, subscribers only need to access vPOST to pay their bills or receive messages or notices from companies. The more subscribers, the more companies and organizations that engage the vPOST service, the more it encourages others to join. This is the network externality effect. The result should be added convenience and choice for individuals, and a more compelling service as it grows.

One element built into the vPOST trial is the Giro-on-Demand, a variation of the usual electronic automatic bill payment system which pays the entire bill at a predetermined dates. Giro-on-Demand allows the subscriber to authorize a specific amount at any time to be paid via vPOST. vPOST will help individuals and organizations to move from the paper-bound, bricks-and-mortar world to the virtual world at their own pace and with ease.

vPOST will be the stepping stone to a deeper involvement in e-commerce, teaming up with partners to develop home shopping services that make use of Singapore Post's back-end systems, logistics, and delivery operations. vPOST will also be a web platform to open up Singapore Post's existing postal services such as the ability to purchase electronic stamps, Post Office box inquiries and rentals, track-and-trace of Speedpost items, local urgent mail and parcels, customer service support desk and many others.

Although this is a very young project, the aim is to seek a System Lock-In positioning.

Application of the Delta Model to the Singapore Post Case

Now we can go back to the framework presented in Figure 9.1, and apply each step of it to the Singapore Post case, with special emphasis on recognizing how the Delta Model generates a full set of comprehensive and distinct metrics throughout this process.

1. *The Triangle: Choosing the Strategic Positioning*
Business segmentation is the initial step required to position the full portfolio of businesses of a firm within the Triangle. The Triangle shown in Figure 9.2 depicts the desired strategic choices that were made for the six businesses of the Singapore Post. Four businesses are seeking Total Customer Solutions, while two are attempting to reach a System Lock-In, including the vPOST business which we will examine closely. These businesses are not pursuing isolated strategies, in fact their complementary nature plays an important role in the overall corporate objectives. The process of business segmentation and the concluding strategic options for the full portfolio is a fundamental cornerstone for the development of Singapore Post's Strategic Agenda.

2. *Task-driven Metrics Emerging from the Business Strategic Agenda*
We now need to translate the business position and its strategic choice into a coherent Strategic Agenda. It is important that the agenda captures a complete set of strategic thrusts that incorporate all the central issues facing the business, identifies the individual responsibilities for the execution of each thrust, recognizes the nature of the business processes that each thrust generates, and, most importantly for our current discussion, assigns clear performance metrics to each thrust. As we explained in Chapter 6, we can summarize these requirements in one single chart. Table 9.1 shows the chart that encompasses the Strategic Agenda of the vPOST business.

The reading of the chart is straightforward. The first column provides the strategic thrusts. The subsequent columns identify the key organizational units of the business. By mapping each thrust into those organiza-

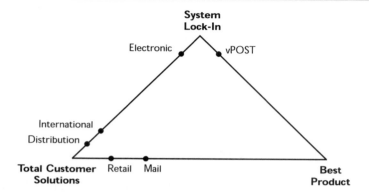

Figure 9.2　　The desired strategic positioning of
the six businesses of Singapore Post

tional units – showing who plays a key role or important supporting role in the execution of each thrust – we address the issues of managerial account-ability. Most thrusts cannot be accomplished by a single organizational unit, which means that they represent a business process. The penultimate column recognizes the kind of business process the thrust generates – OE (Organizational Effectiveness), CT (Customer Targeting), or I (Innova-tion). When the nature of the thrust is of a business kind, meaning that it concerns itself with high level business issues and is not one of the three Adaptive Processes, we designate it as B (Business Model). The final column is the one that singles out performance indicators.

We can see from Table 9.1 that there are two thrusts requiring Opera-tional Effectiveness processes; five thrusts for Customer Targeting processes; and three thrusts requiring Innovation support. This is in line with the desired System Lock-In strategic positioning.

Turning our attention to the metrics, the last column of Table 9.1 gives us a full set of performance indicators that are required to monitor and follow up the progress of each business strategic thrust, which is why we call this type of metrics 'task-driven.' They are generated from the key action programs of the business and should constitute the basis for a high level executive information system. This is the first hierarchy of metrics that the Delta Model framework produces in an almost effortless way.

3. Task-driven Metrics Emerging from the Adaptive Processes
The Adaptive Processes capture the execution commitments generated by each strategic thrust. What is needed at this stage of the process is to

Table 9.1 Strategic Agenda for the vPOST Business

Strategic thrusts	CEO	Mail business	Distribution business	Retail business	International business	Electronic services	vPOST service	Financial and business dev.	Engineering	Property management	Human resources	Communications	Business Processes	Performance measurement
1. Create a trusted Internet brand in Singapore	①	1	1	1	1	1	1	1				1	B	▪ Time to achieve ▪ Transaction vol; no. of hits/month ▪ Market survey
2. Identify key corporate customers that will attract a critical mass of vPOST subscribers	1	2	2	2	2	1	①	①	2	2		2	CT	▪ Customer cost savings/profitability ▪ Number of key customer or services/year ▪ Customer feedback
3. Ensure system integrity, accuracy, and operational effectiveness		2	2	2	2	1	①	1	2		1	2	OE	▪ Unit cost ▪ Life cycle cost ▪ Customer feedback and complaints
4. Set up a competitor analysis team	1	1	1	1	1	1	①	1	1	1	1	2	B	▪ Time to implementation ▪ Determine customer share ▪ Determine market share
5. Establish the business model and identify stable source of revenue streams	1	2	2	2	2	1	①	1					CT	▪ Business model ▪ Revenue stream ▪ Revenue/year
6. Develop excellent expertise in this line of business						1	①	1	1		1		OE	▪ Customer cost savings/profitability ▪ Customer feedback
7. Differentiated service	2	2	2	2	2	1	①	1	1				CT	▪ No. of new services introduced by competitors against vPOST/year ▪ % level of adaptability, affordability and availability
8. Constantly introduce more features and functionalities	2	2	2	2	2	1	1	1	①				1	▪ % sale from new products ▪ Rate of product introduction ▪ Life cycle cost and development cost ▪ Time to market
9. Work with key corporate customers to ensure total satisfaction	1	2	2	2	2	1	①	1	2	2		2	CT	▪ Customer cost savings/profitability ▪ Customer feedback
10. Acquire complementors or seek strategic alliances to expand market share	2	2			2	1	①	1	1			2	I	▪ No. of supplier/complementors ▪ Market share ▪ No. of participating companies/countries
11. Develop new capabilities and interfaces for complementors				1		1	①	1	1				CT	▪ Unit cost ▪ Technology introduced relative to competitors and postal administration
12. Deploy key technology to introduce more business opportunities and move toward System Lock-In	2	2	2	2	2	1	①	1	1				I	▪ Technology introduced relative to competitors and foreign postal administration ▪ Switching costs for complementors and customers

Key
1 Key role in formulation and implementation
2 Important role of support and concurrence
① Identifies the 'champion' who takes leadership for the strategic thrust execution

B   Business model L (process that carries broad managerial activities)
OE Operational effectiveness (cost drivers)
CT Customer targeting (profit drivers)
I   Innovation (renewal drivers)

understand in more detail what the role of each Adaptive Process is in supporting the business agenda. This is accomplished in Table 9.2 for the vPOST business.

We are building a tight relationship between the desired strategic positioning of the vPOST business, its Strategic Agenda, and the more detailed activities linked to the Adaptive Processes.

We have limited ourselves to describing the tactical tasks associated with each Adaptive Process, starting from the role contained in the business Strategic Agenda. If we wanted to complete this stage of the Delta Model, we should develop charts, similar to Table 9.1, for each of the processes. The description of the organizational units could now go further into lower levels of the organizational structure of the firm to bring about players that are involved in operational tasks. The performance measures associated with the action programs of each Adaptive Process provide the second set of 'task-driven' metrics.

4. *Aggregate Metrics: The Overall Scorecard of Business Performance*
The task-driven metrics are tailor-made to monitor the set of action programs that are inherent to the strategic plan. We are still missing two additional components of the full metric systems: Aggregate and Granular Metrics.

If we go back to Figure 9.1, the *fourth* step in the Delta Model is the definition of the Aggregate Metrics of business performance. Aggregate Metrics, as the name implies, are designed to give us, in a concise fashion, an overall picture of the business performance. It has to capture, in a single scorecard, the indicators which are associated with the key drivers of the business, in a way that is consistent with its strategic positioning.

Table 9.3 provides a list of performance metrics for all the businesses of Singapore Post aligned according to the three distinct Adaptive Processes – Operational Effectiveness, Customer Targeting, Innovation. The processes are the ones that define the three sets of relevant drives, that is, cost, profit, and renewal drivers, respectively.

From Table 9.3 we can observe that there is some commonality in the measure of performance for each business. New customer acquisition, key customer selection, number of new and innovative services (through bundling and cross-selling), customer feedback, number of discount schemes that are simple and effective, capacity to attract complementors, are examples of such unit measurement. Most of these measurements focus on customer metrics to give a greater scope of service (broader product range), greater scale of service (bigger customer share especially in the vertical markets), and greater bonding (customization linking to customer lock-in).

Table 9.2 Role of each Adaptive Process in supporting the vPOST Strategic Agenda

OPERATIONAL EFFECTIVENESS	**Objective is to enhance system performance**
	■ Ensure system integrity, accuracy and operational effectiveness
	  – Establish a working operational model
	  – Address all technical issues that arise during the trial implementation (e.g., system response time, ease of use, billing, and so on)
	  – Ensure that features and functionalities operate well according to specifications
	
	■ Develop excellent expertise in this line of business
	  – Create superior technical and operational support team
	  – Establish excellent customer support service
	  – Constantly keep updated with related Internet technology
	  – Build a support chain management and integrate, with the potential of cross-sell, to other products and services

CUSTOMER TARGETING	**Objective is to increase target agency channels and complementors**
	■ Identify key corporate customers that will attract a critical mass of vPOST subscribers
	  – Create economies of scale. The more corporate customers participate with vPOST, the more attractive it is for the public to subscribe to vPOST (because they only go to one web site to perform all transactions, similar to the physical post office). The more transactions vPOST has, the more complementors would like to join vPOST
	  – Create attractive packaging and bundling of services to encourage more corporate customers to participate with vPOST to seek a high level of active subscribers
	
	■ Establish the business model and identify stable source of revenue streams
	  – Identify key revenue, cost and profit drivers for the service
	  – Identify the critical resources required to sustain the service
	
	■ Differentiated service
	  – Track the trends of Internet portals in USA which are usually one or two generations more advanced
	  – Track customer feedback to improve or introduce a differentiated service
	  – Continue to implement strategies that leverage on Singapore Post's strength and to be consistent with the company's mission
	  – Adopt the availability, adaptability, and affordability strategy to embrace vPOST's design and implementation
	  – Produce a one-stop service approach
	
	■ Work with key corporate customers to ensure total satisfaction
	  – Maintain and seek strong relationship with all the corporate customers (e.g., government, public and private companies)
	  – Ensure that there are tangible benefits for corporate customers to participate in vPOST (e.g., cost savings, higher turnaround rate from their subscribers to them)
	
	■ Acquire complementors or seek strategic alliances/joint ventures to expand market share
	  – Seek potential strategic partners or postal administrations that can provide regional or global print and mail operations

INNOVATION	**Objective is to increase Innovation in vPOST service, and enable Innovation by complementors**
	■ Constantly introduce more features and functionalities
	  – Especially where it can leverage on other strengths of Singapore Post's businesses
	  – Seek the right level of return on investment
	  – Establish the product life cycle time and cost
	
	■ Develop new capabilities and interfaces with complementors
	  – Transmitting information via diskettes, dial-up telephone and leased lines, Internet, and so on
	
	■ Deploy key technology to introduce more vertical business opportunities and move toward System Lock-In strategy
	  – Develop new capabilities and interfaces for customers (e.g., transmitting information via Internet, ISDN, and so on)
	  – Develop alternative means to store and retrieve letters (e.g., over CD-ROM, Internet, and so on)
	  – Explore value-added services (e.g., printing of newsletters, color printing, brochures, produce on-demand printing, and so on)
	  – Extend to full value chain of outsourcing which leverages on the strengths of Singapore Post

Table 9.3 Aggregate Metrics for Singapore Post

	Mail Business (Total Customer Solutions)	Distribution Business (Total Customer Solutions)	Retail Business (System Lock-In)	International Business (Total Customer Solutions)	ePOST Business (System Lock-In)	vPOST Business (System Lock-In)
OPERATIONAL EFFECTIVENESS	- Customer savings (through discount schemes) - Years of customer tenure	- Customer savings - Years of customer tenure - # of customer complaints	- Quality of service (queue time) - # of system outages - Costs relative to alternatives - # of automated kiosks deployed - # of agency services introduced - Volume of transactions per service	- Customer savings through discount scheme offerings - # of flexible discount scheme offerings - # of complaints	- Customer savings - System reliability - Quality of service	- Customer savings - System reliability - Quality of service - Measures of affordability, availability, and acceptability of service
CUSTOMER TARGETING	- Relative market share for target vertical market - # of customer acquisitions - Value proposition for key customers	- # of customer acquisitions - # of repeated customers - # of discount schemes (through 'frequent flyer scheme') - Value proposition for key customers	- # of customer acquisitions - # of bundling services - Complementor share	- # of customer acquisitions - # of repeated customers - # of ePOST service offerings - Value proposition for key customers	- # of customer acquisitions - Feedback for improvement - # of bundling services - Complementor share	- # of key customers gain/year - Feedback for improvement - # of bundling services - Profit/complementor - Complementor share
INNOVATION	- # of jointly developed products - Switching costs for customer to change vendor - # of bundling services - # of customers using ePOST service offerings - # of customized products for key customers	- # of bundling services - # of joint development projects - Switching costs for customer to change vendor	- # of alternative means to accept services - Volume transactions for these new alternative means - Switching costs for complementor and customer	- # of bundling services	- # of strategic alliances/acquisitions - # of value-added services - # of alternative means to store and retrieve - Switching costs for complementor and customer	- # of strategic alliances and acquisitions - Technology introduction vs. competitors and foreign postal offices - Switching cost of complementor and customer

5. *Granular Metrics: De-averaging, Learning, and Feedback*

The final set of metrics is captured in the *fifth* step of the Delta Model in Figure 9.1. Instead of producing an aggregate set of performance indicators, characterized by their average performance, our aim now is to select a few critical drivers whose behavior we want to explore in depth. Rather than using averages, we need to understand the full variability of the outcomes associated with the driver, recognize the sources of that variability, and develop proper feedback mechanisms so that learning and change can be accomplished.

Although the subject of Granular Metrics will be covered at length in the next chapter, we would like to illustrate here the use of two useful technologies associated with this topic. One is the cause–effect diagram to identify the performance drivers of a given indicator. This tool is useful to guide us in the definition of the Granular Metrics that are important to encode and analyze. The second tool is the development of feedback mechanisms that are needed to monitor performance against the intended results and make corrections when needed. As actions are tested and their merits or limitations become apparent, managers can understand more deeply the business issues they intend to resolve.

We will now provide a brief illustration of these two tools in the context of the Singapore vPOST business.

The vPOST Business and Cause–Effect Diagram

Figure 9.3 provides a simple cause–effect diagram for the vPOST business. In the case of vPOST, one of the key success factors is to achieve a significant critical mass of subscribers. In order to get high acceptability level, managers need to focus on key issues such as customer interaction (how responsive is vPOST to subscribers' queries), service features (how many services are available to attract subscribers' usage), and ease of use (how easy it is for subscribers to understand and use).

At the bottom of the chart are measures expected to show great variability that should provide clues for improving performance. This segmentation of metrics provides a good insight of how to analyze the key performance drivers.

vPOST Business and Feedback Mechanism

Figure 9.4 describes how a local model can enable adaptation through structured experimentation for the vPOST business. The local model is the

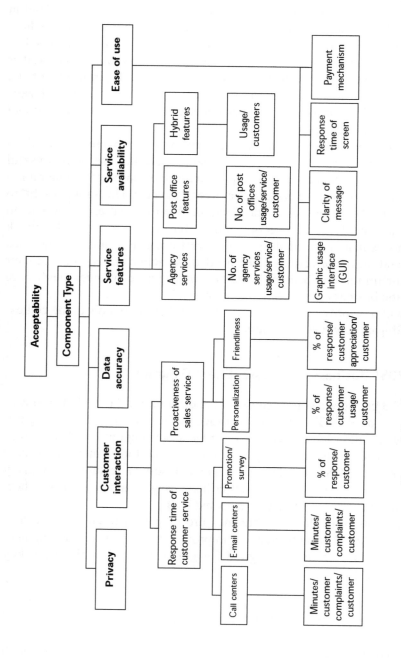

Figure 9.3 A cause–effect diagram for the drivers of acceptability of the vPOST business

engine to screen results. Current variability is not the only source of ideas for improvement; experiments can be structured to explore changes in performance. For the vPOST business, the range of service features should be varied, as should the target customers, the response time for customer care, and so on. Tests can be conducted to collect response data from customers and operations. The model can screen the data, allowing managers to determine what works and what does not in order to select the elements that should be introduced to the broader market. We will discuss this framework in more depth in the next chapter.

First, the range of service features with their corresponding attributes are identified. Second, the core service offer is varied along all the dimensions. For example, the variations for acceptability are privacy, customer interactions, data accuracy, service features, service availability, and end of use as identified in Figure 9.4. Third, a range of customer cells is identified for test marketing. These cells are formed by selected clusters of potential customers whose responses we would like to evaluate. The final step in the process is to screen the results in order to select the service features with the highest acceptability level, measured in terms of net present value so that they capture the full service life cycle profitability. If

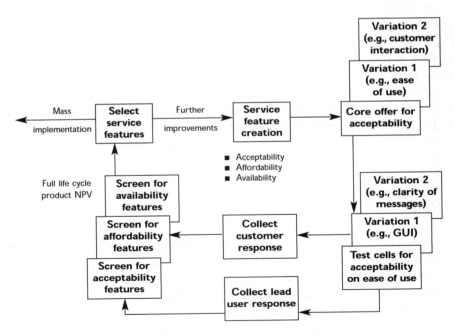

Figure 9.4   The feedback mechanism of the vPOST business

an offer passes the screen, it will be rolled out for mass implementation. Against the background of operating in a highly dynamic environment, a range of offers is designed with the understanding that they will not necessarily be successful, but that they provide the seeds for future success.

The variation in either the service features or customers targeted is important to determine the success of the service. These variations are the key drivers to feedback to the team about what works and what does not. Effective feedback has to incorporate variations in the service and in the customer targets. This information is critical to redesign the service features and dissect customers needs in order to craft a more profitable business.

Reflections

Measure Everything – Judiciously

Measurements are critical for sound, intelligent, and progressive management. A vision, carefully drawn Strategic Agenda, and good metrics to back them up are an unbeatable combination. What we have recommended in this chapter is that a proper measurement system is central to allow us to follow up the progress of our strategic tasks, to get a sense of the overall performance of the business and the firm as a whole, and to go deeply to achieve full understanding of some critical managerial drivers. These tasks could be overwhelming if not properly addressed. We have to exercise a high degree of judgement in the way we deploy the measurement system. One of the salient features of the Delta Model is that it allows us to perform this initial managerial measurement in a fairly systematic and disciplined way. As a result, we generate a comprehensive and well-aligned metric system which is an essential element to successful execution.

Metrics can be an Effective Communication Device

Every executive knows that one of the hardest jobs in strategy is how to communicate it effectively. Brilliant strategies, if they are not propagated throughout the organization, tend to remain isolated, prisoners of the boardroom. Metrics can clearly communicate. When the business agenda is expanded into the multitude of actions embedded in the Adaptive Process – with consistent accountability and measurements – the message begins to disperse throughout the organization. Metrics are not a narrow instrument of management control, rather they constitute a progressive vehicle for communication and shared commitment. Metrics produce congruency in the plethora of actions in which all members of the organization are involved.

Note

1. This case is based upon the MA thesis of one of our students at the Sloan School of Management, M.I.T.: Cheng, Chin Lee, 'An Application of the Delta Model: Developing Strategies for Singapore Post,' unpublished MA thesis, MIT, 1999.

CHAPTER 10

Managing by Averages Leads to Below Average Performance: The Need for Granular Metrics

In most businesses today managers are hostages to two types of information: average data and anecdotal data. The averaged information comes in the form of corporate, business unit, product group, or customer sector data identifying revenues, costs, contribution, and assets regarding actual performance and budgets. Perhaps they also receive market data segmented the same way on share, growth, and competitive activity. Armed with this information executives are asked to improve underlying performance. But, since this information reflects an average across an entire business, product, or customer group, it provides few clues as to what is driving performance. As a consequence, management turns to anecdotes learned from the field. At least this is specific data on a customer or marketing campaign, but it is usually gathered selectively and accompanied by strongly held beliefs. How can executives objectively isolate the critical cause and effect relationships in a business? Managing by anecdote is no better than managing by averages.

In this chapter we will show how average measures need to be systematically disaggregated into Granular Metrics that can reveal spectacular nonlinearities, or concentrations, that are telltale clues to performance drivers. Averages work well as descriptive tools when there is no underlying structure, as with the wind and temperature. In these situations the outcome is truly the mean of independent, random events. However, when the events are interconnected and interdependent, when some crystalline or hierarchical structure is the basis of the emergent property, then the descriptors need to reflect the complexity of the underlying drivers. Averages work well with dead, inert masses, living things within organizations are better described by the concentrations, granular drivers, and reinforcing feedback mechanisms which create the structure.

Businesses are complex, living, interdependent systems characterized by nonlinearity, where small changes can amplify with huge consequences. In contrast, the implied mathematics of aggregate accounting suggests a straightforward linearity, where a 5% change in input leads to a 5% change in output, assuming a certain geometric proportionality. But in fact, it would be odd to expect this to represent the underlying economics of society, since most of the equations that describe the natural world are nonlinear, whether we are looking at immune systems or weather. These are complex nonlinear systems that show sensitive dependence to small variations and which display concentrated, and seemingly chaotic, outcomes. As we dig deeper and deeper into the economics of a business system, we also find massive concentrations in cost, revenue, profits or bonding that are driven and sensitive to Granular Metrics.

Take the example of an executive we know in a large telecom company faced with the task of streamlining the operations of his business, which provides private lines or data circuits. His usual starting point for this would be to analyze the activities of the value chain. The total value chain for a private line, for example a 1.5 megabit or T1 as it is popularly referred to, includes switching or routing equipment, fiber or copper plant, order fulfillment, billing, and other functions. One of the key activities of the chain is order fulfillment, our focus here. The annual cost of a private line is around $400 and the contribution of order fulfillment to that total cost is around $40.

What does that average cost tell the executive? It gives him a sense of the overall importance of order fulfillment in the full value chain, but very little else. Perhaps you could concentrate on the larger parts of the value chain and look at trends in cost over time. If they seem to be rising faster than volume or inflation, you could limit increases. But, yesterday's performance is not necessarily an efficient benchmark. You could collect benchmarks from similar companies and mandate that performance, but that will ensure you little differentiation in the market. With averages at your disposal, it is not surprising that across-the-board cuts are a common resort. It is not possible from averaged information to have a meaningful idea of how well or poorly the company is performing the task of fulfilling orders.

An insight into potential cost performance comes only at a more granular level. When we accurately construct the costs at the level of individual orders, we reveal a wide variability in cost masked by the averages. The highest-cost order is over 10 times more expensive than the lowest-cost order. Also, these high costs are concentrated in a few orders. It is this pattern in the business environment that reflects the nonlinear effects, as shown in Figure 10.1. Twenty percent of the orders generate 75% of the total costs in order fulfillment!

Granular data exposes wide variability that clearly points where to look to enhance performance. You can focus on the 20% of orders contributing

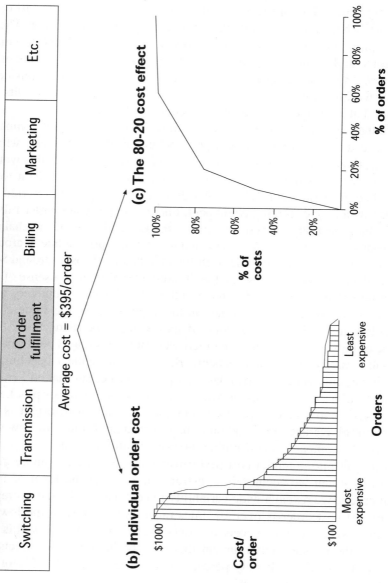

Figure 10.1 The behavior of cost – the case of Business Data Services

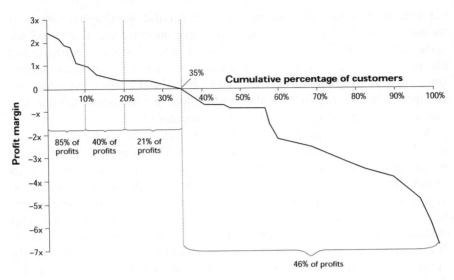

Figure 10.2   Profit margin contribution

Source: Dean & Company analysis

to most of the costs. How are these orders, customers, employees, or processes different? You can compare the most expensive to the least expensive orders to identify best practices, or sometimes wholly new ways of doing business. Sometimes the random, naturally occurring mutations in the operations of the business lead to greatly improved performance.

The same behavior we observed when measuring cost reappears when we look at profit performance. There is marked nonlinearity at a granular level. In Figure 10.2 individual customers are ranked from the most profitable to the least profitable for a financial services company. It shows a huge variation in profit margin by individual customers for the credit card business. This same pattern emerges in all industries, whether in telecommunications, energy, web hosting, transportation, or financial services. This pattern of profitability is typical, but remarkable in its impact.

In this particular example, the top 10% of customers contribute 85% of profits, the next 10% account for 40% of additional profits, and the next 15% of customers add 21% more – this means that only 35% of customers account for 146% of profits, while the other 65% of customers are unprofitable. In the face of this variability, averages are not only unhelpful, they are downright misleading. Yet, this data is not available to most businesses – because they do not measure profitability to the necessary level of granularity. It is a demanding task to accurately construct profits at the intersection of many dimensions: a single customer, buying a discrete service, from a specific channel, in a particular geography. Granular measures introduce a rich set of questions and opportunities that could not arise from looking at averages. Should one eliminate unprofitable customers, or do they help cover fixed costs, contribute to product innovation, or drive organizational learning? Should the price structure be changed? Can we acquire only the most profitable customers? Are our best customers being cherry-picked by our competitors?

Answers to these questions vary with respect to the strategic option. A Best Product strategy might concentrate narrowly on product profitability by customer, and may eliminate those customers who do not contribute to product fixed costs. Even then we have to be careful since there could be unprofitable customers now who might become more profitable in the future. A Total Customer Solutions strategy should emphasize the total customer profit across the offered bundle of products and services. From that perspective, unprofitable products are less important than chronically unprofitable customers. The System Lock-In strategy forces us to consider the implications of customer abandonment, not only to us, but also to our key complementors.

The Delta Model and Granular Metrics

How does a business systematically begin to discover and then harness the value of Granular Metrics? Figure 10.3 gives a succinct representation of

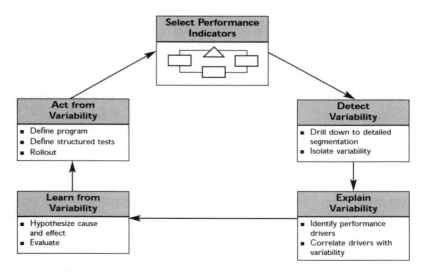

Figure 10.3   The Delta Model and Granular Metrics

the various elements of a complete cycle generated by the use of Granular Metrics. It is anchored in the detection and exploitation of variability to guide us in a learning process conducive to innovation and action. We will illustrate the actual use of this cycle later on in this chapter. First we examine the nature of its key elements, and then we will illustrate the actual use of this cycle.

Select Key Performance Indicators

The rigorous treatment of Granular Metrics cannot be applied indiscriminately to every conceivable performance indicator. We have to select carefully those which are essential to support the desired strategic positioning we have chosen. Table 10.1 shows four of the most important indicators. The first three are logically aligned with the three strategic options of the Triangle: product cost and quality with the Best Product option; customer profit with the Total Customer Solutions option; and complementor contri-

Table 10.1   Drivers of variability for selected performance indicators

Performance indicators	Drivers of variability
Product cost and quality	■ Scale ■ Density – e.g. concentration of service ■ Location ■ Labor productivity – practices and training ■ Equipment productivity – design ■ Process design ■ And so on
Customer profit	■ Customer size ■ Customer revenue ■ Tenure ■ Acquisition cost ■ Channel mix ■ Customer care support ■ Customer investments in relationship ■ And so on
Complementor contribution	■ Size of relevant complementor products ■ Complementor investment in business ■ Relative size in customer value chain ■ Complementor contribution to customer economics ■ Exclusivity of relationship ■ And so on
Business segment economic value	■ ROI (return on investment) – profitability ■ Risk – volatility and covariance ■ Option value ■ Investment base ■ Cashflows

bution with the System Lock-In option. The fourth indicator, business segment economic value, is useful to represent the value implications of the variability found in all of the previous three indicators. Table 10.1 also suggests some of the drivers of variability that can explain changes in performance for each indicator. These drivers are critical for our analysis, as they describe the Granular Metrics that should be collected to expose the nature and intensity of the variability associated with each indicator.

Detect Variability

The drivers are a mechanism to drill down into the economic cause and effect relationships for a given indicator. In the process we create a cause and effect tree and branch diagram. In the last chapter, we illustrated the application of this tool for the vPOST business of the Singapore Post (Figure 9.3). An example for the telecommunications private line situation described earlier is shown in Figure 10.4.

Figure 10.4 shows how the cost of OC-48 (optical fiber carrying 2.4 gigabits per second) broadband capacity is driven by a number of Granular Metrics. The fully utilized cost per mile of OC-48 is around $1500 on average, but it can range from as low as $500 to as high as $100,000. The factors causing this variability first include type of technology, for example ADM (add drop multiplexor) versus WDM (wave division multiplexor). The drivers behind each of these technologies are channel cost, and segment length (the length between the nodes that hold the optical and electronic equipment). Drilling deeper, we find the drivers of these factors include the spare and active channel utilization, routing efficiency, new capacity planning guidelines, and growth on existing segments. This process continues until we find a strong concentration in costs, assets, and quality along some combination of driving factors. Each branch further postulates and, with analysis, confirms or disproves the influence of that driver. The natural state of most economic systems is that all drivers are not created equal; from the many hypothesized at the outset, several are usually found that critically affect the performance of that indicator.

All of this is much more poetically communicated by the fleas of Jonathan Swift:

> So, naturalists observe, a flea
> Hath smaller fleas that on him prey
> And these have smaller fleas to bite 'em
> And so proceed ad infinitum.

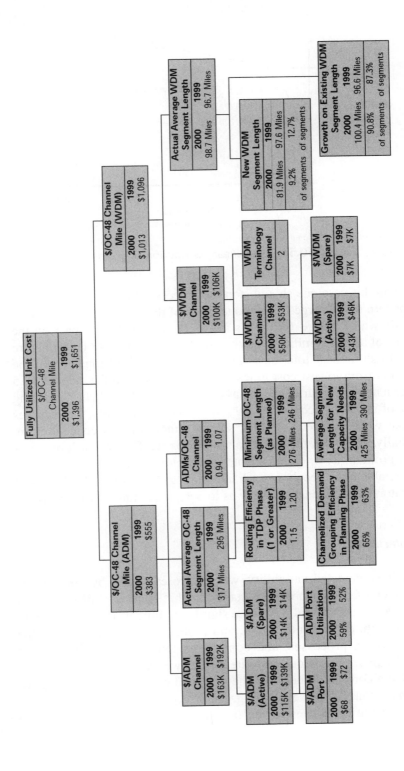

Figure 10.4 Broadband network cost and granular drivers

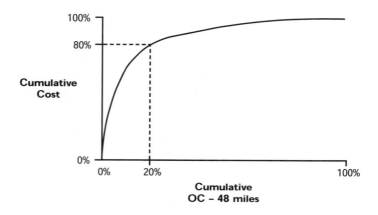

Figure 10.5   Nonlinear distribution of costs

However, in this case one should stop the process well short of infinity.

The pattern that emerges at the conclusion of the process is a concentration, as shown in Figure 10.5. This shows the cumulative impact on the economics of all the significant drivers. In the case of OC-48 costs, Figure 10.5 would show how total costs accumulate as we add together all the OC-48 costs from lowest-cost miles to the highest-cost miles. Figure 10.5 illustrates a nonlinear curve which has exactly an 80–20 behavior, meaning that 20% of the miles account for 80% of the costs. In reality, these curves could take various different forms, showing more or less concentration. Additionally, these are the same relationships we find when looking at customer profitability or complementor contributions. What is important is that we are able to go deeply enough into the segmentation of the drivers of the indicators' performance to allow us to detect meaningful variability.

Explain Variability

Once we have detected variability, we need to explain it by going to its ultimate sources. In our previous example, what generates differences in costs per OC-48 mile? And, given the significant influence on costs due to segment length, channel utilization, and routing efficiency, what are the skills, practices, processes, and constraints that affect these granular drivers? There are numerous hypotheses that we can explore to allow us to establish a correlation between the observed practice and the behavior of the driver that we are examining. At the very least, we can produce similar distribution curves to the one in Figure 10.5 to visualize the impact of individual drivers. More sophisticated statistical analyses can also be conducted.

Learn from Variability

Much has been said about learning and knowledge building as critical determinants of business success. We believe that the learning gained from detecting and explaining the sources of variability constitutes an important, and manageable, source of new knowledge. Furthermore, it is the next critical step to the execution of our desired strategies. A Best Product strategy needs an intimate understanding of individual product, channel, supplier, and supply chain activities. A Total Customer Solutions strategy requires deep and singular knowledge of the customer base; if we observe no significant variability in customer profitability, we have severe limits on the execution of this strategic option. Likewise, the knowledge that we obtain from the sources of profitability of the overall system, and the individual roles played by complementors, will dictate how you can effectively pursue a System Lock-In strategy. From learning comes effective monitoring of progress and programs for improvement.

Act from Variability

All the previous steps have only one guiding objective: to trigger a set of actions that will significantly enhance business positioning. As they say, 'God is in the details.' In order to capture appropriately the opportunities for action, we need to capture the granular details and their corresponding lessons. This will allow us to remove nonperforming entities – such as products, customers, complementors – in order to focus investment in those drivers which are most promising; to target training and educational programs to develop the relevant skills and knowledge base; to foster innovation that corrects weaknesses and promotes the necessary focus of joint development. All these action programs can only be properly realized with the support and understanding of Granular Metrics.

Adaptation and Experimentation

The feedback mechanism implicit in Figure 10.3, to focus, measure, learn, and act, is also the basis of two very important elements of the Delta

Model: adaptation and experimentation. The need for adaptation is born from the unpredictability of our changing environment. If we cannot forecast effectively due to uncertainty, then we have to plan to respond effectively. The feedback process that we have just alluded to gives us the ability to test different approaches to change in a more systematic, scientific way, thus reinforcing our learning capabilities. Most organizations use analytics for policy setting, but not to test the policy. This is why metrics are soon forgotten after the decisions are made and even thoughtful, in-depth, upfront analysis does not provide the continuing guidance that businesses require. Companies then default to the aggregate measures that remain.

Adaptation applies to evolutionary moves that are part of an already accepted course of action. Experimentation, on the other hand, has to do with testing a significant departure from an existing base. It constitutes a major discontinuity that could have longlasting implications for business performance. Figure 10.6 clarifies this point. Businesses contemplate large- and small-scale changes, and they have the option of attacking them slowly or quickly. While we all want to pursue large-scale changes, quickly and with conviction, it is disastrous to do this in light of the genuine unknowns and uncertainty in the market. The other real option is to languish as a distant follower or to systematically experiment. Experimentation is most appropriate when addressing major changes to be done swiftly. It is not prudent to risk the overall business by undertaking such a

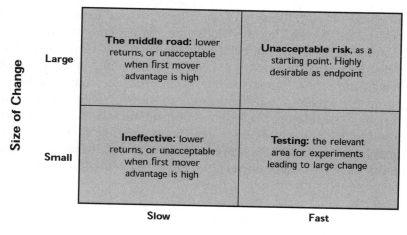

Figure 10.6   Experimentation as the basis for effective change

dramatic change without prior learning. This is when testing and experimentation become relevant.

In the remaining part of this chapter we will illustrate all the concepts expressed above, and the essential nature of Granular Metrics for two indicators: cost and profit. We will 'de-average' these indicators and show how executives are repositioning their businesses using Granular Metrics.

Cost De-averaging: Using Granular Metrics to Drive Performance

We started this chapter showing how averaged metrics are insufficient, or even misleading, to pursue cost performance in the case of a telecommunications business. Let us continue with this example to illustrate the development and application of Granular Metrics. Since the business was following a Best Product strategy in this example, product cost is a fundamental indicator.

Detect and Explain Variability

One of the substantial activities in the value chain is order fulfillment, our focus here. At the beginning of the chapter, we skipped much of this process to show the resulting variation in cost per order. The process of detecting and explaining the variability started with hypothesizing drivers and dissecting the cost into finer elements corresponding to these drivers. Figure 10.7 shows a simplified cause–effect diagram of the cost of order fulfillment recognizing four basic drivers: the location of the working centers, the nature of the activities that are part of fulfilling an order, the differences in productivity of the individual workforce, and the nature of the equipment involved. We will now proceed to analyze the behavior of each driver and infer the true sources of cost variability.

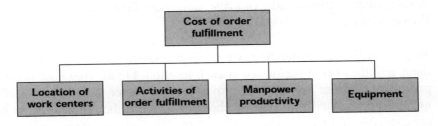

Figure 10.7   The drivers of the cost of order fulfillment

A Granular Segmentation of Cost Behavior: Location

Location is one basis for granular cost segmentation. The telecommunications company in question has five geographically disparate work centers. One would expect these five locations to have different costs because they differ in size, customer mix, type of orders, and culture. After looking across these various factors, however, we found one cost driver that had a predominant influence. The number of orders processed by a work center is highly correlated with the cost per order. Figure 10.8 displays the cost behavior of the five work centers along with the estimated cost position of their competitors.

This curve quantified the impact of scale (as defined by the number of orders) and allowed managers to judge the relative effectiveness of the various locations. We have highlighted a corridor that represents the benchmark of best performers. Information at this level of detail led to a number of useful insights into cost behavior and potential cost savings.

First, if we forget about the curve and simply look at the headcount per order across the first four work centers (Chicago, New York, Tulsa, and Charlotte), we find that the costs are pretty similar. They would appear to be sensitive and internally competitive to relative performance when it has been measured as orders per headcount. However, the performance of these work centers relative to their potential benchmark performance when accounting for their processing size is markedly varied: the Chicago center performs much better than the Charlotte center. The center-specific performance goals and current rewards should reflect these differences. The highest potential for cost savings belongs to Charlotte, if we account for size as a driver and adhere to proven performance levels. At the other extreme, the Kansas City center is the best performer. It might constitute a center of excellence from which the telecommunications company can extract lessons to pass on to improve performance at other centers.

A Granular Segmentation of Cost Behavior: Granular Process Activities

To gain further understanding, we need to disaggregate the order fulfill-ment activities being performed at each location. Figure 10.9 portrays the process or chain of activities for provisioning an order. A number of technicians are involved who start by checking to see if the physical facilities are available in their own network and the networks of other companies they lease. These facilities need to be tested, proper designs created,

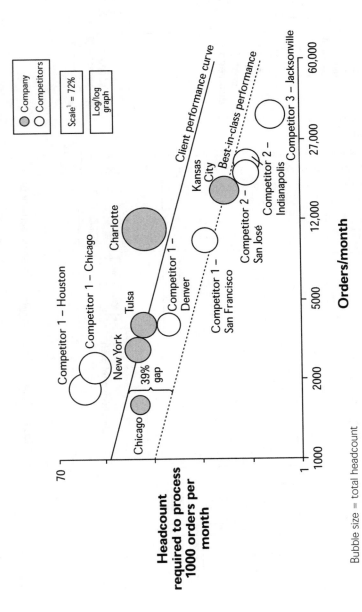

Bubble size = total headcount

Figure 10.8 The behavior of cost by work center

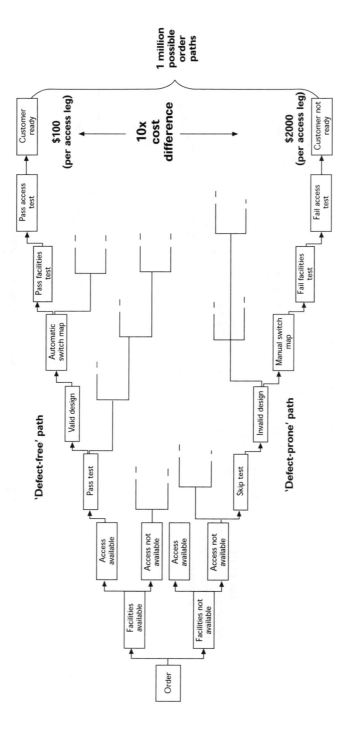

Figure 10.9   The behavior of cost by activity path

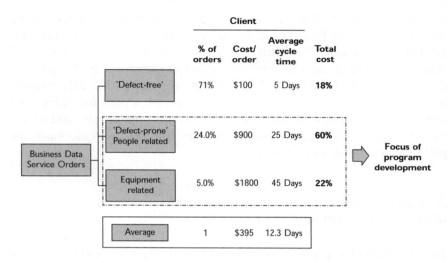

Figure 10.10   The behavior of cost by type of defects

switching or routing hardware needs to be mapped to the logical design of the circuit, and then it all needs to be tested in total and by segment. The upper part of the figure, which we have denoted the 'defect-free' path, describes each of these activities. However, some of these activities are not executed as intended, for a number of reasons. For example, the activity in the order process that involves mapping the design to the available network can be completed quickly if the order is filled out correctly and the network databases are accurate. On the other hand, if the order is incorrect or if the network data is incomplete or wrong, then this step can take hours, delay the order for days, and cause problems further down the activity chain.

At the other extreme, we have outlined the 'defect-prone' path, the outcome of the same process when every step has failed. The combinations that result from the explosion of multiple outcomes lead to one million possible order paths. What appears to be one process turns out to contain one million paths with widely varying cost levels. Fortunately, the probabilities are somewhat linked so that a few paths are more commonly tread than others. The cost difference between the 'defect-free' and 'defect-prone' paths is an order of magnitude. We see here the emergence of an extreme form of nonlinear cost behavior.

Figure 10.10 simplifies the process to show the primary paths. Seventy-one percent of the orders follow the 'defect-free' path and comprise less than 18% of the total order fulfillment cost. Conversely, 29% of the orders follow 'defect-prone' paths and account for 82% of the total cost. Clearly, the place to start looking for cost improvement is in the defect-prone orders. The cost of failure is centered on people-related and equipment-related malfunctions. This provides a clear diagnosis of the source of costs, and suggests areas for further in-depth examination. In this process, defective orders bottlenecked all orders, so, using this information, managers began to segment the process to create a path for defect-free orders. By more deeply understanding what causes the people- and equipment-related problems, they also would have the means to eliminate the problematic sources of cost behavior.

A Granular Segmentation of Cost Behavior: Manpower Productivity

The next logical step was to examine the variability of performance at the level of the individual or case team. Manpower-related defects, it turns out, are the most significant sources of poor performance. Manpower activities involved both technicians in the data centers and field craftsmen responsible for physically reconfiguring the network. Sometimes this physical reconfiguration would require clearing faults to free capacity for new orders. Figure 10.11 illustrates the results of this level of segmentation, where each craftsman is measured in terms of the total hours he or she needs to clear a fault. The figure recognizes five different components of productivity which provide managers with important insights. The bottom portion of each productivity bar shows the number of hours of direct craftsman work it takes on average to fix a fault. There is very little variation here, but these hours do not capture the full contribution to productivity that a craftsman makes. Interestingly however, this is the metric used to evaluate and incent craftsmen. Instead, a craftsman should be evaluated more comprehensively on how he or she affects the overall productivity of the company's operations. In clearing a fault certain craftsmen may frequently choose to call in expensive specialists, or to bypass the problem rather than fix it. While this might keep their personal productivity levels up, it can raise overall company costs. In this particular instance, when we added the other relevant measures of performance, we found that their best performers were three times more productive than their worst performers and 25% of their craftsmen account for 80% of their costs.

The analysis led to very specific recommendations for improving craftsman performance. By being able to properly segment the best performers from the worst, we could compare their work practices, which

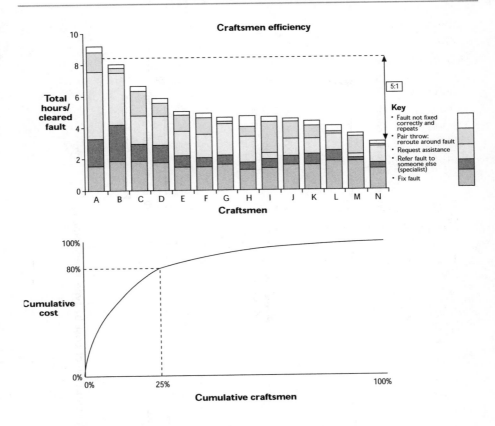

Figure 10.11   The behavior of cost by individual workers

varied widely. The efficient workers had learned shortcuts through the company's information systems, and others had learned to read cable maps more effectively than their peers.

The next step was to map the productivity data to the different practices to see which made the greatest contribution to productivity and to establish priorities in sharing these practices. Based on this the team designed training programs and detailed the skills of the craftsmen, so that individuals could receive the specific training that would be most beneficial to them. The focused training programs were much more effective than the conventional across-the-board training program aimed at the mythical average performer.

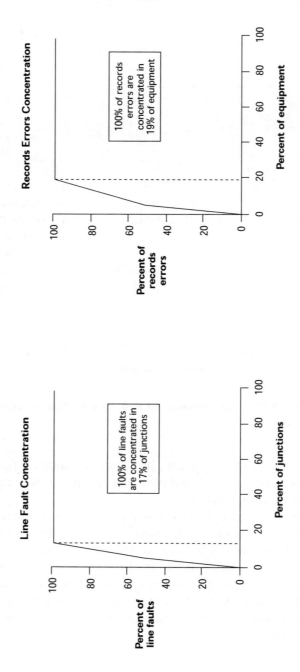

Figure 10.12 The behavior of cost by type of equipment

A Granular Segmentation of Cost Behavior: Equipment

The final part of this cost story in data services involves equipment. After worker productivity, equipment was the most significant source of defect generation and led to unnecessarily high costs. Figure 10.12 identifies two detailed measures of equipment performance.

The equipment was defective either because it was not working, or because the records describing it were inaccurate. The two graphs in Figure 10.12 show equally dramatic concentrations of problems. Roughly 20% of the equipment was responsible for 100% of the errors, which means that the remaining 80% was error free! The company performed equipment maintenance by geographical region. They segmented their service areas into geographies and rehabilitated or upgraded regions sequentially. This would have been the correct practice if failures were uniformly dispersed, but they were not. Through this analysis, managers were able to pinpoint the exact location of the equipment that was consistently problematic and establish maintenance programs targeted at fixing them. The results were again dramatic. There was an opportunity to reduce equipment-related defects by 30% while reducing the investment in maintenance and upgrade at the same time because of the new focus of the program.

Learning and Acting from Variability: Operational Effectiveness

As is evident in the description of the example to date, there was continual learning and implementation of new programs to improve the business at each point in the process. The conclusion of this data services case shows how learning and innovation became embedded in the company's day-to-day operations by using Granular Metrics and feedback to create an Adaptive Process reinforcing Operational Effectiveness. Figure 10.13 illustrates the role played by Granular Metrics in the ongoing monitoring and improvement of performance at all levels.

The data services provisioning group generated monthly Granular Metrics and shared the figures throughout the organization, from senior management to junior technicians. Supervisors, who the technicians reported to, now had the measures they needed to coach low productivity employees and to learn from those with high productivity. Best practices were identified, tested, and shared across work centers as well as within work centers. Results at the work center level were posted for all to see, and results at an individual level were available to supervisors and (on a sanitized basis) to the individuals. Table 10.2 shows the level of granu-

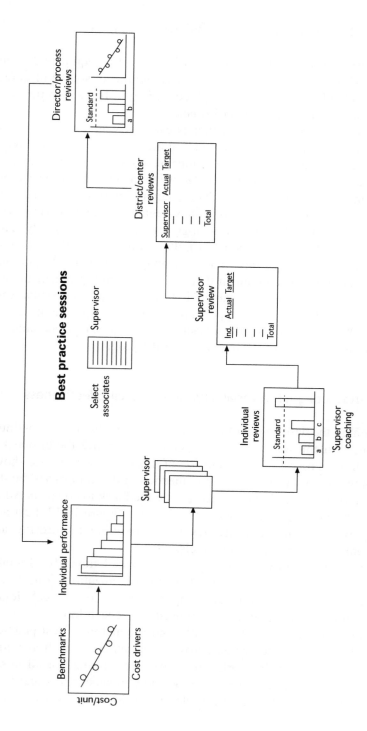

Figure 10.13 Operational Effectiveness: Adaptive Feedback using Granular Metrics

Source: Dean & Company

Table 10.2 Case team productivity reports

SUMMARY PRODUCTIVITY REPORT
February 5–9, 1998
Case team: Alpha

Position	Name	Target	1-week productivity	4-week average	Previous month	Improvement over baseline %
Order entry	A	12.7	15.4	16.4	14.5	-31
Order entry	B	12.7	8.2	10.1	9.0	20
Order entry	C	12.7	12.1	11.2	10.5	42
Order entry	Average	12.7	15.4	21.8	31.5	-31
Design	A	3.8	7.8	6.6	7.0	-5
Design	B	3.8	7.3	N/A	3.0	N/A
Design	C	3.8	6.2	7.3	8.4	-13
Design	D	3.8	8.7	8.3	10.0	-18
Design	Average	3.8	7.6	7.4	8.4	-12
Technician	A	2.8	4.0	5.5	3.3	68
Technician	B	2.8	4.3	5.4	3.9	39
Technician	C	2.8	4.4	7.3	5.4	36
Technician	D	2.8		6.4	6.9	-7
Technician	Average	2.8	2.5	5.9	4.6	28

ON-TIME REPORT
February 5–9, 1998
Case team: Alpha

Position	Name	Due	Missed	On time %
Order entry	A	0	0	N/A
Order entry	B	22	5	81
Order entry	C	15	3	90
Order entry	Average	37	8	87
Design	A	47	2	96
Design	B	0	0	N/A
Design	C	40	0	100
Design	D	56	8	86
Design	Average	143	10	93
Technician	A	34	10	93
Technician	B	33	10	70
Technician	C	31	9	71
Technician	D	16	4	75
Technician	Average	114	33	71

larity shared in the new reports that were now generated at the supervisor level. The outcome was not incremental. Some work centers were consolidated to gain scale advantages, the remaining moved to new plateaus of productivity. The overall gain in performance was over 50% within a year, and further improvements are expected.

Profit De-averaging: Using Granular Metrics to Drive Performance

The same behavior we observed when measuring cost reappears when we look at profit performance. There is marked nonlinearity at a granular level. At the beginning of this chapter we referred to the huge variation in profit margin by individual customer for the credit card business. This financial services company was pursuing a Total Customer Solutions strategy, and a key indicator to explore was customer profit.

Detect and Explain Variability

Many would consider revenue per customer to be the strongest driver of customer profitability followed closely by overall market share as represented by the total number of customers, customer balances, and customer tenure, as shown in Figure 10.14. We will proceed to analyze the behavior of each one of the four drivers captured in the figure.

The Granular Segmentation of Profit Behavior

Figure 10.15 clusters customers into groups based on card usage level and shows monthly profit by group. The average profit climbs slightly with

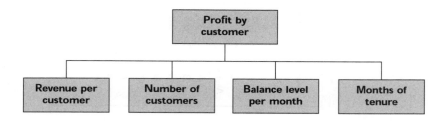

Figure 10.14   The drivers of customer profitability
in the credit card business

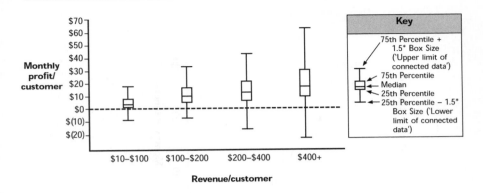

Figure 10.15   Variability of profits by usage levels

usage, but the increase is modest relative to the overall variability of profit within each group. There was a strong belief among managers at the credit card company that revenue is the most important driver of profitability. It was a mistaken belief, however. As revenue increases, variability in profit also increases. There are large numbers of unprofitable customers in the highest usage band, and there are significant numbers of profitable customers in the lowest usage band. In this instance, there are a number of factors driving profitability, one does not dominate.

Figure 10.16 provides a further breakdown of profit drivers. In this particular case, the total number of customers the firm was able to attract had a relatively mild impact on profit margin. Generally, when this is true, product market share is not the dominant strategic variable. There was a different effect resulting from customer usage and customer tenure. In both cases, there is a pronounced effect on profit up to a point, and then profitability begins to increase much more gradually.

This would suggest that the company's top priorities should be to attract the right type of customer, to expand its share of these customers' wallets, and to bond with them for longer periods of time.

De-averaging information allows managers to uncover profit and cost opportunities that their competitors may overlook. The success of Capital One, a major credit card business, is based on their dissection of the market into microsegments that the major banks had averaged together. Capital One segments its customers based on customer profit drivers, which include balances outstanding, usage or transaction volume, default risk, and tenure, among other items. Significant variations in these drivers by customer lead to striking concentrations of profit. Capital One,

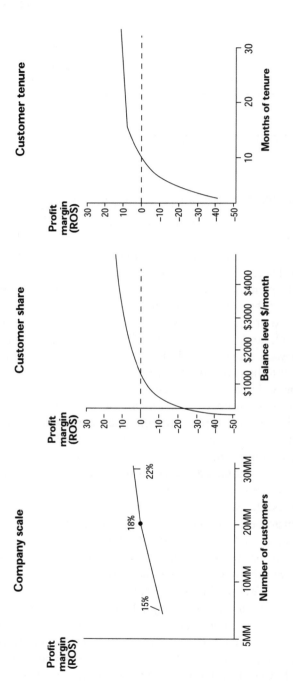

Figure 10.16   Further examination of profit drivers

Universal Card, MBNA and others have excelled at finding and exploiting the profitable niches, and then moving on to a new niche before their competition.

Learning and Acting from Variability: Customer Targeting

Segmentation of profits provides data that allows managers to improve significantly the profitability of their businesses. As a paramount concern, managers must target the right customers to attract and retain.

This is a serious situation because the cost to acquire a customer in the credit card business has grown an order of magnitude over the past 10 years. As mentioned earlier, this is driven largely by the increasingly low conversion rates of direct mail and telemarketing efforts. We can see the effect in our own mailbox, as the number of credit card solicitations increases the odds that we will choose any one solicitation drops proportionally. All of this points to the value of Customer Targeting.

The impact of Customer Targeting in the financial services industry is shown in Figure 10.17. The bottom line shows the effect of a broad-based marketing program that used commonly available demographic information. This 'untargeted' marketing program, it turns out, actually destroys value. The more a company solicits, the more money it loses. The moral of the story is that in today's environment, companies must be focused – in terms of both customers targeted and services offered – to succeed.

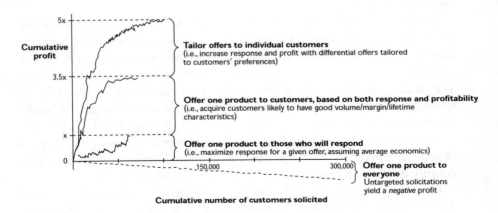

Figure 10.17   The effects of Customer Targeting

Beyond the completely untargeted marketing program, Figure 10.17 shows three marketing programs with increasing levels of targeting. The company achieved the first level of targeting by focusing on actual customer response rates. The marketing programs were conducted in cycles in which information about the first wave was used to refine the targets for the second wave, and so on. Since the response rate has an enormous impact on the acquisition cost of the customer, small improvements made a previously unprofitable program profitable. The second level of targeting was based on the addition of complete measures of customer profitability to the prioritization algorithm. For the third level, the company tested different product variations with different customer groups to optimize the tailoring of products to customers. The company transformed a conventionally unprofitable business into a highly profitable one.

Customer Targeting: The Example of Capital One

The effective use of Granular Metrics, customization, and experimentation can be seen in its entirety in the example of Capital One. Capital One has ably exploited many of the niches in the credit card business and is now among the top ten credit card issuers. In ten years, they have come from nowhere to amass over six million accounts and $10 billion in outstanding credit balances. They have grown sales and earnings per share at 40% and 30%, respectively, over the past five years and have a market capitalization of over $10 billion. Capital One is a Total Customer Solutions firm that has made the Adaptive Process of Customer Targeting its most important weapon.

AT&T Universal Card and MBNA also share a strong emphasis on Customer Targeting that has enabled them to catapult over the once dominant major banks. Capital One uses an information intensive strategy that is based on testing and learning about different consumer credit products. The strategy permits Capital One to leverage massive investment in IT, scientific testing, and a very flexible operating structure to deliver highly customized products to each individual customer segment. The heavy reliance on this data-oriented approach and process is what gives Capital One its advantage in the credit card marketplace. Before solicitations ever get rolled out, they know that the consumer will be profitable.

Capital One is an extremely analytical company with the skill to dissect the profitability of the credit industry down to the smallest microsegment. Profit is a complex equation driven by type of customer, degree and style of usage, customer tenure, and the costs of acquiring the customer, to name but a few variables. Understanding this equation and having the data to use it are clearly important when you consider that customers show a wide range in profitability. Acquiring the average customer will drive you bankrupt, acquiring and retaining the profitable niches creates a cash machine.

Having the right profit metrics, component costs, revenue drivers, and customer information yields a huge competitive advantage. When Richard Fairbanks arrived at Signet Bank, where Capital One originated, he had a vision of building a strategy based upon the rich inventories of data he presumed existed at a bank with so much financial history. To his astonishment he discovered that the computer tapes had been erased so that they could be reused and the bank could save the $30 cost of new tapes. As a result, it took two years to build the customer data that they needed. Banks, and many large companies, have tremendous reserves of customer and operations data fragmented throughout the company that can yield competitive strength if combined and used to drive the business. Capital One's advantage is based, in part, on the fact that the major banks did not use this natural resource.

While the credit card may seem simple – money and interest rates – the potential variations are infinite. Each variation appeals to a different customer and represents a window of opportunity. The challenge is to identify these segments before the competition does, and classic market research is not enough. While it is a valuable tool, market research does not show *actual* buying behavior and false inferences made from it can substantially dilute the profitability of a business. One executive remarked, 'we put together our idea of what would be the most attractive offer for a customer segment, based upon market research, then we deliberately vary the offer off of this "ideal" in terms of rate, price and promotional message. We test all of these variations against different target customer cells. Inevitably, the offer that has the best response was not the "ideal" offer, but one of the variations.'

Capital One's adaptive approach changed the face of the credit card industry. The massive amount of rigorous testing, the number of offers, the granular segmentation of the business and the customer, the central use of data, and the quantitative analysis were a world apart from the conventional financial services industry. The magnitude of change is shown in Table 10.3.

Capital One's capabilities are based upon information technology, scientific testing, and customization. This enables them to get the right product to the right customer at the right time and at the right price. They have made massive investments in information systems and feel that they are so central to their advantage that they will not outsource them. They have a

Table 10.3   Customers' targeting behaviors

Behaviors	Typical competitors	Capital One
▪ Offer	75 products	5000 products
▪ Tests/year	30	15,000
▪ Service tiers	4	13
▪ Key metric	ROE, Delinquency	NPV
▪ Targets	High response likelihood	High NPV potential
▪ Solicitations/year	50 million	400 million
▪ Segmentation frequency	Biannual	Ongoing
▪ Risk orientation	Risk averse	Price for risk
▪ Data sources	80	50,000
▪ Staff analysts	20	150

structure that emphasizes rapid prototyping, modularity, and flexibility. They have invested in the full range of delivery methods, including web-based channels, as well as direct mail and call centers.

This approach has enabled them to be the first to offer balance transfers and secured cards. It is a competence which they feel extends beyond credit cards and which may give them a competitive advantage in other products, such as installment loans, auto loans, mortgages, life insurance, mutual funds, and even telecommunications and energy. They hope to evolve into broad-based, information-based marketing.

Capital One's approach to experimentation and feedback is presented, in a simplified form, in Figure 10.18. This is a Customer Targeting Adaptive Process. The linchpin of the process is scientific testing. First, they brainstorm offers based upon a range of sources. Second, the core offer is varied along all the dimensions – product, price, promotion and channel. Third, and with a high degree of scientific rigor, they identify a range of customer cells for test marketing. The final step in the process is to screen the results in order to select the offers with the highest profit, measured in terms of NPV so that they capture the full customer life cycle profitability – customer tenure is a key profit driver. If an offer passes the screen it is rolled out to the target group as a whole. More importantly, information is generated in the process that yields hypotheses for other offers that may be more profitable.

The offers into the market are not pursued with the goal of 100% acceptability, but rather with the goal of 100% feedback. This notion is perhaps contrary to the wisdom of 0% defects. A range of offers is

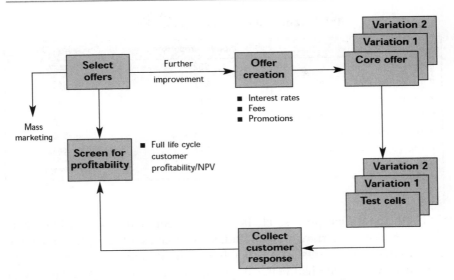

Figure 10.18   Capital One – achieving a Total Customer
Solutions through Customer Targeting

designed with the understanding that they will not necessarily be successful, but that they provide the seeds for future success. According to Kenneth Boulding, 'Nothing fails like success, because we do not learn from it. We learn only from failure.'

There is a key distinction between what we are describing here and what most companies do when they 'trial' a product. Every company we have studied conducts some form of trial. An Internet company we were recently working with was complaining about their product development. A promising network service they had just spent over $30 million to develop had flopped in the market, and they did not know where to go with the business. Their experience was typical of most companies. They took an intriguing product concept, developed it, and then tried to sell it to a sample of customers to test its commercial viability. Although they used the words trial and test, they did not employ a properly structured adaptive feedback mechanism. In their trials only one product variation was tested and it was marketed to a sample of high potential consumers. When the trial failed the only feedback was that it did not work, but there was no information on how variations in either the product or the customers targeted would have changed the acceptance rate. Effective feedback has to incorporate variations in the product and the customer targets. This information is needed to redesign the product and dissect customer needs in order to craft a more profitable business.

Table 10.4   Success metrics

	Typical competitor	Capital One
▪ Customer NPV	$62	$427
▪ Acquisition cost	$77	$67
▪ Activation	58%	79%
▪ Percent with revolving balances	25%	40%
▪ Fee income per account	$55	$73
▪ Charge-off per account	$71	$54
▪ Tenure	4 years	6 years

The Capital One process challenged conventional wisdom. Fairbanks has a 'eureka' chart, which includes the names of people who have contributed outrageous ideas that have failed. For your career to go anywhere your name had better be on that chart; it is safe to assume that success does not hurt your career either.

Capital One estimates the profitability of their trials at the most detailed level. They de-average the customer base, and look into the profit drivers to identify the most lucrative niches. They take pride in being able to calculate the NPV of every marketing and offer decision. The experiments that pass the NPV screens are rolled out. Information from these and the less attractive offers is funneled back into the process for further changes.

The success of their Customer Targeting Adaptive Process is evident across a number of metrics, as shown in Table 10.4. Compared to the typical credit card business, Capital One has achieved significantly higher market value per customer, lower acquisition costs, higher activation rates, more balances and fee income, and 50% longer customer tenure.

Reflections

The Role of Granular Metrics in a Networked Economy

Granular metrics is both a means to cope with an increasingly complex economy and secure bonding.

Jose Scheinkman and Michael Woodford[1] describe the economy as an input-output structure consisting of a large number of layers. Firms which produce the final output are at the top of the pyramid, and they purchase intermediate outputs from the firm in the next layer down. The next firm repeats this process both internally, with other divisions, and externally with other firms. This continues to occur as we work upstream in the economy. An order for a final good will produce a chain reaction for intermediate and raw goods. Complexity arises because a great many of these simple components interact simultaneously.

As the economy grows it adds more components and networks, both human and electronic, to connect these components. The complexity lies in the organization itself – in the myriad of possible ways that the components of the system can interact. Complexity has potential diseconomies of scale. The larger you are the more likely something will go wrong and amplify beyond control. To contend with it requires decentralization, massively delegated autonomy with little recourse by senior management. At the same time, you do not want the components to follow Brownian motion, where individual units move randomly in every direction, leading to anarchy, dissipation, and entropy. Somehow a single sense of purpose with reinforcing strengths needs to be transmitted to the organization via the right incentives while retaining autonomy.

In this context, successful management today is about self-organization – how to put together the components, both internal and external to the firm, consisting of information, people, money, and assets, so that they become a self-sustaining and growing business. The Delta Model reflects strategic positions that describe the self-sustaining elements occurring in a networked economy. The Adaptive Processes are a built-in response mechanism to enable self-organization and create order from chaos. Granular Metrics recognize that businesses, like other complex systems, suffer from sensitive dependencies where small factors can have huge consequences.

The economy is a living system whose properties emerge from the bottom up, from much simpler systems – not from the top down. Color is an emergent property. Sulfur is yellow, but the constituent atoms are not yellow. Profit is also an emergent phenomenon; it is a regularity of behavior that transcends its own ingredients. With emergent phenomenon, local microscopic aspects can determine the big picture. It is important to have global awareness, but things get done due to local causality. Running a company solely with top-down rules is impossible. A meaningful understanding of business requires Granular Metrics and drivers. A meaningful strategy creates local metrics and rules.

Furthermore, bonding has its grip at a granular level. One-to-one marketing, customization, and customer learning need to occur with individual customers, not with averaged business units or typical market segments. Information needs to be collected and acted upon at the intersection of a customer, buying a product, through a channel, in a geography. The self-reinforcing feedback loop with the customer, or with the complementors that sustains bonding needs to be engineered at the granular level. In the example of eBay, systems need to be designed to collect data on specific buyers and sellers to enable lower risk exchanges that will draw new customers to their online auction. In the example of National Starch, joint development is planned separately for individual customers. Generic products designed for the average customer provide little bonding.

Note

1. Scheinkman, J.A., and Woodford, M. (1994). 'Self-organized Criticality and Economic Fluctuations.' *American Economic Review* **84** (May): 417–21.

CHAPTER 11

The Restructuring of the Electric Utility Industry: Applying the Delta Model to an Industry in Transition

Andy Grove, the chairman of Intel, coined the term the '10X force' in his book *Only the Paranoid Survive*. A 10X force occurs when an element of business changes an order of magnitude larger than anything the company has seen before. A 10X force is the impetus for a complete restructuring of the business. Grove suggests potential sources of 10X forces: technological discontinuities, globalization, and regulatory change.

In this chapter we look at the impact on the electric utility industry of the 10X forces of deregulation and technology. The U.S. electricity market has $200 billion in revenue and $550 billion in assets. The market is extremely large in comparison to the much publicized airline sector, which has only $25 billion in annual revenue. The industry is fragmented with thousands of utilities serving a mature, 2%-growth-per-annum market, and the largest utility has only a 4% market share. It is an industry ripe for restructuring and consolidation. In this chapter, we examine how the Delta Model can be applied in support of a better understanding of the strategic changes that are taking place.

This example is particularly relevant and significant because many industries are in the midst of disaggregation, often caused by tumultuous change wrought by the networked economy.

Deregulation in the Electric Utility Industry

Deregulation is transforming whole industries for many developed countries. Every state in the U.S. is engaged in deregulatory activities intended to create open, competitive electricity markets. The Federal Energy Regulatory Commission (FERC) leads this transformation at the national level.

Beginning as early as 1998, fifteen states began to implement open access, which allowed customers to access competitive electricity providers. This regulatory reform covered roughly 38% of the U.S. population. Another 15 states have initiated proceedings on the subject. At the federal level, nine bills have been introduced in an attempt by legislators to be consistent with legislation at the state level. Nevertheless, actions at the state level will unavoidably lead to variations in timing and to a broad range of approaches to the deregulation.

Difficulties in the Deregulation Process

Three primary hurdles must be overcome to ensure an effective, fair, and competitive marketplace. First, the electric utility industry has long had as part of its culture a belief in an 'obligation to serve.' Electricity is seen as a necessity in the developed world and the local utility does not have the option to refuse to provide power (except to customers who fail to pay over an extended period of time). As the industry disaggregates, it is less clear who owns the 'obligation to serve.' Second, most vertically integrated utilities are heavily capitalized in generation, transmission, and distribution assets. If the marketplace is suddenly opened to competition such that any entity can move electricity across existing lines to sell to customers, the issue of 'stranded costs' surfaces. Some experts have estimated that there are up to $125 billion in stranded costs. Every state in the process of deregulating is grappling with this issue in order to protect the investments of the existing utilities while creating a level playing field for all participants in the open market. Third, the mechanism for pricing electricity in the open market is still far from perfect. Several models have been developed in countries such as Chile, Norway, and the United Kingdom but none of these models has been heralded as the definitive solution.

Parallels with the Computer Industry

The computer industry was, until the 1980s, vertically integrated. The major players, including IBM, DEC, Univac, Burroughs, Sperry Rand, and Wang, produced their own chips, developed their own operating systems and applications software, and created their own distribution networks.

A very close parallel can be drawn to the electric industry today. Utilities, in general, produce their own power (generation), transport this power over their own lines (transmission), and distribute the power over local lines to the end-user (distribution).

In the 1980s, the personal computer was not just another new product: it introduced a new architecture that transformed the computer industry. IBM created the dominant design for the PC when it embraced the idea of an open system. IBM served as a systems integrator – purchasing and combining into a single package individual components such as the microprocessor, operating system, hard disk, and monitor. Compaq and the growing hoard of IBM compatibles did this as well. The new architecture of independent component providers and PC assemblers encouraged innovation, lowered the barriers to entry, and segmented an otherwise complex computer development task into tractable pieces. This open design economically stifled attempts by companies such as Apple to gain or retain market share with a vertically integrated architecture. In the end, the computer industry was fully disaggregated (Figure 11.1).

This process of disaggregation is occurring elsewhere in the computer industry. The software market was at one time characterized by large vertically oriented companies such as Andersen Consulting (now renamed Accenture) that provided custom software design, development, and implementation to its customers. As the industry evolved and grew more complex, software products supplanted custom-designed software. Enterprise Resource Planning products, such as SAP, Baan, and People-Soft, began to dominate the software industry. The market acceptance of these products is phenomenal, and they now account for 60% of the market for IT services. These products meet many of the same customer needs that had been addressed by customized systems, but do so at a lower cost, with ongoing version updates and less risk. The risk is lower because the inputs and outputs of the system are predetermined in the product. Taking note of this, Andersen Consulting shifted from developing its own software to implementing the products of others. Andersen evolved into a systems integrator that provides management consulting, training, and facilities outsourcing.

The software industry has vertically disaggregated into horizontal segments that provide software 'products.' The benefit from disaggregation is the rapid innovation that results from the unbridled and independent component providers. Concurrently, the industry demands standards to allow all the components to work together with commonly defined interfaces. The cost from disaggregation is in the growing confusion customers face when confronted with so many choices and networking requirements. As a result of this confusion, demand often emerges for players that pull the pieces back together to provide customers with integrated solutions. Thus, we have disaggregation, concurrent with systems integration, as shown in Figure 11.2.

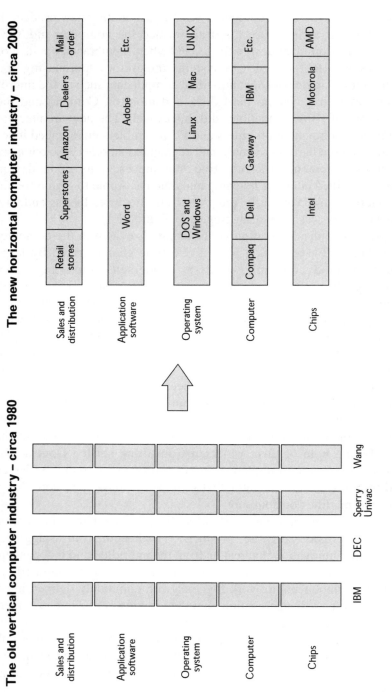

Figure 11.1 The disaggregation of the computer industry

Source: Modified from Only the Paranoid Survive by Andy Grove[1]

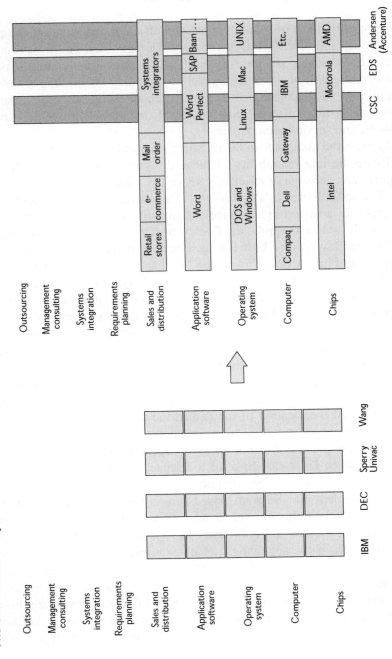

The old vertical computer industry – circa 1980

Outsourcing

Management consulting

Systems integration

Requirements planning

Sales and distribution

Application software

Operating system

Computer

Chips

IBM   DEC   Sperry Univac   Wang

The new horizontal computer industry – circa 2000

Outsourcing

Management consulting

Systems integration

Requirements planning

Sales and distribution

Application software

Operating system

Computer

Chips

Sales and distribution	Retail stores	e-commerce	Mail order	Systems integrators		
Application software	Word		Word Perfect	SAP	Baan ...	
Operating system	DOS and Windows		Linux	Mac	UNIX	
Computer	Compaq	Dell	Gateway	IBM	Etc.	
Chips	Intel			Motorola	AMD	

CSC   EDS   Andersen (Accenture)

Figure 11.2   The disaggregation and integration of the computer industry
Source: Dean & Company

The Effect of Deregulation in Electric Utilities

It is not difficult to imagine the potential effect of deregulation and privatization on the electric utility industry. Deregulation could have a 10X effect, transforming the industry from a vertical to a horizontal structure. Competition will occur at each level of the value chain, among new and established participants. Five segments are likely to emerge: generation companies, transmission companies, distribution companies, power brokers, and services companies.

As with the computer industry, some standards will need to emerge to facilitate the interoperability of these disaggregated parts. The industry requires an exchange to efficiently set prices. One model, which is used in the UK, establishes a 'Poolco' as the exchange for each region. Each generator in a region bids a price and quantity of power for each hour of the day. Based on the bids, the Poolco operator runs simulation programs and selects lowest-cost bids for each hour of demand. The price for that hour is the highest price bid of the last generator to be dispatched. It is effectively a commodities market for electricity. Another pricing model, which can exist alongside the Poolco model, is one of 'bilateral' contracts. It simply allows for buyers and sellers to contract directly with one another for power at whatever price and terms they agree upon. As an additional standardizing force, the physics of power distribution create a need for some central coordination. The Poolco operator or contractor cannot just accept the lowest power bid available. There are constraints on which plants can be dispatched based upon the capacity of the transmission grid and the location of the demand and source of power. 'Independent System Operators' (ISOs) are needed to ensure the integrity of the transmission grid by determining which power sourcing alternatives are feasible. Since ISOs can do a lot to dictate which plant can sell power, their function will likely be regulated.

Each segment may be predisposed to a particular strategic position and the Delta Model helps to explain why. Figure 11.3 displays the transformation of the electric utility industry as well as the implicit strategic position for each of the segments. Let us examine each of the segments in turn. It is important to add here that while we look at the following segments to understand which strategy may yield the most value, this does not mean that other strategies are infeasible. Different strategies may work depending upon the particular skills and circumstance. We aim to show how the different strategies of the Triangle can apply to industry disaggregation.

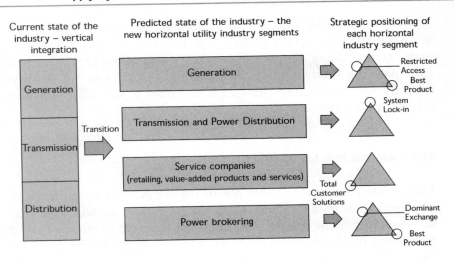

Figure 11.3   The transformation of the electric utility industry

The Generation Companies

Generation currently constitutes about 87% of the cost chain for utilities. Generation companies will build scale by focusing on the production of electricity through fleets of generation plants. They do not necessarily need any ownership of assets further down the value chain. Several companies, such as AES and Calpine, have already begun the strategy of focusing on generation. Enron and other large independent power producers have bought generation assets in order to build credibility and knowledge in certain regions to aid their trading business. Conversely, other companies have already sold, or are in the process of selling, their generation assets in order to dedicate their efforts and resources to downstream activities such as distribution and value-added services.

There will be regulatory limits to consolidation. In fact, larger utilities may be asked to sell off a substantial part of the generation in their regions so as to allow for competition. At the same time, they will have opportunities to acquire generation from nearby regions, from across the country, or from other parts of the world. Consolidation may benefit utilities from both a cost perspective and a revenue perspective. There are scale economies in purchasing and operating skills to be derived from operating a larger fleet of plants focused on one fuel type, such as fossil fuels. By concentrating plants in certain trading regions, competitors may learn about the local supply conditions that allow them to make better investment decisions and avoid marginal cost pricing. Furthermore, consolidating across energy types might allow players to better anticipate the future pricing and availability of fuels. An improved capacity for anticipating changes in the market will allow for better investment decisions.

The Transmission Companies

Transmission accounts for only 4% of the current cost chain, but it is a leveraged point in the system. Transmission companies will own, maintain, and operate the transmission lines that transport electricity from the generation plants to the substations. They carry electricity as high as 765,000 volts and reduce it to lower voltages through the use of step-down transformers that operate on the outskirts of towns. The transmission system in any electric market is the backbone of the industry. All electricity generated must flow over this portion of the system in order to reach the distribution network. Transmission companies have a lock on the system that is not easily bypassed by competition. As one might expect, gaining rights-of-way for new high voltage transmission lines is generally complex and time consuming, if not impossible. Therefore, the owners of the existing systems are in an extremely powerful position. Industry participants and regulators must decide what is the best ownership and regulatory framework to ensure that these owners do not exploit their bottleneck position to the detriment of other participants and consumers.

The Distribution Companies

Distribution accounts for 8% of the costs in today's electricity system. Distribution companies own and operate the local power lines that connect to homes, businesses, and the distribution substations that step down the voltage from the transmission lines to levels appropriate to end-users, typically from 120 to 4000 volts.

The local network portion of the distribution business will probably remain regulated for many of the same reasons that the transmission business will. The local network represents a natural monopoly. It is probably too expensive for any competitors other than the largest industrial customers to bypass. Regulators will probably apply fixed tariffs to all electricity transported over local networks regardless of the supplier. This tariff may also cover stranded cost assessments or costs incurred for the 'obligation to serve.'

The Service Companies

A group of companies may emerge that will excel in their ability to acquire and serve customers. Their ownership of the facilities may be secondary. They can assemble the necessary pieces to bring the complete service to the customer. This could mirror developments in other industries. LDDS (Long Distance Discount Service) began as a reseller of long distance services, buying the facilities from established networks and focusing on marketing and servicing customers. Today LDDS has evolved into MCI WorldCom, a leading bundler of telecommunications services to business customers.

Today, marketing accounts for a negligible 1% portion of the cost chain for utilities. Competition will dramatically expand the role and expense of this activity. In the case of telecommunications, marketing expenses for AT&T expanded from 5% of the cost chain in 1988 to over 14% of the cost chain by 1992. We see the same potential for the electricity market, where the cost of acquiring and retaining customers could rise to 15% of total costs. Utility marketing alone could be a $10–20 billion industry in the U.S.

The activities pursued by these companies will extend from sophisticated mass marketing, billing and call center management for residential customers to in-depth energy management advice for larger customers.

Power Brokering

Power brokering, a growing segment of the value chain, will play a vital role in the newly competitive market. Power brokers are analogous to traders in the financial markets. These companies do not necessarily own any tangible assets involved in the generation or delivery of electricity, but operate sophisticated trading and intermediation systems that match supply with demand either on the spot market or through short- and long-term contracts. Brokers not only match buyers with sellers, they construct contracts that help to shift risk and return to different participants, and they help buyers to hedge against the volatility of electric prices.

Many of these power brokers have entered the electric industry by leveraging expertise through natural gas or financial trading. In 1997, the top U.S. brokers included companies such as Enron, NGC-Chevron/Electric Clearinghouse, El Paso Energy, and Duke Energy.

The next four sections describe how strategic positioning might unfold for the newly established horizontal business segments. Given the changing dynamics of the industry and the creativity of the participants, we may find our thoughts to be only one of many possible scenarios. Nonetheless, it is useful to speculate because it allows us to illustrate how the Delta Model can be used to change strategy and realign execution to better confront market conditions.

The Strategic Positioning of the Horizontal Segments

The division of a vertically integrated industry into distinct horizontal segments leads to new competitive challenges. In addition, the disaggregation of the industry gives rise to new opportunities for intermediation. This phenomenon is typical in industries in transition, where disaggregation leads to the creation of different niches with unique competitive positions with no built-in integration across the resulting segments. The forces of disaggregation and intermediation operate simultaneously in a process that rearranges the industry architecture. People tend to concentrate their attention on one or the other of these effects, but to fully understand the changes in the industry we need to focus on the two in combination. The Triangle captures this combination and the options for strategic positioning that follow from it.

Generation – Best Product and/or Restricted Access

Competitive Positioning for Generation Companies Pursuing Best Product

Mission: We will achieve a leadership position in the regional generation industry and focus on providing a low-cost, reliable product.

Objectives
- Maximize profits by increasing plant availability and plant efficiency
- Build a portfolio of power plants concentrated on one fuel source
- Create the potential for specialized bilateral contracts through interruptible supply options and 'green' electricity
- Adequately hedge our energy positions, so that we do not suffer adversely when prices decline due to supply/demand imbalances.

Profitability in the generation segment of the industry could be driven by a number of factors. Obviously, they could be driven by cost. Players who are effective at reducing generation costs, maximizing interunit synergies, and providing reliable, quality power may be well positioned to compete. The prevailing strategy for these players will be Best Product on the basis of low cost for whatever 'grade' of power, for example environmentally friendly (green) or normal, they can produce.

Unfortunately, to efficiently operate a power plant means that you have to own one (there are some merchant plants that have long-term service contracts, but it is uncommon). To own a plant means taking a long position on the future prices of electricity relative to the fuel costs, which account for the majority of the production expense. Therefore, another factor driving the profitability of generation is price speculation and the raw supply/demand balance of the industry. To the extent that you can predict future electricity pricing, investing in power generation may be a way to take advantage of this. The individuals who should know most about pricing are the power brokers, and this leads to a potential synergy between the generation and the power brokering business. In a sense, the positioning of the power brokering business takes precedence because it is the primary reservoir of the knowledge that makes this synergy work. Consequently, some companies, such as Enron, have purchased power generation to learn about the regional power market and to back up contracts as they get started in trading. As their trading business has grown the generation side has been gradually divested.

A third potential driver of profit is derived from the natural constraints in the business. As mentioned earlier, transmission lines are a scarce item. When a generating plant is on the supply-constrained side of transmission, it may be able to sustain above average returns. This challenges the conventional view that electricity is a commodity, because after all, you cannot differentiate electrons. That may be so, but it is also very difficult today to inventory them. People don't just want energy, they want it at a particular place and time. If the product cannot be differentiated, the place and time can be. Sustainable profits can be found by identifying isolated load pockets not easily served, reserving the geographic locations that can serve them, and building more than adequate capacity to keep future competitive investments at bay. This is not low-cost electricity, but it addresses a premium price market.

Generation can also position itself for premium times as well as premium geographies. Peaker generation plants are designed to serve only the peak periods of demand. They have high incremental costs, but low fixed costs so they are appropriate for short but infrequent use, rather than for continual base load needs. By definition these plants serve a more restricted market. The peaks are rare so there is less capacity addressing this market, and hence fewer competitors. It is a complex market that represents a mixture of insurance, risk hedging, as well as pure generation, which further limits competent competitors. Finally, the peaks also occur when the transmission system is most stressed and supply options restricted.

These strategic options for generation are important to point out because they again demonstrate that no business need be resigned to strictly competing as a Best Product in a commodity industry. In electricity, what appears to be a uniform ocean of electrons traded on the basis of low cost has another side to it. It is a jagged alpine terrain of localized demand available to those with a foothold on the most scenic cliffs. These are System Lock-In strategies based upon Restricted Access.

The Transmission and Distribution Companies – Restricted Access

Competitive Positioning for the Transmission and Distribution Companies

Mission: We will deliver energy services to customers from a strong position of market leadership.

Objectives
- Innovate to achieve greater grid reliability
- Expand customer base by increasing grid capacity
- Lobby actively against adverse government interference
- Be the first to market with digital services over power lines
- Make electric routes, conduits, and poles available for telephone, Internet, line power, and security services.

Both transmission and distribution companies will operate within a natural monopoly, and therefore should expect regulation. In the transmission business, such a regulated monopoly locks out competitors since it is highly unlikely that a new entrant will build parallel transmission lines in an effort to bypass the incumbent. Moreover, there are few short-term technical alternatives to transmission lines. (Perhaps the nearest threat lies in the development of small turbine generators. Allied Signal and others are manufacturing small gas turbines that can be placed at customer sites to produce electricity. Clearly, these could bypass the transmission and distribution facilities.)

Although profitability within this segment will be limited, ownership of these assets will create a stable and predictable income stream year after year. Effective consolidation and cost management may produce higher than market growth rates.

The primary focus of this segment will be to ensure that appropriate levels of capacity are available and to ensure high quality. As in any System Lock-In position, the most important way to sustain profitability is to develop and nurture supportive relationships with complementors. Unquestionably, the key complementors in this case are regulatory bodies (including the FERC, the Public Utility Commissions, and the state and local public officials). It is also important to nurture alternative users of the electricity cable routes, poles, and conduits. Cable television companies and overbuilders, emerging telephone competitors, wireless carriers, and Internet access providers are all looking at different ways to access residences and businesses. The distribution assets can be valuable access paths and, hence, new sources of revenue. Furthermore, if they are not made available to these companies, they may build alternative routes, which later become new competitors to electricity distribution.

The Service Companies – Total Customer Solutions Strategy

Competitive Positioning for the Service Companies

Mission: We will become the preferred interface between consumers and electricity providers.

Objectives
- Provide customized and reliable solutions to the end-user
- Provide a bundle of related services, and/or a complete energy solution
- Acquire a high customer share.

The service sector of this industry will be the most uncertain and dynamic. It needs to draw upon marketing, sales, and customer care skills which are not inherent in most utilities today, so it will require significant investment. Additionally, it is not clear how much margin will be available to a service company. Retail competition is expected to lower prices, but the costs of service, primarily the power, are not subject to any dramatic source of cost decline. To the contrary, marketing and customer acquisition costs will radically increase. Airlines, financial services, and telecommunications have all experienced a magnitude increase in marketing spending with deregulation, and there is little reason to believe it should be different for electricity. This margin squeeze will hit the retailer, so it will take sophisticated Customer Targeting to acquire customers while earning a profit. The prevailing strategy may well be the Total Customer Solutions strategy, and there are at least two different ways to achieve this in this sector. One is to follow the EDS model, which is to focus on larger customers, provide customized services, and integrate with customers' energy management requirements. A second is to follow a combination of the MCI WorldCom and Capital One models, which is to establish a world-class marketing capability, bundle energy (along with other services such as digital data transmission) into one offer, and target only the most profitable customers. The national scale for efficient marketing and product development may ultimately lead to a consolidated field of competitors. Furthermore, the tight margins and huge investment associated with the service sector may give large companies with related skills and with products that could be bundled with electricity an edge. We could see gas, financial services, or even telecommunications companies add electricity as an incremental element in their bundle, since they could consider the addition on incremental costs rather than having to make a fully loaded investment in the necessary infrastructure.

Given the challenges of lower prices and higher costs, if competition thrives in the service sector it will represent expansion and intrigue because it brings a wholly new value-added element to the industry.

Power Brokering – From Best Product to Dominant Exchange

Competitive Positioning for Power Brokers

Mission: We will create the dominant exchange for power brokering. We will also build up a unique network of information sources and develop the ability to analyze market data. The goal is to gain profits through arbitrage opportunities.

Objectives
- Create a real-time information network that accesses and analyzes information
- Ensure rapid conversion from data to knowledge
- Use the knowledge to provide hedging and risk shifting opportunities for customers
- Gain dominant share in the focused regions and products that we serve in order to secure the most knowledge about prices in that segment and to be clearly recognized as the dominant location for buyers and sellers to meet.

One approach to the emerging power brokering segment is to build scale through a Best Product strategic position based upon first-to-market, low-cost, high volume activities. However, as more entrants emerge, margins could be squeezed. Growth options are focused on innovative product introduction (such as new types of trading and risk management products), acquisition of new customers through mergers or acquisitions, and creative marketing and sales efforts.

Brokers may find another opportunity, however, to build System Lock-In over time. If power brokers gain significant regional share, they could become de facto regional exchange floors for power. Even if a Poolco existed in a given region, the dominant power broker could be the de facto exchange for more complex deals. A de facto exchange exercises lock-in in that buyers want to go to the exchange with the most sellers and sellers want to go to the exchange with the most buyers.

The Role of the Adaptive Processes in the Horizontal Segments

Up to this point, we have described likely strategic positions of each horizontal segment. Achieving these different positions requires radically different sets of actions. To describe the specific nature of these actions we again turn to the Adaptive Processes: Operational Effectiveness, Customer Targeting, and Innovation. Table 11.1 summarizes some of the more salient features of these processes and how they change by segment and strategy.[2]

Even a cursory examination of the industry makes it clear that to achieve success, companies operating in the five different sectors – generation, service, power brokering, transmission and distribution – must approach each sector with a different mindset. For purposes of simplicity we will only discuss the Best Product strategies for generation companies. In this case, they must prioritize cost and quality. The service companies must focus on customer economics by building a completely new set of skills to identify, understand, and serve customers better. The distribution companies will appeal to some of the traditional regulatory competencies to protect the franchise, but with a new desire to consolidate fragmented local networks in order to lower costs and grow earnings under a price cap. Adapting to these new requirements will be an enormous challenge for the existing utilities, which have cultures anchored in a protected, public service environment.

Furthermore, the generation companies and brokers have different processes even when both are pursuing Best Product strategies. Generation follows a classic low-cost formula with an emphasis on Operational Effectiveness. Generation companies must minimize fuel and labor costs, and maximize utilization, and efficiency. This implies an emphasis on opera-

Table 11.1 The role of the Adaptive Processes in supporting the strategic positioning of the electric utility horizontal segments

STRATEGIC POSITIONING

ADAPTIVE PROCESSES	Generation companies — Best Product	Power brokers — Best Product to System Lock-In	Service companies — Total Customer Solutions	Transmission/distribution — System Lock-In
Operational Effectiveness	▪ Minimize fuel costs ▪ Minimize labor costs ▪ Maximize plant utilization ▪ Maximize quality ▪ Adequately hedge to limit exposure to volatile energy prices	▪ Minimize backroom trading costs and overheads ▪ Flexible systems to allow for feature proliferation ▪ Scale partnerships to reduce risk positions ▪ Aggregate loads for smaller customer groups	▪ World-class billing and customer care capabilities ▪ Flexible 'gateway' fuction for all kinds of services ▪ Partnerships to efficiently source value-added extensions	▪ Control operating and maintenance costs to ensure that there are no surprises ▪ Efficient provisioning of common services ▪ Ensure lower cost than alternatives
Customer Targeting	▪ Maximize regional scope to reach the most demand ▪ Develop tight linkages with a wide range of ISOs, distribution and service companies ▪ Explore range and depth of bilateral contracts	▪ In target regions expand share of market to become dominant exchange point ▪ Robust customer interfaces to improve bonding ▪ Locate pockets of market inefficiency, whether by region or by customer ▪ Scope adequate to improve, maintain market knowledge	▪ Identify most attractive and profitable vertical markets ▪ Extend and enhance customer interfaces through new media and project management add-ons	▪ Strong relationship with all complementors, including regulators, generators, service companies, ISOs, and so on ▪ Help proliferate complementors ▪ Extensive linkages and interfaces with generators and service companies
Innovation	▪ Alternative low-cost fuel ▪ Onsite power generation ▪ Quality and reliability features ▪ IT linkages with ISOs for real-time data exchange of pricing ▪ Forms of bilateral contracts ▪ Bid to optimize price	▪ First to develop new trading products and services ▪ Risk management systems for managing internal exposure ▪ Maximize connectivity to all regions	▪ Develop customized bundle of products and services (e.g. gas, water, telecom) ▪ Joint development projects with key customers ▪ Outsourcing of customer energy-related processes ▪ Skills and project database for effective organizational learning	▪ New capabilities and interfaces for complementors ▪ New mechanisms to enhance capacity ▪ Closely monitor breakthrough technologies such as 'power line carrier' or 'resident generation equipment'

tions as well as on engineering. Utilities today have a strong engineering-centric culture, in which teams are well trained to optimize and plan. Adopting an operations capability will mean recognizing that engineering only has some of the answers and that improved operating practices can bring greater leverage. Nucor may provide a valuable model to address these challenges. At Nucor, each plant is viewed as a laboratory for best practices with performance measurements and consistent performance-based rewards. Nucor's experience might even suggest that it is dangerous to overengineer when entering a very competitive environment because it limits flexibility while adding cost and time. With the Customer Targeting process, the focus is on generating volume and accessing more market share in order to obtain best price and consistent demand.

Power brokers adhere to a Best Product position that emphasizes Differentiation and market share, but have the potential to develop System Lock-In. They make money in two ways. First, they offer products that others do not yet have, whether in risk management or in some financial derivative related to energy transactions. Second, they also locate and arbitrage market inefficiencies by acting as an exchange point for energy transactions. The brokers with better market knowledge (how energy prices may vary over time, by geography, and by energy type) will achieve better returns. It is reasonable to expect that this market knowledge may be enhanced through market share. As they gain market share, there is the potential to become a Dominant Exchange as buyers flock to the source of most sellers and vice versa. This may be a natural migration path; however, there are inherent trade-offs to resolve. A broker determined to achieve a Dominant Exchange may trade-off current profits for future positioning through deep discounting, and may wish to simplify and demystify the trading process. Best Product destined brokers will wish to make money as they develop the business and may benefit from a more secretive book of knowledge.

The service companies have Total Customer Solutions as their prevailing strategic position. Operational Effectiveness requires the creation of a world-class billing, call receipt, and customer care center. Rather than reducing costs, service companies are enhancing functionality. For example, bundling requires tremendous flexibility in these systems; they must be able to add and integrate services, such as gas, water, and perhaps telecommunications. Customer Targeting places great emphasis on understanding customer economics and profitability by customer, rather than simply seeking volume. In deregulating markets, most money is made through cherry-picking. For example, MCI WorldCom's market share of their long distance business and international traffic, where the margins are much higher, is almost twice their share in the lower-margin domestic residential market. MCI WorldCom puts a premium on segmenting customers, building databases, and generating analytical mechanisms to determine which customers are attractive and how to find them.

Experimentation has never been a priority for utilities, and perhaps it should not be in certain segments (nuclear reactor construction, for example). Innovation in other segments, however, now depends critically on trial and error, and working jointly with customers. Large customers, in particular, present opportunities to extend energy services from selling kilowatt-hours to selling related services, whether it is heating, chilling, or some mechanical operation. Determining which related services to pursue will require experimentation and adaptation. National Starch, for example, could not have anticipated its role in gluing wings to the fuselages of airplanes before it began to work closely with Boeing.

The transmission and distribution companies have a form of System Lock-In, but not one likely to generate high margins. We mentioned that lobbying skills will continue to be critical to success in transmission and distribution, but the characteristics of System Lock-In suggest that a very different angle must be added to this focus on the regulatory process. This new approach is tied to the central role of complementors in the sustainability of System Lock-In. Traditionally, the regulatory effort focuses on the customer and the regulatory bodies. With System Lock-In, the distribution/transmission companies need to nurture the support of all generation, brokers, and services companies, and not just the ones with which they have historical ties. Locking in these complementors means creating tight interfaces with their systems and processes so that they find it difficult to switch to emerging alternatives (such as building their own distribution for large customers or installing small turbines onsite). It also means that the complementors may find it more difficult to complain to the regulators about the distribution/transmission companies. There are numerous interfaces that are important to the seamless operation of a power service. These can include power reliability, cost-effective meter reading, and efficient billing.

Performance Metrics in the Horizontal Segments

Table 11.2 summarizes the performance measures required to monitor the performance of each of the Adaptive Processes. Clearly, there are more metrics than those listed here, but these characterize the key differences among the actions behind the different strategies.

Table 11.2   Performance measures associated with the Adaptive Processes of the horizontal segments

PERFORMANCE MEASURES

ADAPTIVE PROCESSES	Generation companies — Best Product	Power brokers — Best Product to System Lock-In	Service companies — Total Customer Solutions	Transmission/distribution — System Lock-In
Operational Effectiveness	■ Cost/kwh ■ Effective capacity of plant relative to the investment ■ Availability ■ Utilization ■ Return on assets ■ Unit cost by activity adjusted for cost drivers	■ Cost per kwh traded ■ Total kwh sold per day, month, year, relative to competition ■ Relative risk and costs of funds ■ Relative price of power compared to competition	■ Customer savings through service offerings ■ Cost per acquisition ■ Customer tenure ■ Cost of customer care	■ Cost per unit transported ■ System reliability ■ Schedule vs. unscheduled maintenance time ■ Costs relative to alternatives
Customer Targeting	■ Addressable market size ■ Price per kwh ■ Load forecasting accuracy ■ Share of regional power pool	■ Share of market, share of customers in targeted region ■ Share of contracts/volume of contracts ■ Arbitrage profits vs. exposure profits	■ Share of customer's energy purchases ■ Customer profitability ■ Relative market share for target vertical market ■ Share of national market, absolute and relative competition	■ Number of complementors using the system ■ Average sales of complementor ■ Kwh sales relative to added feature sales ■ National market share, absolute and relative to competition
Innovation	■ Bilateral contract features ■ Bidding practices ■ Quality and reliability improvements	■ Number of new services and products ■ Degree of customization, switching cost	■ Percentage of jointly developed products ■ Switching costs for customer to change vendor ■ Scope of services available	■ Number of new capabilities for complementors ■ Switching cost for complementors

To succeed, generation companies will need to track ever more detailed metrics of unit cost performance. Today, the range in operating cost performance by plant is significant. The most efficient plant in the U.S. operates at 50% lower cost than the least efficient plant, even after adjusting for fuel type, size, and utilization. Variation in cost will not be tolerated in a competitive market. To address the cost opportunities, metrics need to transcend average cost per kilowatt-hour (kwh) to address each activity that goes into the development, construction, and maintenance of power generation. As important, they will need to benchmark these same performance metrics at their competitors' facilities. Finally, there is the link between rewards and compensation, which is complex but key to having metrics drive continual performance gains.

Generation companies with large investments in power production and supply contracts may end up with massive exposure to power prices. The question arises over whether the profits from generation are from long positions in energy or cost effectiveness in production. With competencies in cost efficiency rather than in price prediction, there arises a need to hedge the exposure so that margins can be preserved despite the volatility in energy prices. Properly hedging the energy exposure requires a broad set of metrics on risk management. It may also lead to the development of new and innovative financial instruments to shift risk.

Power brokers may focus on measures of market share and innovation. Market share helps to keep costs down, but more importantly, it may eventually enable some lock-in. Brokers may take a regional focus in trying to build dominant market share for power exchanged within its borders. Innovation, in terms of the number of new offers or the range of services, will help to differentiate the product. Brokers are in a position to make bets on the future price of energy and may organize their books of business to manage these bets. Enron, has a 'book' as a tool and major competitive weapon. The book organizes their positions and guides the individual actions of the traders and dealmakers who arbitrage the market to take the net exposure the company desires. Enron's profit from trading now exceeds its profit from generation.

Distribution and transmission companies will manage traditional utility metrics associated with reliability, customer satisfaction, capacity utilization, and cost. Metrics will help to avoid future rate cases or 'show cause' investigations. Additionally, these companies should measure how many complementors (generation and service companies) they serve and how tied the complementors are to the network. The switching costs for the complementors is a function of the number of services they receive from the network and how tightly intertwined their systems and processes are with those of the distribution and transmission companies.

Service companies will focus on customer metrics. These include their share of their customers' expenditures (on energy and related services) and their share of the profitable customers (which requires a measure of customer profitability). Rather than the cost per kilowatt-hour, they will measure efficiency in terms of the cost per customer acquisition and the customer churn rate. Their profit hinges on improving customers' economics through either bundling or service extension. They therefore need comprehensive measures of customer economics. They need to measure how they might reduce their customers' energy costs without simply lowering the price of power itself. Certain vertical markets may emerge as the most attractive, and the service companies will measure the number of innovations, service offerings, and customer satisfaction in these segments.

Creating a Strategic Agenda

The strategic agenda brings the strategic thrusts, Adaptive Processes, and performance measurements together in one blueprint for strategic change. The strategic agenda speaks to the question of which departments and organizational leaders are responsible for the tasks necessary to accomplish the organization's goals. Individuals and departments primarily responsible for a specific goal receive a '1,' while individuals and departments that play more of a support role receive a '2.' The individual or department in charge of a specific goal – who we refer to as the 'champion' – receives a circled '1.'

Rather than review the Strategic Agenda for each business as we have done before, let us look at the real case of an emerging Service Company business. This Service Company is pursuing a Total Customer Solutions strategy and is establishing itself in one of the newly deregulated regions. They are buying electricity from the local utility's power plants, independent power producers, and from brokers. The fundamental task ahead of them is to build a customer base. While they address both the residential and business markets, for the purposes of this example we will focus on the consumer market.

The key thrust is centered around acquiring customers and sustaining the relationships (Table 11.3). Customer Targeting is among the foremost Adaptive Processes. While marketing has many leadership roles, the thrusts necessarily involve multiple divisions.

Table 11.3 The Strategic Agenda for service companies

Strategic thrusts (examples)	ORGANIZATIONAL STRUCTURE								Business Processes	Performance measurements (examples)
	CEO	Consulting	Customer Care	Human Resources	Customer Research	Marketing	Communications/PR	Finance		
Retain customer base by strengthening the relationship with the consumer	1	2	(1)	2	1	1	1		CT	■ Customer market share growth ■ Customer retention rate ■ Percent of customized service arrangements
Establish process for offer testing and customer acquisition	1		1	2	1	(1)		2	CT	■ Customer profitability ■ Customer acquisition costs ■ Number of tests, success rates
Develop a new energy tracking system	2			1	(1)	2	1	2	I/OE	■ Number of licensees ■ Number of web page visitors; duration of visits ■ Percent of customers using new system
Build a reputation in energy marketing and establish an energy consulting department	2	1	2	2	1	(1)	1	2	CT	■ Image perceptions in opinion polling as compared to the image perceptions of competitors ■ Percent of potential customers switching from rival consulting firms
Quantify customer economics	2			2	(1)	2	2	2	CT	■ Consumption of each consumer ■ Price elasticity of consumers ■ Environmental elasticity of consumers
Customer education	2	1	1	1	1	2	(1)	2	CT	■ Number of customer workshops per month ■ Volume of requested information material ■ Improvements in customer awareness in the latest surveys ■ Resources spent on joint product development with customers
Recruit high-quality engineers	2		(1)	1	1			1	OE	■ Percent of offers accepted at the top schools

Granular Metrics

Granular metrics are essential to survival in the unregulated energy market. Let us continue with the emerging Service Company illustration, and look at the actual underlying variability that drives its performance. A critical underlying indicator is customer profitability.

Profits in the regulated market vary by customer. Customers have different costs to serve because they are at uneven distances from electrical substations, which drive distribution costs, and they have variable load shapes. Load describes the power consumed throughout the day and the year. If a customer consumes most of their power during hot summer days, then their costs will be higher than the customer who consumes their power during temperate autumn evenings. This is because the hot summer day is typically a period of peak load when all the facilities of power production need to be dispatched. During an autumn evening little overall power is in demand and only the cheapest base-load plant needs to be in operation. Furthermore, for a given load shape the customer who uses more electricity will have a lower per kilowatt-hour cost to serve. Since prices have been averaged the differing costs lead to widely differing profitability.

Profits in deregulated markets show double the variability of regulated markets. In addition to the factors noted above, competitive markets add variability from customer acquisition and retention and from alternative product offers. Acquisition costs vary because some customers have a propensity to switch from the incumbent provider, and some have longer tenure. Alternate offers provide different price structures and add some features, such as power from ostensibly cleaner, 'green,' sources, that can add to the profit margin. Offers also need to account for different customer price elasticities and product perceptions. Some customers will always select on the basis of price, but a growing number will select on brand and on value. Value customers will spend more per kilowatt-hour when they perceive a better value proposition due to some feature, customer service, or whatever.

Two of the key parameters driving profitability are mapped in Figure 11.4: consumer propensity to switch and usage. High home market value, early adopter of competitive services, and, electric heat customers were cheaper to acquire and had four times the usage of other segments making them very profitable customers, especially relative to low home value, late adopter, gas heat consumers. From this, and other factors not shown in the figure, optimal customer targets can be identified and different programs crafted that can be expected to optimize the profit from each viable customer. Accurate measures of profitability have to be developed at a

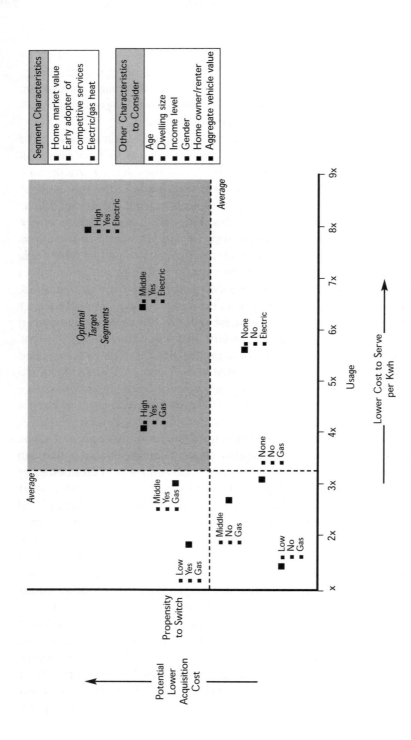

Figure 11.4 Residential segmentation

Source: Dean & Company research and analysis

very deep level to capture the interaction of load shapes, acquisition, retention, usage, distribution, features, and so on. This information is critical to the success of Customer Targeting.

At the outset of competition, little is known about customer behavior other than through market research regarding an abstract set of trade-offs. As competition ensues and consumers become engaged in real decisions, more can be known and the data changes. Consequently, it is imperative to systematically test alternative offers and measure the response. This Service Company tested hundreds of offers that varied by price, promotion, feature and customer target. Over time we discovered that optimal pricing alone could double the profits for many customer segments. Due to tight margins, the sensitivities were enormous. Being only 0.3 cents per kilowatt-hour below (or above) the best price tripled the profit for the low income renters with gas heat, and increased by 30% the profit for high income home owners with electric heat.

This business established a Customer Targeting process much like that referenced earlier with Capital One for credit cards. They regularly tested different offers, rigorously measured the outcomes, calculated customer profitability down to microscopic levels, and expanded the offers that proved in analytically.

Information Disaggregation and the Internet

While deregulation draws attention to the physical disaggregation that is separating the power generation from distribution and retail customer services, there is an associated information disaggregation that is being propelled by the forces of the new Internet infrastructure. Each horizontal business is a new locus of specific and valuable information, as well as the focal point for certain physical goods. The Internet is a means to instantly transport this information to the relevant community. To be a viable competitor in any new sector of the electricity industry, the Internet has to be a central mechanism in your strategy. Conversely, to employ the Internet without the vision of the strategies outlined above can dissipate energy and capital and gain no specific advantage.

Service companies have to consider online portals and Internet-based customer relationship management[3] to competitively serve and lock in customers, as well as to mitigate costs. Brokers provide an even clearer illustration. The network is a critical tool to facilitate a Dominant Exchange between buyers and sellers. Enron is a leading broker and has made Enron Online a central part of their overall strategy. They enjoy 2.5

times the trading volume of any other energy broker and command a 10–1 lead in trading volume over any other energy-related web site. Not only are they able to expand the volume of trades in raw energy, they are using the Internet platform to expand the portfolio of products traded. To deal in energy, there are a multitude of related services that can help to allay or shift risk, ranging from price futures to weather insurance. Enron is seizing a Dominant Exchange position from every vantage point available.

Reflections

The electric utility industry is a stunning example of transformation. While the patterns have and will continue to occur elsewhere, nowhere else is the metamorphosis more astonishing. From the seed of one single, monolithic, and homogeneous utility, we will see a diverse garden of businesses begin to bloom. This diversity is as profound as you would find in comparing credit cards to custodial services, as has occurred in the banking industry; or, as you would find in comparing routers to wireless data services, as has occurred in the telecommunications industry. It represents the endless evolution of business. Firms mutate in the heat of competition that is fueled by growth, and then seek out shade within ever more specific market niches. These different niches reflect the wide range of strategies described by the Delta Model. Each of these strategies requires a unique combination of Adaptive Processes, Aggregate Metrics, and Granular Metrics to survive, let alone succeed.

Notes

1. Andrew S. Grove *Only the Paranoid Survive* (Currency Doubleday, 1996).
2. Notice that we are departing from the methodology that we described in the case of Motorola Semiconductors in Chapter 6. In employing the Delta Model, a business must first define its strategic thrusts. These thrusts capture the agenda that enables a company to achieve its desired strategic position. The thrusts need to be tailored to the individual firm's circumstances, which are a function of its competencies and the specifics of its market. Because we are not describing the strategy for a specific company, but the prevailing strategies for a segment, we are not addressing the strategic thrusts here.
3. We more fully discuss electronic customer relationship management in Chapter 8.

CHAPTER 12

Toward a Unified Framework of Strategy

We started this book with the claim that the two most celebrated and influential business strategy frameworks – Michael Porter's Competitive Advantage and the Resource-Based View of the firm – are fundamentally incomplete, both in explaining sources of profitability and guiding managers to superior strategic options. Although these frameworks have often been presented as conflicting views, we feel that they share a similar management philosophy. Moreover, it is our strong belief that the Delta Model has the ability to complement the perspectives of both frameworks and provide the integrative glue that may result in one unified strategy framework.

We will now briefly describe the two frameworks.[1] Our treatment is not intended to be exhaustive. We will deal with the frameworks at a level sufficient for the reader to understand the implications of our claim regarding unification. We urge the reader to go to the original sources in order to gain a deeper appreciation of their contributions.

Porter's Competitive Positioning Framework

According to Porter, there are two basic determinants of the profitability of a business: the structure of the industry in which the business operates and the competitive positioning of the business within that industry. These are the inputs that determine the Strategic Agenda of the business and lead to the formulation and implementation of its strategy. Figure 12.1 captures the essence of the framework.

Industry structure explains the value generated by the economic activity of the industry participants, as well as their ability to share in the wealth created. Michael Porter postulates that there are five forces that typically shape industry structure: intensity of rivalry among competitors, threat of new entrants, threat of substitutes, bargaining power of buyers, and bargaining power of suppliers. These five forces determine prices, costs, and investment requirements, which are the basic factors driving long-

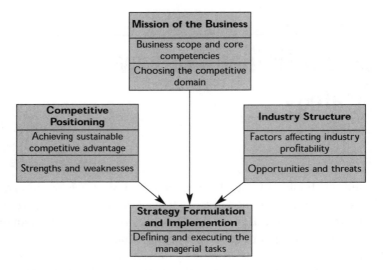

Figure 12.1   The basic framework for explaining
the profitability of a business

term profitability, and hence industry attractiveness. Figure 12.2 illustrates
the generic structure of an industry as represented by its main players
(competitors, buyers, suppliers, substitutes, and new entrants), their interrelationships (the five forces), and the factors behind those interrelationships that account for industry attractiveness.

The competitive position establishes the basis for achieving a sustainable advantage, which is a business' relative standing against its key
competitors. According to Porter, the value chain model is the guiding
framework for assessing the competitive position of a business. The
underlying principle is that all the tasks performed by the business organization can be classified into nine broad categories, five are *primary activities* and four *support activities*. Figure 12.3 provides a full representation
of the value chain.

The primary activities involve the physical movement of raw materials
and finished products and the marketing, sale, and servicing of these products.[2] They can be thought of as the classical management functions of the
firm, where there is an organizational entity with a manager in charge of a
very specific task, and a balance between authority and responsibility. The
support activities are more pervasive. Their role is to provide support not
only to the primary activities, but to each other. They provide the managerial infrastructure of the business: all processes and systems intended to

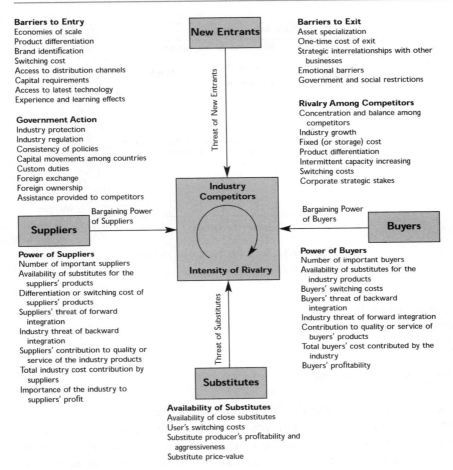

Barriers to Entry
Economies of scale
Product differentiation
Brand identification
Switching cost
Access to distribution channels
Capital requirements
Access to latest technology
Experience and learning effects

Government Action
Industry protection
Industry regulation
Consistency of policies
Capital movements among countries
Custom duties
Foreign exchange
Foreign ownership
Assistance provided to competitors

Power of Suppliers
Number of important suppliers
Availability of substitutes for the
   suppliers' products
Differentiation or switching cost of
   suppliers' products
Suppliers' threat of forward
   integration
Industry threat of backward
   integration
Suppliers' contribution to quality or
   service of the industry products
Total industry cost contribution by
   suppliers
Importance of the industry to
   suppliers' profit

Barriers to Exit
Asset specialization
One-time cost of exit
Strategic interrelationships with other
   businesses
Emotional barriers
Government and social restrictions

Rivalry Among Competitors
Concentration and balance among
   competitors
Industry growth
Fixed (or storage) cost
Product differentiation
Intermittent capacity increasing
Switching costs
Corporate strategic stakes

Power of Buyers
Number of important buyers
Availability of substitutes for the
   industry products
Buyers' switching costs
Buyers' threat of backward
   integration
Industry threat of forward integration
Contribution to quality or service of
   buyers' products
Total buyers' cost contributed by the
   industry
Buyers' profitability

Availability of Substitutes
Availability of close substitutes
User's switching costs
Substitute producer's profitability and
   aggressiveness
Substitute price-value

Figure 12.2   Elements of industry structure: Porter's five forces

Source: Adapted from Michael E. Porter, *Competitive Advantage,* New York: Free Press, 1985

ensure proper coordination and accountability. Examples include human resource management, technology development, and procurement.

Since the value chain is composed of a set of activities performed by the business unit, it provides a very effective way to diagnose the position of the business against its major competitors, and to define the foundations for action aimed at sustaining a competitive advantage. As opposed to the forces that determine the industry structure of the business – which are largely external and not controllable by the firm – the activities of the value chain are factors that companies can control as they strive to achieve competitive superiority. By analyzing these activities, managers can identify the success

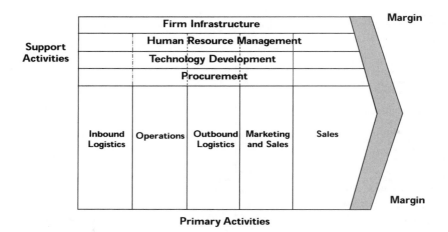

Figure 12.3 Porter's value chain

Source: Michael E. Porter, Competitive Advantage, New York: Free Press (1985)

factors central to competing well and understanding how to develop the unique competencies that provide the basis for sound business leadership.

The Winning Formula

Porter's framework offers a simple approach to business success: pick an attractive industry in which you can excel. The framework and the language Porter uses to describe it stress rivalry and competition. Therefore, an attractive industry is one in which a business can achieve as close to a monopolistic position as is possible. The message of the value chain model to managers is that they must achieve sustainable advantage by beating their competitors in as many key activities as possible. According to Porter, then, strategy is war!

The Resource-Based View of the Firm

The Resource-Based View of the firm represents a major departure from Porter's approach that is based on market-driven factor considerations. Porter posits that industry structure plays a central role in creating opportunities for superior profitability. The Resource-Based View, on the other hand, argues that the central forces of competitive advantage are factor-driven; that is, they depend on the firm's development of resources and

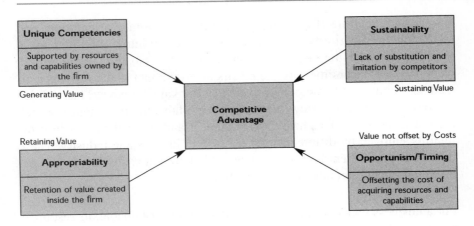

Figure 12.4 The Resource-Based View – elements of competitive advantage

Source: Adapted from Margaret A. Peteraf, 'The cornerstones of competitive advantage: a resource-based view', *Strategic Management Journal* (March, 1993), pp. 179–92

capabilities. Porter's basic framework identified in Figure 12.1 tacitly assumes that industry structure and competitive position contribute equally to the profitability of the business. The Resource-Based View pushes the explanation of superior performance to the competitive positioning side. Figure 12.4 illustrates the essence of the Resource-Based View, which has four key components:

1. Competitive advantage is created when resources and capabilities owned exclusively by the firm can generate unique core competencies.
2. The resulting advantage can be sustained due to lack of substitution and imitation capacities by the firm's competitors.
3. The benefits derived from these advantages are retained inside the firm: they are not appropriated by others.
4. The timing of the acquisition of the necessary resources and capabilities is so opportune that their cost will not offset the resulting benefits.

If all these conditions are met, then the competitive advantage that is created will generate economic value for the firm.

Building on Figure 12.4, we will now explore the components of the Resource-Based View in more detail.

1. *Unique Competencies*

The firm's resources and capabilities are the sources of its unique competencies. Resources can be tangible (for example financial and physical assets) or intangible (for example reputation, customer orientation, and technological superiority). Resources are converted into capabilities when the firm develops the necessary routines to use them effectively. Often, resources and capabilities are the results of investment in durable, specialized, and nontradable factors. This is what Pankaj Ghemawat[3] has defined as commitment. In his view, commitment explains the persistence or lack thereof in an individual firm's performance, and the differences in profitability enjoyed by different firms competing in the same industry. These investments represent both sticky factors that are not easily lost to competition, and major bets that are not easily reversed.

2. *Sustainability*
For a business unit's competitive advantage to be sustainable, its resources must be valuable, scarce, and difficult to imitate or substitute.

3. *Appropriability*
A strategy that is both unique and sustainable generates significant economic value. The issue of appropriability addresses the question of who will capture that value. Sometimes the owners of the business do not appropriate all the value created because of a gap between ownership and control. Nonowners might control complementary and specialized factors that divert the cash proceeds away from the business. This type of dissipation of value is called *hold-up*. A well-known example of hold-up took place in the personal computer industry, in which Intel and Microsoft captured 80% of the total market value of the industry, value lost to the computer manufacturers themselves.

The second threat related to the appropriability of economic value is referred to as *slack*. It measures the extent to which the economic value realized by a business is significantly lower than it could have been. Slack is often the result of inefficiencies or unwarranted benefits that prevent the accumulation of economic rents by a business. One of the major sources of slack in the U.S. has been confrontations between management and labor unions. It has been reported, for example, that General Motors loses $2 billion annually to its bottom line due to strikes.

While hold-up changes the distribution of the total wealth created, slack reduces the overall size of this wealth.

4. *Opportunism and Timing*
The final condition necessary for competitive advantage comes (or fails to come) prior to the establishment of a superior resource position. The cost incurred in acquiring the resources must be lower than the value created by them. In other words, the cost of implementing the strategy should not offset the value generated by it.

Core Competencies and the Resource-Based View of the Firm

C.K. Prahalad and Gary Hamel popularized the Resource-Based View of the firm, particularly with their prominent article in the *Harvard Business Review*.[4] They established three main ideas in their paper. First, that competitive advantage derives from an ability to build, less expensively and more rapidly than competitors, the core competencies that spawn unanticipated products. The real source of advantage is to be found in management's ability to consolidate company-wide technologies and production skills into competencies that empower individual businesses to adapt quickly to changing opportunities. Second, the tangible link between identified core competencies and end products is what they call the core products, the physical embodiment of one or more core competencies. And third, senior management should spend a significant amount of its time developing a corporate strategic architecture that establishes objectives for competency building. Strategic architecture is the road map to the future; it helps to determine which core competencies to build and to identify their constituent technologies.

The Winning Formula

Based on the original Resource-Based View unmodified by Prahalad and Hamel, the winning formula is very simple:

- Develop resources and capabilities that are unique, valuable, and non-tradable, and that constitute the unique competencies of the firm
- Make the resulting advantages sustainable by preventing imitation or substitution by competitors
- Appropriate the resulting economic rent by preventing negative hold-up and slack conditions
- Ensure that the implementation process is done in such a way that its associated costs do not overwhelm the resulting benefits.

In other words, it is strategy as real estate.

If we further extend the winning formula to account for Prahalad and Hamel's message, we would add three more elements: develop core competencies at the corporate level; apply them to create core products as opposed to end products; and use a strategic architecture to guide competence building.

Porter's framework and the Resource-Based View differ in explaining the sources of profitability. Porter associates it with monopolistic rent that flows from industry structure. The Resource-Based View of the firm ties it to the corporation's internal capabilities. They share the perspective that business is akin to war and that designing business strategy is akin to playing a zero-sum game. Profitability accrues to those who are superior to their competitors. The Delta Model takes issue with this almost obsessive focus on competition.

As importantly, there is vagueness regarding the treatment of resources to create competitive advantage. This is magnified when the resources are held at the corporate level. The core competencies, core products, and strategic architecture devoid of content become elusive and hard to apprehend in pragmatic, meaningful terms.

The Delta Model: An Integrated Framework for Strategy

We will now show how the Delta Model answers some of the questions unanswered by these two frameworks. The resulting integrated framework makes the three approaches – Porter's framework, the Resource-Based View, and the Delta Model – complementary to one another and therefore stronger. From this perspective, the Delta Model serves as a unifying framework that starts with a vision statement that captures the essence of how the business positions itself and culminates with the tactical means to adapt continuously to an ever-changing environment.

Why consider an integrated framework? After all, a business cannot follow a rigid, predetermined formula for running its organization and expect to succeed in today's fluid world. At the same time, if each individual within the organization follows random 'Brownian' motion, only chaos will result. A well-designed integrative strategy provides a coherence of action throughout the business that connects decisions in the boardroom with behaviors in the field.

The Delta Model framework is an integrative process for formulating and executing strategy. The elements of the process are described in Figure 12.5.

The Triangle: Capturing the Business Vision

The first and most critical task for any business is to capture the essence of its strategic position, in other words, the development of a business vision.

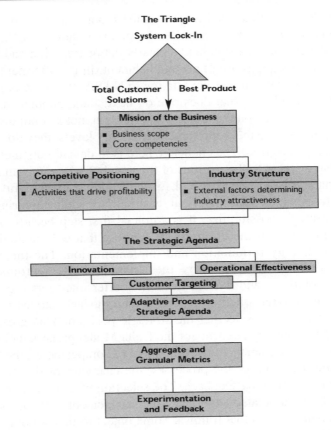

Figure 12.5   The Delta Model – an integrative strategic framework

Unfortunately, most managers find this an elusive task, often ending in empty slogans and platitudes.

One approach to defining the vision that has produced an enormous amount of attention is called 'strategic intent.'[5] This is an active management process that creates a sense of urgency, focuses the organization on the essence of winning, and motivates people to act. Examples of successful expressions of strategic intent are those of the Apollo Program – 'Landing a man on the moon;' Komatsu's drive against Caterpillar 'Encircle Caterpillar;' Canon's determination to surpass Xerox 'Beat Xerox;' and Honda's aspiration to conquer the American auto industry – 'Become a second Ford.' While these can be inspiring and serve as a rallying cry throughout the organization, they have limitations.

One could argue that 'land a man on the moon' had both the best and worst consequences for NASA. On the positive side, it mobilized the whole of American society behind a clearly defined mission and helped to produce a remarkable sense of accomplishment. In the aftermath of going to the moon, however, it was devastating to NASA. It left the organization empty and rudderless. What does one do next: 'land another man on the moon?' Putting a man on the moon was a mission, not a continuing vision. While slogans inspire the troops and raise energy levels, they do not represent a strategic position. The challenge here is to develop distinct business options that respond to the realities of the new business environment.

The Triangle is an effective tool for describing a meaningful strategic position. Its power resides mainly in its simplicity while capturing the full range of strategic possibilities. It is a crucial first step because it defines the central purpose of the business, the purpose that will guide the whole process of strategy formulation and implementation. The three distinct strategic alternatives offered by the Triangle – Best Product, Total Customer Solutions, and System Lock-In – offer managers a contrasting set of options through which to reflect on their business strategy.

They must start by selecting the strategic position. This greatly influences all the remaining elements of the Delta Model process including the scope, the way to compete, the development of competencies, the Strategic Agenda, the definition of the processes, the character of the metrics and the methods of obtaining feedback. The selection of a strategic position is based on the accumulated experience of management without the benefit of the detailed analysis that follows. Some object to this, arguing that one should collect the data first and then select a strategic option. But, if so, what data should they collect? This is a chicken and egg problem and managers need a starting point. As the process evolves and new information is generated, it is important for managers to reexamine their assumptions and modify or recalibrate their starting point. The Delta Model process makes explicit a practice that many companies carry out implicitly. Most senior executives today make their most important decisions without explicitly raising the question of which strategic position the business is striving to achieve. This has serious drawbacks; it leads to fuzzy and unclear thinking, and prevents the strategy from being developed and communicated through a process that leads to a clear consensus among the key players.

The Mission: Defining the Business Scope and Competencies

The mission of the business should make concrete the strategic option that managers have identified using the Triangle. The mission includes two key decisions: defining the business scope, which determines where to compete; and developing the core competencies of the business, which determines the resources and capabilities needed to succeed.

Consequently, there are two sets of information in a well-defined and well-articulated mission of the business. First, the business scope must include a view of the competitive domain of the business, both for today and the future, as described by its overall portfolio of products, market coverage, customer focus, complementor focus, and geographic presence. The business scope is informative not only for what it includes, but for what it leaves out. Second, the core competencies should include the tangible and intangible resources necessary for reaching the desired competitive position.

The selection of the strategic option using the Triangle has a profound impact on the mission. Adopting the Best Product option, for example, makes the product the most critical dimension of business scope; the core competencies are those required to achieve cost leadership or a highly differentiated product offering. The Total Customer Solutions option makes the customer the most critical dimension and requires competencies that focus on customer bonding. The System Lock-In position introduces complementors as a new dimension of business scope and requires the competencies needed to develop the proper architecture and complementor lock-in.

The mission should highlight the *changes* that the business is seeking to realize. If there are no changes in the mission, there is little chance that the business will succeed in a dynamic world. Strategy is fundamentally about dealing with change, which is why the mission must deal with the contrast between the business' existing scope and its future scope. These changes ripple through the subsequent process steps and the Strategic Agenda that allows the business to move forward.

Managers often think of the mission as a broad statement of purpose, similar to those appearing in annual reports. These are typically polished and cosmetic in nature, driven by public relations objectives. This trivializes the special nature of strategy.

The Industry Structure: Understanding and Negotiating External Forces

Sound analysis of industry structure captures the principal external forces, their future trends, and their impact on a business. Porter's five forces model helps managers to understand the strategic implications of industry structure. The Delta Model gives rise to a number of critical modifications to the five force framework. First, the question of rivalry and the focus on the 'winner takes all' mentality. With two of the Delta Model's three strategic options (Total Customer Solutions and System Lock-In), rivalry is replaced by bonding as the critical lens through which to observe industry structure, bonding of customers in one instance and of complementors in the other.

Second, the question of which industry structure managers should analyze. In the Porter model, they must look at the industry in which their business resides. Obviously, that industry always remains relevant to the business; however, managers using the Delta Model do not stop with their own industry. They extend the analysis to include the industries of their key customers and complementors and seek insights to achieve the desired bonding. As a result, the nature of the industry analysis is greatly affected by the selection of the strategic option. Finally, the five forces are replaced with a six force model in which complementors are added to Porter's competitors, suppliers, buyers, new entrants, and substitutes. (This last force should constitute a category of analysis that includes not only replacements for the products that a business unit sells, but the disruptive change that can radically modify the rules of the game. This is what Andy Grove called the 10X force.)

Competitive Positioning: Building the Activities to Drive Profitability

Having analyzed the external forces that are part of the industry structure, and reached a clear understanding of the opportunities and threats presented by the business environment, we need to establish a strong competitive position that responds to this environment. Again, Porter's value chain is a useful starting point. The value chain allows us to identify the activities that are most important to achieve competitive advantage, and to develop action programs to enhance the desired capabilities. However, the Delta Model necessitates a significant expansion of the conventional analysis. Rather than concentrating exclusively on the internal value chain of our own business, we need to include the value chain of all external relevant parties.

In the Total Customer Solutions option we look for the proper integration of our value chain with key suppliers and customers, searching for complementary assets that substantiate and enrich the relationships. National Starch looked beyond adhesives to Boeing's airplane industry. AT&T needs to understand the industries of its clients and how its capabilities enhance their competitive advantage.

In the System Lock-In option, we look beyond our immediate industry to the system as a whole with all its relevant complementors. Microsoft needs to look beyond the operating system industry to the industries of the application providers. Coca-Cola needs to look at the industry of the fountains and grocery stores. The challenge is to create mechanisms where the linkages across those value chains originate the ultimate bond. Once more, the strategic focus is away from rivalry and competition and toward cooperation and bonding.

As we can see, the steps in the Delta Model process involving the industry structure and competitive positioning map directly to Porter's framework, but make it more relevant to a wider array of strategic options. The fundamental methodology proposed by Porter – the five forces and the value chain – are greatly expanded in scope to include the customer and complementor dimensions, enriched by bonding as an economic force.

The Strategic Agenda: Specifying the Key Business Tasks

The previous steps of the Delta Model – selection of the preferred strategic options, mission of the business, industry structure analysis, and competitive positioning – provide the relevant background for the development of a comprehensive Strategic Agenda. These should include pragmatic, action-driven tasks that in totality will accomplish the strategic objectives of the business. Earlier in the book, we provided various examples on how to describe the Strategic Agenda. Here, it is enough to say that the agenda should define each task with sufficient clarity to communicate it across the organization. It makes explicit the role to be played by every manager involved in its execution, including the nature of the Adaptive Process it might generate. It also should identify the necessary indicators and targets associated with each task in order to monitor the business. We have two additional observations. First, the agenda is dynamic, which means that it is the subject of continuous revisions. That is what is meant by the comment: 'Plans are not made to be followed.'

Second, it must be communicated throughout the organization. We have encountered numerous situations where management is hesitant to share the strategy broadly either because it raises competitively confidential issues, or it contains bad news for some business segments. Both are usually bogus concerns. The competitively sensitive information is typically in the tactical elements of execution and the bad news for individuals is better addressed head-on. Communication is essential to energize the organization and ensure congruence between the business purpose and the individual actions of all the participants.

The Adaptive Processes: Aligning Strategy with Execution

The Strategic Agenda integrates all the necessary tasks required to set the overall direction of the business. The Adaptive Processes go further. They go deeper into the organization and into the details of execution. This guarantees the alignment of strategy and execution in an explicit and direct way.

Every Adaptive Process in turn produces its own Strategic Agenda that has the same format characteristics as the business agenda but more localized and detailed. With these steps finished, the strategy formulation is complete.

The Resource-Based View of the firm calls for the nurturing and appropriation of key resources and capabilities as the source of competitive advantage. We complained that the vagueness of this statement impairs the usefulness of this framework in the pragmatic world of management. There are, however, two steps within the Delta Model where the Resource-Based View concepts are a natural fit.

In the mission statement we call for the specification of the required core competencies that the business needs to achieve its desired strategic positioning. These core competencies might not be exclusive to a given business unit within the overall corporation. Indeed, the most desirable situation exists when the competencies reside at the corporate level – as the Resource-Based View insists – and are also distributed throughout the entire business portfolio. In this manner the corporation creates additional value through the businesses, which legitimizes the corporate structure as an added-value entity. In that sense, core competencies are the critical focus of the corporate strategy.

The definition of the Strategic Agenda of the Adaptive Processes is the second step in the Delta Model where issues of capabilities are confronted. Now we go from the broad statement of core competencies that are part of the business mission to the skills that are needed in the Operational Effectiveness, Customer Targeting, and Innovation processes.

This sharper focus of requirements breaks the ambiguity inherent in the abstract Resource-Based View. From this perspective core competencies support the development of the strategic positioning of the business; and resources and capabilities are the skills required in the Adaptive Process that are needed in the implementation.

The intersection of the Resource-Based View and the Delta Model occurs in the mission and now in the Adaptive Processes. The Adaptive Processes link strategy with execution and link the broad competencies at the corporate level with the specific activities required at the business level.

The Metrics: Aggregate and Granular

Three sources of metrics are generated by the Delta Model. One set emerges from the Strategic Agenda, and is developed for the business and each supporting Adaptive Process. These metrics have great importance because they monitor the progress against the most important business tasks, and also guarantee alignment between the strategic option and its execution.

The second source is Aggregate Metrics, which permit a coherent monitoring of the overall business performance. Instead of talking about the inputs, which relate to the tasks, we turn our attention to the outputs, the key indicators of success for the business.

Granular Metrics comprise the third set. These metrics detect variability in performance with the intent of learning about the performance drivers so that improvements can be made in both continuous and discontinuous ways.

Experimentation and Feedback: Creating Adaptive Mechanisms

Strategy is based upon the best available data and analysis, but should explicitly acknowledge the unknowable and changing market. Experimentation and feedback are structured into the processes, generating tasks to test the assumptions and learn about the market. If the strategy or elements of its implementation do not change, then the odds of its success drop considerably. Experimentation ensures change.

The Delta Model deals with the large and the small, with the strategic direction and the key elements of execution that enable that strategy. Where the metrics allow us to go from the aggregate to the granular, experimentation and feedback connects the detailed 'in-market' tests to the adaptation of the grand strategy. These are not dealt with explicitly in the leading strategy frameworks, nor do methods of execution include strategy frameworks. Hence, the natural gap in alignment that we have referred to throughout the book. Execution has many elements, but metrics, experimentation, and feedback are the most critical.

A schematic of the full Delta Model Process is shown in Table 12.1.

Reflections

Managers Need to Reflect, But Seldom Do

Executives are trapped by the need for action. A focus on the immediate can easily become all-consuming, limiting the time and distance necessary to reflect on the business. As a result the entire organization can often end up with no clear, explicit sense of the business or corporate purpose. Without this sense of direction, the business is ill equipped to decentralize and respond to the market. Flexibility and empowerment are lost, putting even greater demands on short-term senior decision making. Much is to be gained by spending high-quality time among key managers to build a consensus around the business strategy.

The Process of Reflection should be Rigorous, Systematic, and Holistic

It is always best to start at the beginning. The process of reflecting on the strategy and how it is implemented needs to be led by the top executive. The process then engages the total organization – guided by a coherent framework – that then cascades to it individuals parts. In this way the strategic tasks gain the proper interdependence and gather the necessary detailed character at each level.

It is important to recognize the four levels of strategy: corporate, business, process, and functional. Corporate strategy has a unique vantage point for identifying all major new opportunities and the creation of value across businesses. Business strategy should mobilize all the capabilities of the corporation toward the pursuit of profitability. The process and functional strategies are responsible for nurturing and applying the capabilities. In the end the process should envelop the entire set of activities in the firm. The processes need to include the Adaptive Processes: Operational Effec-

Table 12.1 The Delta Model and the three strategic options

The elements of the Delta Model	The three strategic options		
	Best Product	Total Customer Solutions	System Lock-In
The Triangle: the source of strategic options			
Business mission	Driver		
Product scope		Driver	
Market scope (customer, consumer, channel)			Driver
Complementor scope			
Geographical scope		(Either local, regional, or global)	
Core competencies		Align with strategic option	
Industry structure: relevant industry focus	Business industry *plus*	Customer industry *plus*	Complementor industry
Competitive positioning: relevant value chain focus	Internal value chain: business	Integrated value chain: business and customer	Systems value chain: business, complementor, and customer
Business strategic agenda	Align with strategic option	Align with strategic option	Align with strategic option
Adaptive process priorities			
Operational Effectiveness	1st	2nd	3rd
Customer Targeting	3rd	1st	2nd
Innovation	2nd	3rd	1st
Aggregate/Granular Metrics	Align with strategic option	Align with strategic option	
Experimentation and feedback	Align with strategic option	Align with strategic option	

tiveness and the supply chain, Customer Targeting or relationship management, and Innovation or renewal. The functions need to include activities such as finance, IT, R&D, and human resources.

The Content Should be Based on a Sound Methodology

In order for the output to be superior performance measured in bottom line economic returns, the methodology used in the strategy development process needs to be spelled out in an equally tangible and explicit fashion. The process ends with Granular Metrics and experimental testing in order to align and direct the business. There is the additional benefit in that this approach provides a quantitative discipline to strategy development.

The Process Should Not Stop with Strategy

Many companies have a compelling conceptual strategy, but lack the means of execution. Many companies have a tremendous focus on supremely efficient execution, but lack the connection to strategy. Designing success into the business requires a process that does not stop with strategic development or start with execution, but that spans strategy to structure, to coordinated business processes, to metrics, and to adaptive response. This is what the Delta Model provides. As a result, it necessarily involves all the key players, is widely communicated, and places a strong emphasis on educating the rank and file on the specifics of the strategy.

Notes

1. Our presentation follows closely that offered by Arnoldo C. Hax and Nicolas S. Majluf, *The Strategy Concept and Process*, 2nd edn (Prentice Hall, 1996).
2. This applies to services as well as products.
3. Pankaj Ghemawat, *Commitment; The Dynamics of Strategy*, (New York, Free Press, 1991).
4. C.K. Prahalad and Gary Hamel, 'The Core Competence of the Corporation', *Harvard Business Review*, May–June 1990, pp. 79–91.
5. Source: Gary Hamel and C.K. Prahalad, 'Strategic Intent', *Harvard Business Review*, May/June 1989, pp. 63–76.

INDEX